By
Robert E. Levinson

GARRETT PUBLISHING, INC.

by Robert E. Levinson

Published by
Garrett Publishing, Inc.
384 S. Military Trail
Deerfield Beach, Fl. 33442

Tel. 305-480-8543 • Fax. 305-698-0057

Library of Congress Cataloging-in-Publication Data

Levinson, Robert E., 1925-
Robert E. Levinson's super savvy: how to get, how to use it, how to make a fortune with it!
p. cm.
ISBN 1-880539-29-2: $14.95
1. Executive ability. 2. Management.   I. Title. II. Title: Super savvy.
HD38.2.L48   1994   94-14016
658.4—dc20   CIP
Previously published by REL Enterprises 1973: The Knack of Developing and Using Management Savvy.

Printed in the United States of America
10 9 8 7 6 5 4 3 2 1

To my mother

> *who encouraged and*
> *guided my first young*
> *business ventures*

and my father

> *whose example has*
> *inspired my entire*
> *business career*

What Management Savvy

Can Do for You

Management is people

The real manager *works with people*. That's what this book is about—*people*.

The real manager is the one who knows how to get the job done profitably and brilliantly *with* people, and *through* people. Because when you boil it all down you find that management *is* people! It's that simple.

A knowledge of people is a knowledge of management. And the combination of the two is *Management Savvy*.

Management savvy is something else, too. It's the art—*yes, the art*—of inspiring new heights of achievement in people by showing them how, through example, to *draw multiple value out of every action they take!* The ability to do this is worth a million dollars, plus a wealth of satisfaction.

How does one go about getting management savvy? This book will show you how. Better still, it will work with you to build and develop your savvy instincts. How? *By osmosis*. This book won't merely *tell* about management savvy, or explain what it is. It will *show* you management savvy in action. You will see it applied on the firing line, right on the job where it is really meaningful. You will be an on-hand witness.

As you read this book you will relate the live, dynamic, nuts-and-bolts examples which are given to your own job and your own experience. You will build savvy by example. You'll absorb it into your personal management philosophy. You'll make it a new and richly rewarding way of life.

Is this going to be easy to do? Frankly and bluntly, no! You're going to have to work at it, and work hard. And remember this. If anyone tells you management savvy is easy to acquire, take care. He's out to bamboozle you.

That's why this book doesn't deal with the *easy* way to acquire management savvy. It deals with the *only* way! It explores the nuances and ramifications. It lays the facts on the line.

Let's get started

Want to draw top value from this book? The secret is to assume an attitude. Don't think of yourself as reading a book. Think of yourself as participating in it. Because the stuff in this book is anything but play acting. This book is life. It's firing line action. In the office, in the warehouse, on the shop floor. In short, this is the real thing! And the principal player is YOU!

Now here's what to do. As you re-live the real problems and human interactions illustrated, keep your own job and your own people in mind every step of the way. Imagine *yourself* in the midst of each situation. Anticipate each action, each development. Decide what *YOU* would have done in each situation. Then see what was *actually* done. This, my friend, is the way to acquire management savvy. Not by lecturing, not by remote control, but *by live, on-the-scene osmosis!*

Here's a fact. There is no truly successful manager who is not also a savvy manager. If you acquire management savvy in one business, you will be able to apply it to *any* business.

Whom do you work with? Ralph, Bill, Ann, Harry, Carol, Al, Jack? It makes no difference. This book will help you decide what to do when a subordinate asks for a raise, whatever his name happens to be. You'll know what to say to George when you fire him. You'll know how to make a production meeting more effective, and teach Ray to do the same. You'll find out how to get more work done through Dick in the Order Department. You'll develop powerful new skills in selling your company, its products, its image, its service, its people. Most important, you'll develop powerful new skills in selling yourself!

How are you going to do this? There's one way only. By facing up to real issues. Live issues. Let's stop theorizing, and start "people-izing." It's time to stop beating around the bush with dull management principles and platitudes. It's time to replace ancient book sense with modern horse sense. It's time to put positive, field-tested techniques to work.

That's why this book has been written. By the time you finish this book, you too will understand the secret of getting multiple value out of every action you take. You'll know how to tackle thorny problems and solve them through your people—then turn around and convert the problems into dramatically effective teaching examples. You'll know how to uncover and exploit the untapped talents of your people; to excite profit-building ideas; to spark each working day with stimulating new "Job Variety" and an invigorating sense of job fulfillment.

You will learn all this and more. But I repeat—it won't be easy. In plain talk, all this book can do is half the job. It will provide the live examples, the working tools of your savvy search. But the other half of the job—the most important half: *applying* the examples—is up to you.

And the best time to start is now!

STOP!

This book is different. It won't lecture or preach. It's not designed to curry favor, amuse, or entertain. This book is different because it is all business. Literally, *all business*. It reveals the practical business experiences of the author as they take place on an everyday firing line basis—experiences you can relate to your own job, your own problems.

This book has one goal only: *To develop YOU into a savvy manager*—a manager who, by effectively working WITH PEOPLE AND THROUGH PEOPLE, will achieve and surpass *your personal profit objectives* and *the profit objectives of your company.*

That's one aspect. Most of all, what makes this book different is YOU! Working with this book you will be more than a reader. You will be a *participant!* The idea of this book is to bring you right smack into the middle of the picture where you belong. When? Starting *now!*

The Big Question is this: *do you have what it takes to be a savvy manager—right at this moment?*

The following quiz will answer this question. Before you can measure the savvy you acquire, you must first measure the savvy you possess right now. *The trick is to be as self-critical as you can.* This quiz is intended for you, and you alone. The more candidly you respond, the more benefit you will derive.

Now—pulling no punches on yourself—here's the way to score:

Rating	Score
Excellent	5
Good	4
Fair	3
Poor	2
Bad	1
Hopeless	0

IMPORTANT: This is a *double* rating system. It measures your savvy potential today. It also measures your savvy *growth* over a six-month period. Now, read the following instructions with care:

STEP ONE—Complete the quiz now. Score yourself in Column A.

STEP TWO—Complete the quiz *a second time* six months after completing this book. Jot down a reminder on the last page to mark your calendar six months hence. Don't be afraid to write in the margins. The book is a management tool in your hands to be used in any way you see fit.

Your personal management savvy quiz

NOTE: The quiz assumes that you currently supervise one or more people. *Do not bypass any question!* This would unfairly lower your score. If a question refers to a supervisory function you do not presently fulfill, rate yourself on *your ability to perform the function* should you be called upon to do so.

PART I—SELECTING AND DEVELOPING PEOPLE

	A Today	**B** In 6 Mos.

1. How good are you at picking winners when you hire people?
2. How effectively do you train your people? (Do most of them grow under your supervision?)
3. How well charged with job interest and enthusiasm do you keep your people? How skillfully do you motivate them to surpass their past achievements?
4. How careful are you to give your people *full* credit and recognition for their achievements?
5. How well do you encourage qualified subordinates to percolate on their own steam (by fueling their self-confidence with your faith and trust)?
6. How effectively do you prevent "Talent Erosion" and track down hidden abilities (by finding new ways to use your people's talents to keep them from rusting; by throwing people into unfamiliar situations, giving them a chance to show their mettle in hitherto untried areas)?

PART I—TOTAL SCORE   _____   _____

PART II—EXPANDING YOUR KNOWLEDGE AND EXPERTISE

1. How do you rate as a generalist? (Does your storehouse of knowledge extend beyond your company and special field of endeavor? Do you attempt to sharpen your savvy skills away from the shop as well as on the job?)   _____   _____

2. How *actively* curious are you about what makes people do what they do?   _____   _____

3. How much savvy restlessness do you possess? (Does an inner voice keep goading you to improve yourself, your people, your operation?)   _____   _____

4. How aggressively do you attempt to find out about and understand the key functions and events of your company?   _____   _____

5. How well do you profit from mistakes (by tracking down error causes and putting mistakes to use as training tools)?   _____   _____

6. How do you rate as a constructive snooper? (Do you ask the right questions of the right people at the right time?)   _____   _____

PART II—TOTAL SCORE   _____   _____

PART III—YOUR OPERATING EFFICIENCY

1. How well organized is your time? (Do you find enough time to really *manage?*)   _____   _____
2. How well do you delegate?   _____   _____
3. How fast do you "blast off" in launching a project or crusade? (Do you ever require a prod to spark your ignition?)   _____   _____
4. When problems erupt, how successfully do you track them to their root?   _____   _____
5. How accurately do you evaluate performance and progress (your own, as well as your people's)?   _____   _____
6. How hard do you work at selling ideas you believe in (by fanning lagging interest, dreaming up new sales strategies, recruiting allies to your cause)?   _____   _____
7. How well do you "people-ize" your management techniques? (With shirtsleeve, on-stage management, not "ivory tower" supervision.)   _____   _____
8. How well do you simplify, and trim fat from, communications?   _____   _____
9. How patient and persistent are you? (Do you remain calm even in impatience-provoking situations? Do you fight "can't do" skepticism with "must do" urgency?)   _____   _____

PART III—TOTAL SCORE   _____   _____

PART IV—YOUR PROFIT AWARENESS

1. How lean do you keep your operation (by trimming waste, inefficiency, excess paperwork, labor costs)? How quickly and effectively do you spot profit leaks? _____ _____

2. How aggressively do you seek profit opportunities? (Do you make your own breaks, or wait for them to come to you? Do you agitate your people to explore profit prospects and plan profit actions?) _____ _____

3. How strong is your resolution that, no matter what, the customer must be kept satisfied? _____ _____

4. Do you think like the owner? (Are the boss' profit interests _your_ profit interests?) _____ _____

5. How effectively do you put the "Multiple Value" concept to work? (Deriving a variety of extra benefits from a single management action.) _____ _____

6. How impressive is your output of profit ideas? (How freely do they flow? How often do they click?) _____ _____

PART IV—TOTAL SCORE _____ _____

PART I _____ _____
PART II _____ _____
PART III _____ _____
PART IV _____ _____
GRAND TOTAL _____ _____

Hundreds of threads are woven into the fabric of which management savvy is composed. This quiz does not include every one of them. But the sampling included here is broad enough to give you a fairly comprehensive idea of how you stand.

The final figure in Column A represents your management savvy rating today. The final figure in Column B represents your management savvy rating six months after completion of this book. The *difference between the two figures* represents your management savvy GROWTH after you have had the chance to apply what you learned from this book.

Result evaluation

Score	Significance
135	Perfect. Attainable by one kind of manager only, the wishful thinker.
120 or higher	You're loaded with management savvy and should be *writing* a book like this instead of *reading* one.
95 to 119	You're well stocked with savvy, but could use plenty more. This book will help you immensely.
below 95	Congratulations on your forthrightness and objectivity. You have a long savvy building row to hoe. This book will do wonders to shorten your trip.

The real test

Above all, don't forget to mark your calendar and retake this test *six months after completing this book.* What you learn from this procedure can shortcut the achievement of your goal by 30 to 50 per cent. It will tip you off as to how well you understood, absorbed and *put into practice* the savvy techniques spelled out in the book. Most important, it will help you pinpoint specific areas of management where—*in your own judgment*—you show a weakness and need for shoring-up action.

Contents

The Knack of

Developing and Using

MANAGEMENT SAVVY

1

What Is Management Savvy, and
How Do You Get It?

I'll let you in on a secret.

While this book was still in the spawning stages, I was trying to dream up a good name for it, and an associate suggested, "The Mystery of Management Savvy." I hit the ceiling. He should have known better.

"That's the worst possible title," I said. "There's no *mystery* to management savvy. It's the simplest thing in the world. That's why it eludes so many people."

"Okay," my friend wanted to know, "then what *is* management savvy?"

Good question. The *American College Dictionary* defines savvy as, "Understanding, intelligence, sense." Add the word "management" and you've got a fair definition.

Except for one thing. It doesn't tell you very much. It tells you nothing you didn't already know before you opened this book. Understandably, too. Because—and if anyone tries to tell you otherwise you can pass him a dark and dirty look—*no one* is going to make you understand what management savvy is by tossing a definition at you. Simple as it is, there's just too much involved.

True, management savvy *is* business understanding, business intelligence, business sense. So what? This doesn't tell you how to apply savvy on your job or in your shop. No, there's only one way you can get to know what management savvy is—only one way to understand it so you'll be able to use it.

That's by seeing it applied *right on the firing line* in day-to-day job situations, and more particularly, finding how *you* can apply it in your own job situation.

Want to know what management savvy really is? All right. We will start by looking at practical, down-to-earth situations. That's the way to see what management savvy really means to a company, to a department, to a manager or to any employee.

Management savvy—the big payoff

• *The savvy executive knows how to promote ideas and finally get them across.* Here's a situation. Jones is an executive and he has an idea to improve a process, make it simpler, faster, cheaper. He takes it to the president. The president looks it over. "This has possibilities, but . . ." The president starts knocking holes in it and in the end the verdict is, "Not interested. No dice." Now, here's where you separate the real executives from the wishful thinkers. A no-savvy executive would be content to let the idea die right there. He would give up and move on to another area and forget the whole incident. A savvy executive would realize that perhaps he did not present the idea properly. Maybe it was a bad day, or the timing for his idea was not right. A savvy executive, if he was convinced his idea had real merit, would figure ways to present the idea in a different way, at a different time, with a new approach. And the president would be delighted, because this would show that the executive possessed intuition, dedication to his ideas, and constructive drive. Remember this: eventually, if your idea is sound and is properly presented, the boss will accept it and you will become a hero.

QUESTION: How does a man convert a lukewarm reception to red-hot approval? In a subsequent chapter we will plunge right into the nuts-and-bolts specifics of exactly how this is done. For the moment you can accept one thing as gospel. The ingredient that makes the difference is *savvy!*

• *A savvy manager knows people—how to pick them, how to keep them.* Bill Smith needs an assistant. He starts interviewing men. Does management savvy apply here? It most certainly does.

In spades! Take the no-savvy manager. He *might* end up with the right man. But only if he's lucky. It's more likely the applicant would wind up interviewing *him* (more on this later) and he'd wind up with the wrong man. But for Bill Smith with the magic touch it's a different story. With Bill there'd be no maybe's about it. He'd be *sure* to end up with the right man. He'd get his man. He'd develop his man. He'd keep his man. Because if there's one thing that management savvy does for you that's more important than any other thing, it's this—*it people-izes you!* More on this, too. Much more.

• *The savvy manager makes short shrift of problems, and teaches his people to do the same.* An employee comes to Ed Brown for advice. Should we handle the job this way or that? How would the savvy manager field this one? By brushing him off? Saying he doesn't know the answer? Probably not. What's more likely is that he would make the man think, he would probe the particular problem with the employee. He would try to get the employee to come up with the answer himself—try to instill confidence in the employee by proving to the employee that he could answer the problem. Depending upon the seriousness of the problem, the savvy manager might let the employee come up with the wrong answer and find through experience how wrong the answer was. If the problem was very serious and important, the savvy manager would not let the employee leave with the wrong answer, but would try his best to have the employee think out with the boss the right answer. Next time the same problem came up, the man would be able to tackle it on his own.

• *The savvy manager makes managing a full-time job.* Let's take a walk through the office or plant with savvy-starved Simpson. He passes people, desks, machines. Nothing registers. Simpson is merely on his way from this place to that place. The only benefit he gets from his walk is exercise. Good benefit; but it's not enough. The savvy manager gets *much* more. His walk through the shop is an interesting experience, stimulating, rewarding. He spots a problem here, an opportunity there. As he walks he thinks. He manages. The ideas hum. What does he have that the other fellow lacks? One thing. Savvy.

• *The savvy manager recruits fans for his company.* A customer visits the plant. Adams, a manager without savvy, is assigned to show him around, take care of his needs. The customer returns home unimpressed. Just another company. Just another routine visit. Next year he comes back again. This time Wilson, whose middle name is Savvy, takes care of him. This time the customer goes home with a positive charge. What a company, he thinks! What a product line! What people! P.S.—What a difference savvy makes!

• *The savvy manager fuels his people with job interest and enthusiasm.* Take a look at Tom Carleton's department. Carleton himself is off on a trip. So you spend some time with his people. You're a customer, let's say, or a supplier. "What can we do for you?" his people want to know. "How can we make *your* problem *our* problem?" Their eyes sparkle with interest—interest fueled by the "Job Variety" program (just wait till you see this one in action later in the book). Tom's people are anxious to please. They conduct themselves in good taste. They're pleasant, cheerful, friendly. They bubble with enthusiasm and zest; they radiate "sell." QUESTION: What does this tell you about Tom Carleton? That's right; you've guessed it. Tom made his people the way they are. He is a savvy manager.

• *The savvy manager is alive to profit opportunities.* A manager thumbs through a business magazine. He scans the words. He looks at the pictures. If he's a man without savvy, that's *all* he does—scans the words, looks at the pictures. But not Jack Miller. Jack is charged with savvy. He doesn't just "thumb through" a magazine. *He's on a profit excursion!* His mind is sharp, alert, triggered to snap at each profit opportunity like a shark at bait. An ad strikes his eye: *spray-on packing fill.* ("Just what we need for the new 15B.") An article: *Internal Communications Set-Up.* ("Could this relieve our over-taxed switchboard?") Get the picture? The man has savvy.

• *The savvy manager makes time to manage, and manages his time.* Poor Davis. Look at him after a hectic day. He's a sorry sight. All day long he's been waging a losing war with the clock. Now he drags himself home with a briefcase full of work. Haggard, worn, irritable. Davis is short on two key necessities of management life: time—and savvy. Not so Al Silver. Savvy Al has a different slant on life. Compared to Davis, he's twice as busy, half as hectic. He comes home with a newspaper and a smile, plus energy to spare. How does he manage it? Simple. He *manages!*

Just as you'll know how to manage by the time you're through with this book. For one thing, instead of trying to solve every problem himself, Al trains his people to solve them. He begins by working with them, getting them off on the right course. Then he leaves the time-consuming wrap-up to them. Twice the achievement; half the time. Next comes a brainstorming session. Same technique. The savvy manager revs the engine, gets the movement started. He stimulates, prods, provokes. He whips up interest, excites discussion. When the ideas start popping like corn, he leaves the session. Next problem; next project. Get the idea? The savvy manager is not a do-it-yourselfer! He stimulates. He motivates. *He gets things done through people.*

• *The savvy manager chops problems to size by getting in on the act.* Here's another situation. A subordinate, after years of satisfactory work, suddenly stops producing. What's the problem? Is it the work? A personal predicament? What do you do? One man who'll ferret out the answer is the savvy manager. He'll "me-too" his way into the problem by getting in on the act. He'll work with the man, talk with him. He'll sit down alongside him at his desk. He'll join him in the field. Approaching the situation from *his* point of view, he'll find out, "Why this? Why that?" He'll delve. He'll probe. He'll build. He'll develop. And he'll do it all in a constructive, helpful, *savvy* way, that will win him gratitude instead of resentment.

• *The savvy manager knows how to organize others into profit action.* Remember some of the cracks you must have heard about meetings? "A meeting's like a steer: one point here, another point there, and a lot of bull in between." Or, "They open at 9:00 sharp, and close at 12:00 dull." Well, little wonder. A meeting run by a no-savvy manager can be a harrowing affair. Inadequate planning. Poor organization. The meeting drones on and on. People become bored. They know what to expect. Discussion bogs down, rambles off track, lacks profit direction. But when a savvy manager takes over, forget the cracks. This fellow keeps proceedings on target, spices them with variety. Excitement runs high. Ideas fly. Problems dissolve into action and commitment. The meeting starts sharp, and ends the same way—on a high note of achievement. Achievement through planning. Through organization. Through—that's right—*savvy!*

Organization + people

This, briefly, very briefly, is what management savvy is all about. This and a good deal more. Boil it down and you might say that management savvy is about two key factors primarily: *organization and people*. It always gets back to this.

Management savvy is about organizing the job to prepare it for people, and organizing people to prepare them for the job.

Understanding. Intelligence. Sense.

The manager with savvy understands organization, understands people, and knows how to blend the two together. Nothing is more important to the businessman than to build and upgrade this understanding. John Locke once put it this way: "The improvement of understanding is for two ends: first, your own increase of knowledge; secondly, to enable us to deliver that knowledge to others."

This book is your gateway to management savvy. *With your active participation and cooperation,* it will give you understanding—the kind of understanding you can translate into profit action for company growth, for people growth, *for your personal growth!*

Look at it this way. Mrs. Albert Einstein was once asked if she understood her husband's theories. "I understand the words," she replied, "but I don't understand the sentences."

With management savvy you'll understand the sentences too.

How do you get it?

What are your aspirations? Top executive job? Plant manager? General manager? Chief executive in 15 years? An income of $50,000 a year?

All right, here's a $50,000 question. *Management savvy—how do you get it?* Where does it come from? How important to you is the answer to this question? Maybe this will give you an idea. *Without* management savvy, you can forget about your aspirations.

It's important to get one thing straight from the start. I've said it before, and I'll repeat it now. *There is no brief, simple shortcut to the development of savvy!* But there is a *long* and simple shortcut. That's why this book has been put together. Sound paradoxical? It's not.

This book can cut your groping upward climb in half or better—providing you participate. Providing you cooperate to achieve your own objectives, your own rewards.

Step one is to resolve not to be Mr. Average Manager. Make this resolution now. Because Mr. Average Manager is going to plod the long, wearisome road to management savvy. Perhaps he'll make it. More likely he won't. In any event, his indoctrination is going to be by trial and error, trial and error, again and again, over long, tedious years.

Well, here's a big plus in your favor. It's true: trial and error *is* essential to the development of management savvy. But it doesn't have to be *your* trial and *your* error. It can be anybody's trial and error. Do you get the distinction? Your objective is to take the short road.

Someone once said: "Learn from the mistakes of others—you can't live long enough to make them all yourself."

Good advice. We tried to trade on this advice in planning this book.

With *you* at the scene of each incident, playing the active role of involved observer, this book is going to point up wrong moves as well as right moves, pitfalls as well as powerful management techniques. You are going to see management savvy applied to correct poor judgments, shore up weak decisions, clear away indecision—as well as to tackle problems, motivate and develop your people, sell your ideas, your products, *yourself*.

You're going to learn management savvy by osmosis! And once it sinks in, it is going to stay sunk.

Getting started

By the time you finish this book you are going to be two giant steps ahead of where you are right now.

1. You're going to know exactly what management savvy is, what it means to you, your people, and your company.
2. You're going to know how to apply management savvy successfully on your job—the same way you're going to see it applied in scores of live case situations throughout this book.

But first things first. The objective now is to get a better depth idea of just what management savvy really is in specific, nuts-and-bolts terms; in terms you can relate to the job. Here's a chart that will help you to understand what it is we're going to be talking about throughout this book. The chart sketches in thumbnail form the key ingredients of management savvy. It makes no attempt to give you a complete picture, because only the chapter-by-chapter osmosis can do that. The idea is to give you an advance feel for the subject, to know what to expect.

As you read over the chart, keep in mind those two *master ingredients*—people and organization—and the relationship of one to the other.

INGREDIENTS OF SAVVY—A THUMBNAIL SKETCH

Your Main Goal	Actions to Further	Techniques
To become a self propelling management force.	To take off on my own without the boss' prodding.	"Agitator Method" "Self-Starter Checklist"
	To spot and remove quick-start roadblocks.	"Multiple Value Concept"
	To encourage my people to become self-starters, and develop them along these lines.	
To supplement well honed specialist skills with carefully cultivated generalist know-how.	To be the one they come to for advice.	"Auditor's Query Technique"
	To act as consultant to superiors and associates as well as to subordinates.	"Plant Walk-through" "Telephone Self-Audit"
	To stock my mental storehouse to overflowing.	

Your Main Goal	Actions to Further	Techniques
To develop a proprietary point of view.	To make the boss' profit goals my profit goals.	"Proprietor's Checklist"
	To build my company's "image" wherever and however possible.	"Profit Agitation" "Career Investment Appraisal Technique"
	To convince the boss that he can place absolute reliance on my shoulders.	
To persuade my people to help me grow by making a sincere and concerted effort to help them grow.	To develop avid "me-fans" and to keep them loyal.	"Mr. Steelcraft Loyalist Technique"
	To shore up my people-to-people skills.	"Measured Pressure"
	To spark profit action through planned motivational techniques.	"Management Theatrics"
	To profitably utilize abilities and thought patterns that complement my own.	
To keep my own and my people's job interest high.	To achieve maximum job competence and job satisfaction through planned diversification.	"Job Variety" "Sink-or-swimsmanship"
	To expand the skills of myself and my people.	
	To make an organized search and discovery of hidden talent among my people.	

YOUR MAIN GOAL	ACTIONS TO FURTHER	TECHNIQUES
To make the most profitable use of my own time and my people's time.	To pinpoint and eliminate time waste factors. To plan my working day efficiently. To learn when and how to turn down a project. To build an inventory of problem-solving short-cuts.	Mental "Shorthand" Techniques "Checklist of Unessentials" "Constructive Ball Passing Technique"
Become a master at initiating, and adjusting to, change.	To learn how to skillfully originate and put across a change. To sharpen my skill at squelching "hem-and-haw tactics. To learn how to keep ideas alive.	"No-man Throttlers" "Mental Outlining" Idea Brainstorming
To pinpoint and develop the true profit makers.	To learn how to spot the characteristics that mark the real contributor. To sharpen my skill at distinguishing between the natural leader and the appointed leader—and profitably blending the two. To "people-ize" my hiring and firing techniques.	"Chemical response-ability" "People-ized Talent Exploitation" "Response Factor Chart"

YOUR MAIN GOAL	ACTIONS TO FURTHER	TECHNIQUES
On-hand involvement and participation.	To learn how to quickly spot and stop a "man-slide."	"Quick Alert Technique" "Why-man Probe"
	To cash in on my mistakes, and help my people do the same.	
	To set realistic goals, and swiftly pinpoint goals that are unrealistic.	
	To maintain an effective running appraisal of my own progress and my people's progress.	
To become a master salesman.	To apply tested selling techniques to win cooperation, achieve goals, motivate people.	"Enthusiasm Feedback and Chain Stimulation" "Magic No. 7" Selling Technique "Topdogsmanship"
	To continuously come up with new ideas to generate interest and build excitement.	
	To learn how to whittle objections down to size.	
To develop a reputation as a problem-solving "whiz."	To "sherlock" for trouble, and track it down on a day-to-day basis.	"Constructive Meddling" "Prospecting Techniques" "Trouble Shooter's Checklist" "Leading Lines"
	To spot and plug profit leaks before they become significant.	
	To train my people to become expert trouble shooters.	

YOUR MAIN GOAL	ACTIONS TO FURTHER	TECHNIQUES
To convert profit thinking into profit action.	To eliminate "noise" when I write, talk or listen.	"Audience Pulse-taking"
	To learn how to size up a speaker and "listen between the lines."	"Shorthand Thought Transmission"
	To track down profit opportunities in my daily mail.	"Firing Line Test" for company literature
	To heighten the effectiveness of meetings by spicing them with variety.	
To stand out from the others as a supermanager.	To remove the "im" from impossible when it is practical to do so through techniques encompassing swift action, efficient organization, applied motivation.	"Yes Determination" "Action Thrust Technique"
	To learn when to refuse to take "No" for an answer.	
	To learn how to recognize when a goal is truly impossible.	
To make management savvy a way of life.	To make my personal life an asset to my business life—and vice versa.	"Image Building Blocks"
	To take advantage of my wife's career-building abilities to her advantage and mine.	Career growth pitfalls: "Scale Tipping," "Back Seat Management"
	To build a reputation for service and contribution in the community as well as the shop.	
	To develop generalist skills on and off the job.	

Now, suppose you succeed in accomplishing all these goals—in becoming a savvy manager—what then? What's in it for you?

Absolute security, for one thing.

Assured career growth, for another.

Security plus growth. It's a tough combination to beat.

Here's a fact of business life. The manager with savvy doesn't have to scrounge and struggle to ferret out career opportunities. That's where the security and growth come in. The opportunities seek him out.

Business Week puts it this way: "The biggest demand now is for men with overall management ability, even in a specialized industry . . . 'Companies consider managerial skills over any specialty today,' says James A. Clark, consultant to the oil industry."

What the man is talking about is management savvy.

It's rare. It's precious. It's in demand today like it has never been in demand before. *Management savvy!* The man who acquires it is headed no place but *UP*.

Who is that man going to be?

You?

Why not?

Your Turn

At this point you have a rough idea of what management savvy is all about. You can see how all-encompassing it is, how it touches upon any and all aspects of your job, how it even goes beyond your job.

Thus far we have dealt with highlights only. Fine. All we're doing at this juncture is to give you a feel for the subject, create a savvy-oriented atmosphere, so to speak. Don't worry about the details and refinements. The diamond will be well-polished in chapters to come. Osmosis. Remember?

All right, now for some self-involvement. Take a pencil and paper. Get into a comfortable thinking position, and make a list of all the ingredients you can dream up which go into management savvy as you understand it at this point. Do it now, before you read on. The exercise will do you good. It will entrench the ingredients of savvy more solidly in your mind. It will help the osmosis to work.

All done? Good. Now we will check your rundown against the

one that follows. This will further reinforce the ingredients of management savvy in your mind, strengthen your feel for it.

Management savvy is:

- Knowing you are never too old or too smart to learn.
- Being constantly on the alert for new approaches, new ideas, new techniques.
- Knowing how to motivate—rather than force—top performance from your people.
- Continuously searching for problems to solve; not waiting around for others to bring them to your attention.

Management savvy is:

- Giving your people full credit and recognition for their contributions and achievements.
- Being unshakably convinced that your company, its people and products are the greatest, and doing your utmost to convince others of this conviction.
- Deftly nailing down abstract ideas and relating them profitably to the specifics of your job.
- Wading with gusto into challenging problems and projects; matching the toughness of your "can-do" determination to the toughness of the task at hand.

Management savvy is:

- Focusing on "What's next?" after you've done a superior job, instead of waving flags in front of the boss to show him how good you are.
- Doubling up on your personal profit performance by deriving multiple benefits from your key management actions. (Make a special note of this powerful management technique, and put it at the top of your list. You'll find numerous examples of how the "Multiple Value Concept" pays off woven throughout the entire book.)
- Realizing that the best way to develop profit growth is to develop your people into highly qualified profit contributors.
- Realizing that your personal profit and progress growth is tied directly and unmistakably to the contribution you make to your company's profit and progress growth.

Management savvy is:

- Using on-hand observation techniques to gauge your personal progress, your people's progress, and the realism of profit goals.
- Translating thoughts quickly and effectively into profit action through the sharpening of "noise-free" writing, speaking, and listening techniques.
- Using daring and imagination to spark job interest and enthusiasm.
- Searching endlessly for the hidden talents that lie latent in all of us, and putting the best capabilities of your people to the most profitable use in your company.

Management savvy is:

- Regarding the word "impossible" as a double-barreled challenge to succeed.
- Applying savvy techniques to manage your life to the best advantage of your company, your family, your community, *both on and off the job*—and knowing that when this is done it must inevitably work to *your own* best advantage as well.

You're on your way

"Management savvy," says the board chairman of a large power company, "is nothing more than experience with the 'won't work' elements filtered out."

We're ready now to delve into the nuts-and-bolts specifics of "will work" management savvy in action. And launching pad number one is geared to make you more reliant on yourself, less reliant on the boss.

It is all spelled out in the next chapter: *How to Stay a Giant Step Ahead of the Boss.*

Interested?

Fine. It's time to get strapped in—and to blast off!

2

How to Stay a Giant Step Ahead

of the Boss

Pick a working day. A manager spends eight hours on the job. If he's a genuine savvy manager, this represents *eight hours of profitable performance.*

Now, suppose on this same day an assistant takes an hour of the manager's time on a problem, which, with a little initiative, he might have licked on his own. What does this mean to the manager? Doesn't it cut his profitable performance span from eight hours to seven? Doesn't it, in a sense, rob the manager—and the company—of one hour of valuable time? And can you think of anything *more* valuable than time?

The point is this: The more problems, decisions, and actions you can accomplish on your own, the less time your boss will have to spend helping you accomplish them and the more valuable *you* will be to your boss and your company.

Simple? Sure. But how easily overlooked.

Want to build your savvy rating? Here's one powerful way to do it. *Resolve to take off on your own, more often, and with more determination.*

The easy way—and admittedly, at times, the *only* way—to lick a problem, is to run to the boss. But the way to *become* "the boss" is to tackle problems and solve them on your own.

The self-starter in action

Kicking the Door Open

It happened about a year ago: I get a call from the lobby; a visitor to see me. Names aren't important. We will call him Sam Miller from XYZ Company. Something about a materials handling system I can't afford to miss. Am I interested?

Sam Miller. The name rings a bell. Letters, phone calls. Requests for an appointment. Yes. I'm interested. Only problem is I have at least 25 more pressing matters on my mind and on my schedule. Isn't this always the case? All right then, Miller wants to know, could I spare him just 30 minutes of my time?

The man flew 200 miles to see me. How can I refuse? I agree to the 30 minutes, knowing it could be an hour or two. Or three. Or four. The moment I spotted Miller, there was something about him I liked. His appearance, the way he carried himself, the taste he displayed in his manner and dress. First impression, true, but he built on the impression as he went along. The chemistry between us began to percolate. He had a way of talking profits, relating them to our operation. Profits. My number one responsibility. How could he miss? He couldn't miss. He didn't miss.

Tactfully, he edged into a discussion of his equipment, relating his product to our system. And I can tell you this. He knew his product. And he knew our system.

Thirty minutes passed. Miller drew pictures as he spoke. Word pictures. I could almost visualize his equipment handling our products. An hour passed. Two hours. So what? "This equipment will pay for itself in one year." He backed his claim with proof. With profit results. I had questions. He had answers. I had reservations. He had convictions. Strong answers. Positive convictions.

Well now. We were long into the discussion, and I was hooked. It would mean revamping our old established system, I pointed out. He nodded. Well now. The moment of decision. "What would we have to do to get this project off the ground?"

No hesitation. No delay. Miller was waiting for this moment, and he was ready. He started to outline a plan, step by step.

Break! Suppose we pause right there to get our bearings. What are we talking about? Self-starting in action. Let's review what happened, and see how the self-starting ties in.

One: I'm stingy with minutes, a hard man to see at times. This didn't faze Miller. He is pure-bred self-starter all the way. Letters didn't work, phone calls didn't work; he came down to see me personally. The non-starter or slow-starter wouldn't have done this. He'd have reported to his boss a long time ago that Levinson couldn't be reached. But Miller made it his business, *on his own,* to get the audience he required to fulfill his goal. And he got it.

Two: Getting the audience wasn't enough. Miller knew he had to *hold* the audience. And he did. He invested time and effort in learning our system upside down and backwards. He took time to learn about me and find out what would make me respond. *And he did it on his own.* No one had to hold his hand and say, do this, or do that.

Three: Two businessmen in a room with a money-making idea bouncing around between them. How would a slow starter react? "Hmmm," he'd say, "let me mull this over a week or two," and the "week or two" would drag into five or six. He'd get nine associates in on the act, and five committees. By the time they got finished beating the idea to death, the excitement would be sapped out of it.

The proper approach: "Here's what we have to do to get this thing off the ground." Movement! Action! Do you get the distinction? The self-starter pounces on a profit opportunity like a frisky kitten on a spool of yarn. He multiplies enthusiasm. He makes things hum. *This does not mean he acts rashly or is foolishly impulsive.* But when it's time to convert profit thinking into profit action, he does so. His philosophy is, "Let's go!" instead of, "Well, maybe."

I think it was Emerson who said: "In every work of genius we recognize our own rejected thoughts: they come back to us with a certain alienated majesty."

The point is this. If *you* don't go with the idea, someone else will.

Running with the Ball

The other week I threw Fred, one of our self-starters in the plant, a short lateral pass. The idea: to put price tags on our materials and supplies. If people see what the items cost, they may be more careful. Fred thought about the idea, and liked it.

All right, Mr. Would-be Savvy Manager. How would an ambitious self-starter respond to such an idea from his boss? In short, *what, exactly, was that ball I passed to Fred?* Think it over, and answer in your mind.

Time's up. If your answer is, "Getting the price tags on those supplies," your answer is wrong.

The right answer is *"cost reduction."* What plagued me at the moment was finding new ways to chop costs. Here's a priceless tip: This is *always* plaguing the boss! And self-starter Fred was quick to respond.

A couple of hours later he came to see me. *On his own!* "Bob," he said, "I've been thinking about all the different tools and materials we use." He dumped some stuff on my desk: a drill, a tap, emery cloth. "In working with those price tags, I got to wondering. How much would this stuff cost if we bought it at the local hardware store? So I sent Eddie down to check."

Fred picked up the drill. "We pay a buck-fifty for this. Eddie bought one for 90 cents. The emery cloth costs us 30 cents for a big piece, 20 cents for a split piece. It takes three splits to make one big piece. If we buy all big pieces and tear them into splits ourselves, we'll be way ahead of the game. On the tap, the price is right, but we're buying twice the quality we need. We're working with specs that are 12 years old."

That was enough for me. I picked up the phone and called Purchasing. Before long a control system was set up so that in the future reviews of this kind would be automatic.

QUESTION: What's the point to all this? What does it all add up to? For one thing, thousands of dollars saved. For another, increased confidence in Fred's judgment and initiative. Plus a new respect for company assets on the part of the crew.

Here's another worthwhile point. Fred scored in "his own backyard" so to speak. He used the resources available to him on a day-to-day basis: the tools of his job, the ingenuity of his mind.

Alson J. Smith lays special stress on this in his book, *Live All Your Life.* "The little fellow didn't have much," he writes, "while the big fellow seemed to have everything. He was heavier, taller, and had the latest and best equipment. Moreover, he was the champion.

"The little fellow didn't have much, but he did have something.

A stone. He picked it up, did the best he could with it, and two minutes later there was a new champ. The biblical story of David and Goliath is the very best possible illustration of what can happen when, instead of wailing about lacks and handicaps, we take whatever is at hand and put it to work."

It makes good solid sense. David was a self-starter. He picked up a stone. Fred was a self-starter. He picked up some tools. What about *you?*

The agitator method

Here's a premise to mull over. Half your job as a manager consists of developing yourself; the other half consists of developing your people. This task will be a great deal easier if you use the "ditto" approach—whatever *your* general aspirations, ditto for your people.

You're determined to become a high-powered self-starter. Make the same determination for your people. Simple? Not so simple. You have to work at it. But remember this: *To a large degree your reputation will mirror the progress of your people.* Build your people tall, and you yourself will tower.

Now, back to the nuts and bolts. How can you motivate and spark self-starting profit performance on the part of your people? There's a one-word answer. *Agitate!* It's one of the most powerful words in the savvy manager's lexicon.

Keep Stirring the Pot

ON-SCENE OBSERVATION. It's time to get on scene. Our objective is to get right into a savvy manager's mind, to observe him in action.

At the moment he is leafing through a plant magazine. No, not just "leafing," but *prospecting!* He's prospecting, and he is about to agitate. He turns one page, another page, another . . . Suddenly—contact! His eyes spot a product, a tan spray that makes used cartons reusable.

Profit *opportunity.* Immediately the wheels start spinning. He makes pictures in his mind, pictures of how the warehouse operation is now, pictures of how it might be with this new spraying system added. He asks himself, "How much could we save?" It's the savvy manager's perennial question.

He takes the magazine. He takes a walk to the warehouse. The warehouse supervisor is going over some papers. "Pete," the manager says, "you get this magazine. Have you seen this ad?"

Pete looks at the ad. "No, I just skimmed past it," he admits.

"Well, what do you think?" Pete takes another look at the ad, a better look. Suddenly, what had struck the manager at once, starts to dawn on him. "Hey," he says, "we could. . . ."

Pete's interest mounts. He starts embellishing, elaborating, adding his own ideas to the manager's. The ideas multiply. After all, he's the man with the real on-hand know-how about the operation. He's the one who lives with it on a day-to-day basis. "You know," he raves, "this is great. This is just what we need." Interest lights his face. His mind is running on all cylinders.

At this point the savvy manager bows out. His job is done. The pot has been stirred.

Now for that point we referred to earlier: the *"Multiple Value"* concept. You're going to hear a lot about this. And here's a perfect illustration of it. *One single pot-stirring action—but look at all the gains derived:* (1) Warehousing cost reduction, (2) The company buys magazine subscriptions for key people. This action will encourage Pete to use his subscription more creatively and profitably. It stands to reason. Everyone wants to keep a step ahead of the boss. (3) Pete was being trained by this action to think and plan on his own. By exposing Pete to self-starting techniques, Pete will learn to become a self-starter himself, and in time, hopefully, he will transfer this skill to others.

A single seed. A triple harvest. Get the idea?

Steer Your People into New Areas of Thought

Sometimes agitation means leading your subordinates into new ideas of problem solving.

Recently I entered one of the shop offices. A meeting was in progress, with several production supervisors and one production manager. The problem at hand was to fit a special government job into our already too-crowded schedule. I listened in a few minutes to get the drift of the conversation. Then I chimed in: "Since this job involves a large quantity of the same items, maybe it would be smart to run it on a series of Saturdays, or even Sundays."

The words sunk in gradually. No one had even considered this idea because of the overtime premium pay. But now the thought struck home. It excited interest. Here was a new approach that hadn't even been considered.

Moments later I left the meeting, my purpose achieved. Now it was up to the production manager to follow through.

The manager immediately started to put the figures together. He checked with Accounting. After a period of study it was determined that the job could flow through the plant faster and more efficiently on weekends, in spite of the extra labor costs. The increase would be more than compensated for by other considerations.

Nothing earth-shattering about this. But it's the old story. It shows what happens when you agitate, throw in ideas, keep the pot boiling. Your actions, brief, timely, and to the point, can lead to the better training and development of your key people—and yourself.

Train 'em and Trust 'em

"You cannot help men permanently," William Boetcker once said, "by doing for them what they could and should do for themselves."

Chet is a young manager-in-training, a recent addition to our traffic department. He's ambitious, intelligent, hard-working. But there's one problem. He's too much accustomed to having the boss think and act on his behalf. We talked about pitfalls that serve to throttle savvy rather than promote it. Well, this is one that ranks high up on the list.

A man needs a chance to think and act on his own. Lacking it, he's likely to become a leaner instead of a stander, a no-starter instead of a self-starter.

One day, "prospecting" as usual, I clipped an ad from a trade journal. The product was a canvas balloon used as a wedge in the packing of freight cars. In the past we used dunnage blocks for the purpose, pieces of wood cut to size and inserted between cartons and crates to keep them from shifting in transit. There was a good deal of labor to this method, cutting up two-by-fours, stocking the lumber, etc.

What this ad proposed was to use the canvas balloons instead, insert them in place, then blow them up to size. The idea looked promising. Handing the ad to Chet, I asked him to look into it. A couple of days later he called me on the phone. "That salesman you wanted to see about the dunnage balloons is here," he said, "should I send him in?"

"Not a chance," I countered. "It's your baby. You see him. Study his product. Check out the costs. Discuss it with Production. If you think we can save money on this, let me know, and we'll place an order." Then I hung up.

Do you see what I'm driving at? It's just another every-day routine incident. But take a second look and you'll see that it's a form of "agitation."

You've observed it yourself. Some people require a gentle push now and then to impel them to act on their own initiative. It varies from person to person. You may take one man and push him all his life, and he still remains a leaner. You push another man once, three times, five times, and *then, all of a sudden, you realize that you don't have to push him any more.* You've developed a self-starter. If you've never experienced it yourself, I can tell you this. It is one of the great gratifications of management.

Joe's Idea

It finally happened. Two months ago Joe, one of our office employees, presented an idea to his boss. For Joe this was something of an event.

The idea, or more correctly, the *germ* of an idea involved our accounts payable procedure. It wasn't much, but for Joe it was a beginning. The trick was to inspire Joe to produce more of the same in the future.

Now, we're talking about developing self-starters, motivating initiative. Here was a fine opportunity to put all the preaching into practice. This, incidentally, is a vital part of management savvy—*the ability to spot a development opportunity such as this one*. The question is, where do we go from here? No problem. The direction is clear.

"There's some good sound thinking here," Joe's boss said. "Let me give the idea some further thought. Maybe we can develop it into something worthwhile."

Joe beamed. He was obviously flattered. Step two. Remember, we're building and developing Joe. Joe's boss sat down with the idea and worked it over. What evolved was a far cry from Joe's suggestion, but using the original idea as a launching pad, he was able to come up with *something*, a way to save us money.

The boss sat down with Joe and reviewed his findings. At one point there was a small decision to make. "It's *your* idea," the boss said. "Whatever you think." By this time Joe was half convinced. Of course, the boss had one strong plus working in his favor. Joe *wanted* to be convinced. Everybody wants to be convinced about how good he is.

When the refinements were all worked out the boss started talking up "Joe's idea" all over the shop. Needless to say, Joe was delighted.

The point is this: The savvy manager doesn't require polished ideas to trigger improvements. *All he needs are thought starters.* To convince Joe of this took some doing. As yet he is not exactly what you would classify as a top "idea-man." But he's getting there. Two suggestions last month, entirely on his own. That's exactly 200 per cent more than the entire previous year.

Recognition! Inscribe that word in bold print on your management savvy list. Then underscore it. Recognition will turn the trick every time. "They that value not praise," Thomas Fuller once said, "will never do anything worthy of praise."

It is a rare individual who does not welcome, even long for, recognition. You may have heard the story of the well-known artist who was admiring a famous Sargent picture in a New York gallery. Next to him, a husky fellow was admiring the same picture.

"They've given me a good place at last," the husky murmured.

The artist eyed him narrowly. "This picture happens to have been painted by Sargent," he said in a cold tone.

"Who's talking about the painting!" the man said haughtily, "I was referring to the frame. It's mine. Ain't she a beaut?"

"It's mine!" Recognition. Show me the man who doesn't want it.

As long as I live, I'll never forget the period in my life when, as a youngster, I had decided to become the world's foremost magazine salesman. It was an all-out effort, and it paid off in a myriad of prizes ranging from skates to a bike.

But the biggest prize of all was the one awarded by my mother.

Thinking back, I feel that her field should have been management development. She heaped on that recognition like a pro. When she described my achievements in the "publishing field" with glowing pride to neighbors and friends it was worth all the bikes in the world. Recognition can take many forms. Money, prizes, and the like is only one. Recognition can be a hand shake or a nod of the head. Or seeds of tribute and praise sown down the line. My mother taught me a valuable lesson when I was a child. Recognition is the most powerful management development—and *savvy development*—tool in your kit. It's a lesson I never forgot.

Make your middle name "Profits"

A stockholder makes an investment. What does he have in mind? The chairman makes a decision. What is he gunning for? What is foremost in the thoughts of the chief executive, the directors, the top officers of the company? That's right, you guessed it.

The name of the game is profits!

The 100-proof savvy manager never forgets this fact of business life. Instead, *he aggressively remembers!* How? One method has proved extremely helpful to me.

A manager usually has, depending on where he lives, from 15 to 40 minutes of traveling time getting to work in the morning, coming home from work in the evening. It makes no difference if he drives a car, takes a bus, or rides the subway. He has this time to be alone with himself. He has this time to ask: "What can I do to improve my operation?"

These are good times of the day—at least I find it so from my experience—to indulge in some honest self-appraisal with the profit objective in mind. It's a time to evaluate what has been done, what is being done, what *should be* done to make things better, smoother, more efficient.

One management expert states the case in this way: "If you have nothing else to do, look about you and see if there isn't something close at hand that you can improve! It may make you wealthy, though it is more likely that it will make you happy."

Happy or wealthy. Either way, how can you lose?

I like to think of this morning and evening time as my special question-and-answer periods. Strictly solo. I ask the questions. I give the answers. What develops is a plan—a *savvy* plan, I like to believe—for profit improvement.

Questions? What kind of questions?

Any kind of questions on *any* aspect of the job. The priorities will come to you automatically as the questions pass in review in your mind. Eventually you'll decide, "today is going to be my Order Department day." Or, "this will be my day to attack maintenance costs." Whatever you decide, it will be your day to improve *something*.

Another useful tactic is to review in your mind decisions that you made during the day. Relive the action that took place and explore other decisions that might have been made. Re-enact situations and re-evaluate the reactions and judgments of the people involved. By restaging and role-playing actual situations in your mind, you will sharpen your savvy experience and your savvy awareness.

Getting Down to Specifics

Here's an indisputable fact. Neither I, nor anyone else, can tell you what questions to ask yourself. Because nobody knows your job as well as you know it. But thinking of my company I can give you a rundown of the kind of questions a savvy manager at Steelcraft might ask:

- What can I do to relieve that bottleneck in the Receiving Department?
- Are we taking full advantage of the various telephone services most economically suited to our special operation?
- What can we substitute in Assembly Unit 175B that would do the same job for less money?
- What can be done to simplify the filing system in the general office?
- How can I cut down the amount of scrap in Department 6?
- How can I speed the flow of orders going to the Shipping Department? (Where have you heard that one before?)
- What can I do to spark increased interest in our exhibit in the forthcoming trade show?

- What new motivational technique can I dream up to trigger fresh enthusiasm on the part of the sales force?

Once you ask a question, what then? This is the way it works for me. Here is one question I actually asked a few weeks ago. I'm purposely picking a tough one to give you a better picture. "How can I cut down on the time of long distance phone calls?"

I asked myself this question one day on the way home. And I searched my mind for an answer. It didn't come. Sometimes you ask a question and the solution bounces right back at you. Other times you have to go back to the shop. You investigate. And still no answer. But that doesn't mean the question is gone. What happens is that it hangs around your subconscious. It waits for a signal to shoot back to the surface.

A few days later I was thumbing through a magazine, and up popped the telephone question again. What touched it off was a story about a company that used a three-minute egg timer on employee's desks to keep the calls trimmed down to size. Hmmm. It was an answer. I kicked it around my mind for a while. Then I rejected it. Not for us.

The following week another item came to my attention and the question was back again. This one called for keeping a small time clock at the switchboard, stamp people in and out when they start and finish a call, and set up a record that way. Another answer. More thought. Another rejection.

Today the question has surfaced again. The telephone company, I've been told, has some kind of deal whereby long distance callers are assigned individual numbers. At month-end a listing spells out just who made what calls, pinpointing the source of the high toll costs. I don't know. This may prove to be the answer for us. Maybe not. It's still under consideration. But the point is this: *A question, once asked by a savvy manager, stays alive until it is answered.*

Now You

The thought of profit-appraising your job to and from work may appeal to you or not. In any case, *when* you ask the questions isn't important. It's the *asking* that counts. I have found— and any top consultant will back me up—that *the probing ques-*

tion to the self-starter is like a wrench to the plumber. It's like turning the key in the ignition. It's the quickest way to get going.

Now let's give that key a twist. Get yourself a pencil and pad. Now, step one. Start thinking about your company. Focus on trouble spots, bottlenecks. Where are the most delays? The most complaints? The most irritation and dissatisfaction?

First, identify profit roadblocks. Then gear your questions to ram right through them. Jot down each question as it comes to mind. Think in pictures. Think systems. Think materials. Think people. Frame a question, if you can, about every part of your operation that doesn't fully satisfy you in every way.

Now rate the questions in their order of importance. Where is the need for improvement most urgent? When the top priority question is singled out, pencil in a big fat asterisk alongside it. Give this one your attention tomorrow, or sooner. And keep the others in reserve. *Resolve not to let a single day go by without taking special action in some key area of profit improvement.*

What's in it for you? Once your boss gets wind of this new approach, you'll find out soon enough. Inevitably there will be only one possible conclusion that he could draw: *That you are a 100 per cent super-charged self-starter!* Your reputation will be made, your future assured.

And you will rest secure in the knowledge that you are managing to stay a giant step ahead of the boss.

What makes your engine conk out?

The head of an oil company was once asked, "What reason, more than any other, keeps employees from advancing in their jobs?" His answer: "The inability to get going without the boss' help."

What produces this inability? That's what we're interested in. We've talked about roadblocks. Let's identify a few. Let's pinpoint some of the pitfalls most likely to keep you and your people from wading into projects and triggering actions on your own initiative.

Following are six of the most common pitfalls. Study them carefully. Then make an honest "Me too?" analysis to spot for shoes that fit.

Self-starting roadblocks

• *Lack of training.* Think of projects you should be moving ahead on, but are not moving ahead on. Then ask of each task: "Do I *know* enough about this subject to go ahead with it?" If the answer in any case is "No " concentrate your self-starting effort on registering for that course, reading that book, boosting your knowledge.

• *Failure to analyze fully.* Ever watch a person trying to solve a problem without being fully acquainted with the facts? It's usually a sorry sight. The truly savvy manager squints into every nook and cranny. He explores in depth. He works with the guy in the plant, sits down with the gal at her desk. He *finds out.* The failure to analyze in depth will confine you to the ranks of bum starter or no-starter.

• *Lack of profit awareness.* Picture a football game. Ten men devote their total energy to scoring a touchdown. Number 11 is determined to get the batter out at home plate. Is somebody balmy? No question about it. Obviously Number 11 doesn't know the name of the game. The manager who loses sight of the importance of profits is in precisely the same position. He'll be thinking balls and strikes while the quarterback is calling signals.

• *The waiting game.* A bad habit to get into. The manager who plays this game is usually a person who for years has been stifled by a boss who did little to fuel his self-starting inclinations. The victim of such supervision is so accustomed to having his decisions made for him, his starts sparked by the boss, that he has come to believe that this is the only way to operate. This is a good issue to square up to without flinching. If you, or any of your people, have fallen into the habit of waiting for a push from the boss before tackling that problem or project, it's time for a change.

• *Fear of idea rejection.* This fear, though widespread, is usually unfounded. Speaking on the subject, a utility's board chairman put it this way: "In business today, coming up with a good idea is a big feather in your cap; coming up with no ideas is no feather in your cap." Here's the point: ideas are so urgently needed today, you'll get an "A" just for suggesting them.

• *Belief that the job is too tough.* This belief is valid only if it stems from lack of training or the failure to analyze fully. Have the confidence to do the job. More often, there is only one sure way to dispel this belief, and that's by taking that all-important *first step.* Then watch those apprehensions dissolve.

Staying ahead of the boss—summary roundup

1. Resolve to take off on your own more often. Go to the boss for help when you have to, but only after you have exhausted all possibilities of solving the problem by yourself.

2. Be constructively aggressive. *This does not mean pushy!* But resolve to double your pioneering initiative during the next six months—without treading on the next fellow's toes or violating your range of authority. The trick is to test your boss from time to time. See how far he'll permit you to proceed into new areas without stepping in to curb your actions. Most bosses welcome pioneering initiative on the part of their subordinates. But you will never find out if you don't venture forth.

3. The best way to destroy an idea is via the route of negation. The self-starter does not express a blah reaction to ideas—even those he is not totally sold on at the start. He injects enthusiasm into ideas to keep them alive. He does not permit idea foundations to crumble. Instead, he helps to reinforce them with a positive, profit-directed attitude. Then, he helps to build on the foundation by instigating forward action and movement.

4. Inspire and motivate self-starting profit performance on the part of your people. One good way to do this is to keep constantly aware of their expectations and desires. How can you determine this? The answer is simple. What do *you* wish for and hope for yourself? Chances are that their desires and aspirations, though more limited in degree, are not much different from your desires and aspirations. After all, they are people, too.

5. Self-starters don't simply materialize. As a savvy manager, you *cause them to be developed.* The strategy is to analyze all of your subordinates on an individual basis. Some people, you'll find, need a gentle push now and then to set them into motion. Others propel themselves more readily. Your responsibility as a savvy manager is threefold: First, *train 'em.* Then, *trust 'em.* Finally, prove to them that you trust them by giving them the impetus

and the faith to act on their own. Don't rely on *their* initiative for this. Your job is to imbue them with *your* initiative.

6. Ideas are more precious than pure white gold. The novice subordinate who never tried his wings doesn't appreciate this yet. The super-sensitive subordinate is probably too reticent to think about it. The subordinate whose thought wheels have grown rusty may have known this once, but has long since stopped thinking about it. All of these people lack the confidence to really dig in and mine those precious pure white gold ideas. But the savvy manager is skilled at making first rate "mining engineers" of all his people. He makes a "big deal" out of every idea proposed. He helps his people to convert small ideas into big money savers. Most important, he spells Recognition with a capital "R," and heaps it on his subordinates "R"egularly.

7. Practice "dollar diplomacy" to the hilt. Make no bones about it. The savvy manager not only knows that the name of the game is PROFITS—he's an expert at playing the game as well. He tracks down profit opportunities *on his own*—without needing to be prodded by the boss. And he trains his people to respond in the same way.

8. Don't let your moments of think time trickle down the drain. Every hour of every day contains 60 minutes worth of potentially profitable think time. Don't disconnect your mental apparatus when you leave the office or plant. Stay alert to profit-building ideas on a round-the-clock basis. Cash in on all the potentially productive time at your disposal—traveling to and from work, sitting in the barber's chair, waiting for the dentist, walking through your plant or in the street. Any time, and all the time.

9. Adopt a constantly questioning attitude towards your job and towards life in general. Analyze all operations within your province that give you less than absolute satisfaction. Resolve to find out all of the why's, where's, when's, how's, what's and who's. If you get in the habit of posing the right questions, you'll be sure to come up with the right savvy answers. Remember, a question asked by a savvy manager remains alive until it is answered.

10. Stay alert to self-starting roadblocks in your department. Search your mind regarding each individual under your supervision. Ask yourself: Is he being fully and properly trained? Does he get all the facts he needs to do his job? Does he use them effectively? Might a gentle nudge from you set him off into profitable motion? Does he fail to come up with ideas because he fears rejection from you? Does he lack the vital confidence which a little help and encouragement on your part could provide?

Almost every self-starter was a slow starter until a savvy superior happened along to inject the super-octane fuel which helped to power his engine into an independently operating unit.

3

Be the Man They Come to

for Help or Advice

Take any company, any city, any state. How do you pinpoint the manager with savvy? Simple. He's the one they run to when trouble strikes, when the problem becomes too thorny for the ordinary guy to handle. When you encounter such a man you can be sure of two things: he's a manager who commands top respect, and he's a man on his way up.

I run into firing line proof of this every day in the office and in the plant. In my view, the fellow who wins the Most Valuable Employee award is the one you can step up to and say: "Jim, here's a problem. Handle it." "Bill, sales and production can't agree on this issue. What do you think we should do?" "Fred, the supplier says he can't deliver. Please straighten it out."

It's a fact of business life: The man who means the most, climbs the most, and earns the most in any organization is the manager who can cope single-handedly with his own responsibilities and help others to cope with theirs. Fireman. Counselor. Problem-solver. He's the man they come to for help and advice.

In short, he's the manager with knowhow!

Knowhow! It's the heart and guts of management savvy. Are you gunning for a $50,000 job? Then knowhow is a $50,000 word.

And the $50,000 question is: Where does it come from? How do you get it?

Mostly from *wanting* it. Knowing what it means to you and wanting it. Not half-heartedly. Not wishfully. But *hard*. Drivingly, greedily, compulsively hard. Wanting to learn. Wanting to become a better manager. And wanting, once you become a better manager, to become even better than that.

Here's another fact. Desiring knowledge, of itself, implies humility. It implies the realization that you're never too old to learn, never too mature, never too smart. It implies that you're man enough to look yourself over critically and objectively and admit to yourself that no matter how great you think you are there is still room for improvement.

You know, there is no better way to make satisfying progress than to be dissatisfied with the progress you've made. If you are content, if you think you know it all and have no faults, then that is your biggest fault.

An old proverb says: "The first step to self-knowledge is self-distrust." The soundest answer to self-distrust is self-appraisal. And there's no better time than *right now* to start this process.

Your personal knowhow profile

Let's face a hard, unyielding fact. There's only one way to hoist your knowhow rating to the savvy manager class. That's through planned, positive, aggressive action. Step one is to construct your "Personal Knowhow Profile." Learn how you stand today. For this you will need three simple tools: a pad, a pencil, and your conscience. Now, here's what to do.

First, set down in writing a capsule summary of your strengths and weaknesses as they relate to your job and your company. The format you use is unimportant, so long as the following is covered. It may be difficult and even painful to make this list. But no one will see it but yourself, and what you reveal may be priceless in value.

YOUR STRENGTHS (LIST ON SHEET NUMBER ONE)

1. The tasks and responsibilities you enjoy most. (Almost invariably, these will be the ones you do best and know the most about.)

2. The problems and decisions most often brought to you for help and advice.
3. Your most significant profit contributions.
4. Any other talents or outstanding skills that come to mind, used or not.

YOUR WEAKNESSES (LIST ON SHEET NUMBER TWO)

1. Tasks you avoid or palm off because you dislike them, or because they're difficult or confusing to cope with.
2. Problems you most often need help with because you lack confidence in your ability to tackle them on your own.
3. Added responsibilities you could be taking over, but are not because of the mental acrobatics involved.
4. Tasks which take too long to complete, or cause you too much mental strain to complete.

Now, on another sheet of paper, list as many business functions as you can call to mind that you are indirectly involved with, but which do not fall under the direct scope of your responsibility. One by one, evaluate your understanding of these functions. On your "Strength" sheet number one enter those functions you understand thoroughly—not the minute details, but their purpose and their bearing on your company's profit goal. List the other functions, the fuzzy ones, on your "Weaknesses" sheet.

Once this is done your Profile is complete and your work cut out for you. The next step is to rate all of your strengths and all of your weaknesses in order of importance. This will hinge on the degree you are being advanced in your job progress by your understanding, or hindered by your lack of understanding.

Your goal is to fortify your strengths even further by refining your knowledge in each area. Dissatisfaction, remember? Don't settle with merely being an "expert." Resolve to be "expert number one." Resolve to make yours the first name that would come to mind if an associate, your boss, or the president of the company needed information or advice on the subject.

Regarding your weaknesses, the requirement is obvious. Tackle the most important one first, the one that is hurting you most. Take positive steps to change the impediment into an asset. Read up on the subject. Take an evening course. Get personal instruction from an authority on the subject. Find a person whom you respect and who has the quality you need, then study this person and try to copy him. Do whatever is necessary to barrel through that progress-defeating barricade of ignorance. The ultimate objective is to clear sheet number two and load sheet number one. When this is done you'll be most pleasantly surprised. You will be deriving an immeasurably greater amount of satisfaction from your work. You'll be a manager with real knowhow and real savvy.

You may even be president of your company. Why not?

Blast out of your cocoon

The truly savvy manager is both general and generalist. He commands his troops with wisdom, forcefulness, tempered judgment. He knows the business inside-out, upside-down and back-wards. He is a man who wears many hats.

What's your job? Engineer, accountant, production manager, personnel head? Well, here's a blunt fact. No matter how good you may be at your specialized calling, this will not make a savvy manager out of you. It may qualify you as a savvy engineer, or a savvy accountant—but not as a savvy *manager*. Not until you blast out of your cocoon and expand your scope.

Here's why. The savvy manager is just that. Part accountant, part production man, part engineer, part human relations expert, part diplomat, part everything. The strategy is clear. *Do anything and everything you can to break your accustomed, well-ordered, specialist-oriented routine.* And not on the job alone. Travel. Read. Contact a diversity of people. Line up a diversity of interests. Involve yourself in community affairs. Each additional role you play will help in some measure to broaden your know-how and outlook.

The objective always is to learn, to take an active part in all types of projects, to stock your mental storehouse, hungrily, greedily. "He who adds not to his learning," the Talmud says, "diminishes it." But *the way* you learn is vital; your *philosophy* of learning is all-important, because real learning—savvy-directed learning—like perpetual motion, is a never-ending process.

The idea is to expose yourself—*and your people*—to as many varied situations as possible.

Your People

There's a great need in business today for managers with growth flexibility.

Too often, as Paul Goodman stresses in *Growing Up Absurd,* an effort is made to make the man a little bit rounder to fit him more comfortably into the round slot that has been designed for him. In our company we take the reverse approach. We try, where possible, to fashion the job to the man, to bring his latent talents to the surface and shape his responsibilities accordingly. We do this by exposing our people to as many different tasks, functions and areas of the business as possible.

I have found that too many young fellows today, in applying for a job, or making their ambitions known, will tell you: "I want to be a product engineer," or, "My ambition is to become an advertising executive."

Too few will say: "I want to learn as much as I can about the business. I want to grow with the organization."

What we seek, and many other employers seek, is the man who wants to learn as much as he can wherever he can. He may wind up product engineer or advertising executive. But if we've done our job properly, he'll wind up a savvy manager, too.

How does it work? There's no better way to find out than by positioning yourself on the firing line. Sometime ago we hired a young fellow named Mike. Mike was intelligent and personable. He made a fine impression on us. But what was he good at? What could he do? This was the key question. His application and background gave us a general idea. But it didn't give us a real insight into the man. It didn't tell us how his mind worked, or what he was like inside. One learns that by observation, by evaluation and re-evaluation. *By analysis.*

So we started Mike off in Shipping. We switched him from one department to another. We watched him. We analyzed him. We found him hard-working and conscientious. Gradually we learned more. Mike possessed an inquisitive nature. He wasn't satisfied to just do a job, carry out a procedure. He wanted to know WHY. He wanted to know how it tied into the rest of the operation.

At one point he wound up in the Purchasing Department. One assigned task was to rubber stamp the word PAID on hundreds of invoices. Dull. Boring. Enough to put the average fellow to sleep. But not Mike. Mike was quick, alert. Before long he came to us with an idea.

"Why stamp each invoice individually?" he wanted to know. "Why not tie four rubber stamps together and stamp four invoices at a time?"

Get the picture? Do you see the profile of the man emerging? Systems talent. Savvy potential.

Now here's the point. Suppose, as happens in so many companies with so many managers—suppose Mike had been put in Shipping and left in Shipping? What would we have known about his systems talent and potential? Oh, it probably would have come to the surface eventually, with luck. But why depend on luck?

The savvy manager makes his own luck. *He develops himself and his people aggressively, according to a well-formed plan.* He exposes his people—and himself—to a variety of jobs, a variety of situations. He analyzes. He observes.

He uses the shelf to store reference books, not people.

Auditor's Query Technique

"If children did not ask questions," someone once said, "they would never learn how little adults know."

And if adults did not ask questions they would never find out what their children have already learned about how little they know.

Questions! Yes indeed. They are remarkable instruments of the mind. Ever watch a crackerjack auditor at work? His job is to check controls, track down discrepancies. And questions are the tools of his trade. They spotlight checkpoints to cover, areas to probe.

Let's make our purpose clear. Once again we're on the trail of management savvy shortcomings; the search is for weaknesses in need of shoring up. But keep in mind that the list which follows is by no means complete. It couldn't be because, in large measure, self-probe questions are a highly personalized and individualized matter. So the following list is intended as a starter only. The finishing is up to you. After working through these questions, the idea is to compose a supplementary list of your own.

Do this on a running basis on and off the job. When a question comes up about how to handle a person, solve a problem, make a decision, or whatever, jot it down. If you're not sure of the answer, check it with someone older, wiser, or more experienced than yourself. Like the auditor, you too will be "tracking down" shortcomings and discrepancies, in your operation, in your understanding, in your management philosophy. While you're doing it, here's a tip. *Don't be any easier on yourself than your boss will be when your name comes up for a promotion or salary boost.*

When you pinpoint a shortcoming in your make-up, flag it with a star or by underlining it. Then work at correcting the fault. And don't cross it off your list until you are positively certain that the savvy lapse has been plugged.

Okay, let's go. But remember, this is just a starter.

Questionnaire: Operation Soul Search

- When a subordinate comes to you with a suggestion, do you say: "Hey, that's a great idea; let's talk about it?" Or do you come up with a blah reaction that makes him regret having approached you? Do you enjoy giving credit to other people and do you make it your business to do so?
- When the boss hands you an assignment, do you carry it out in routine fashion; or do you make every effort to supplement his requirements with ideas of your own?
- After attending a fruitful meeting or seminar, or after reading a meaty magazine article or report, do you come right back and apply what you have learned to your company or department?
- Do you devote enough time to the problems of your people? Are you properly sympathetic? Do you offer guidance and help when it's needed? Do you make time to talk with your staff?
- Do you consciously try each and every day to improve some aspect of your company's operation?
- At this moment, are you holding up any decisions, projects, pieces of paper, that you know you should not be holding up?
- Do you ever fail to go along with another person's idea because of vanity, politics, jealousy, or for any other negative reason?

All right, from this point on, you're in charge. It is up to you to get that personal self-probe questionnaire into shape, to chop those shortcomings down to size.

One of the hardest realities for a man to face is that he is less than perfect. So, above all, be honest with yourself. Face up to your own faults, and concentrate on ways to eliminate them. It will take time, and it won't be easy. But I can guarantee this: it will be well worth your effort.

Be your own man

There's one thing I want to get across if I haven't already. I don't want anyone to get the idea that acquiring savvy is an automatic procedure, that you're going to get it by reading a book or by abiding by a set of rules. The rules may help, and the book will give you guidance and shortcut your trip. But in the end the savvy you acquire will be the product of X hours of experience, X number of experiments, X number of mistakes.

Do you see what I'm driving at? Without experience, without experiments, without mistakes, there can be no management savvy. "Teach yourself by your own mistakes," Faulkner said. "People learn only by error." And don't permit mistakes or failures to slow you down. Think of mistakes as stepping stones. As somebody once said, "There is only one true stumbling block to success. It's the one we hide under our hat."

How true! The men with the greatest amount of savvy and the leaders in their fields are the men who, armed with knowledge and training, are least afraid to try and try and try again.

The story is told of Thomas Edison that in his quest for a material for a filament he tried 50,000 different tests and failed 50,000 times. "Why do you go on?" an assistant asked. "Look at the results."

"The results!" Edison exclaimed. "The results have been wonderful. Look what we learned. We now know 50,000 things which won't work!"

Why experiment? The reason is clear. You never know. Experiment 50,001 could just be the one that pays off.

All right then, the point is this. The savvy manager, above all, is *his own man*. He's a pioneer, a thinker, an innovator. He is never a me-too manager, a rubber stamper, a play-it-safer.

You know, you will often find, in your journey through management, that it's easier and more comfortable to agree than to disagree. And by all means, you *should* agree when agreement is in order. But not because the other man is your boss, or talks louder, or is a better politician, or has seniority, or won't react too kindly to your disagreement. If you do agree it should be for one reason only. Because, *in your carefully considered judgment,* you feel that this is the right course of action to take.

The idea, in short, is to be natural. Be yourself. And encourage your people to be *themselves,* not carbon copies of you.

How can you achieve this goal? Here's a technique that we find helpful. Try to determine how it sits with you. Our plant, as you know, is in Cincinnati, and customers from all over the country come in for special training in the use, sale, and assembly of our products. When a customer visits our plant he usually wants to discuss his problems, air his views, talk about his operation, find out about our operation.

Most companies, to satisfy this need, would make some sales department ear available. We try to be different. We'll send a man out from Research, from the office, from Engineering, from Shipping, or from anywhere else. More often than not, we'll send a man who is normally nailed to his desk. And here's why:

First and foremost, in line with our objective to shape knowledgeable and well-honed individuals, we seize on the opportunity to get a man out of his shell, to broaden his perspective. We give him a chance to express himself, and we take note of his talent in this area. We expose him to fresh ideas, a fresh point of view, the other fellow's problems. We give him an on-the-scene chance to learn first-hand about the business.

Not only that, but when you put a desk man in charge of an important customer (and there's no other kind), it builds his ego and does wonders for his self-confidence. This is important to us. From the employee's standpoint, it's development with a capital "D." From the company's point of view, it's the old familiar theme, the one we're going to hammer away at in chapter after chapter.

Multiple Value! Double, triple, quadruple gains from a single profit action. What happens in this case? (1) We build savvy individualists. (2) We achieve much needed ego build-up. (3) We develop poise, personality, communicating skills. (4) We measure progress and uncover hidden abilities.

In short, when you boil it down, we just can't miss. And neither can you. So why not give it a try? Experiment. See how you fare.

Become a knowhow addict

Ever run across a man who said he didn't want to learn? Unlikely. Most people will swear that they want to learn and intend to learn. The only problem is, in the savvy-boosting struggle good intentions don't count for much. Neither does lip service.

What does count is aggressiveness. Go-out-and-get-it-ness. *Addiction,* if you will!

Ugly word? Not at all. Not if it's used wisely and positively. What applies to man, applies to manager. "I think; therefore, I am!" I learn; therefore I earn. And one thing is certain. You don't gain knowledge by waiting for it to happen. You have to *make* it happen. So, beginning today, make your quest for knowledge compulsive. *Become a knowhow addict!* Get yourself "hooked" to a promising future.

The following savvy-boosting techniques will serve as a starter.

The Plant Walkthrough

My brother, Charles Levinson, who is the president of our company, has a favorite saying: "Don't walk through life with your blinders on." In short, keep the input hoppers of your mind active and ready at all times to register and record facts, ideas, information.

Example: You work, let us assume, in the production department. Executive. Manager. Supervisor. It makes no difference. You walk through the plant four times, nine times, 20 times a day. Deliberately, to make sure everything's in order. Or as a matter of course on your way from one place to another.

Whatever the reason, this is a plant walkthrough. You pass people at work, machines in operation, materials in stock. Things are happening. For the savvy manager, the plant walkthrough is an educational experience. His eyes are alert, his profit wheels are spinning, his mind is active and prospecting for ideas. For the no-savvy manager it's a nothing experience. He roams the plant with blinders on.

Let me give you a small example of how useful and educational a plant walkthrough can be. And this is by no means an isolated example. It is one of many. A couple of weeks ago I walked through our plant with my blinders off, as I have trained myself to do. My eyes were peeled for profit ideas, signs of waste. My mental pad and pencil were poised and ready for note taking. Then suddenly, *poing! Spray cans.* The item struck my eye. The profit bell rang.

Spray cans. Twelve or 15 of them in the finishing department. The kind we supply as a service to customers. Cost, about 75 cents apiece. What were they doing here?

I soon found out. They were being used by the men for touch-up. Hmmm. That's what I'd been afraid of. Expensive touch-up. It's like an outfit that requires pots and pots of glue and goes to the dime store to buy small jars. At the moment I was in a hurry, just passing through. But the mental note was made: "Discuss with Production. Suggest using automatic sprayer or something else in place of the expensive cans."

Each day as I walk through the office and plant, I make it my business to observe people at work. I look for items out of place, for systems that are not working properly, for equipment that is not functioning as it should. I walk through the shop with a three-fold purpose in mind: (1) To spot problems, (2) to uncover problem causes, (3) to call both problems and causes to the attention of the individual best qualified to institute corrective action.

Get the idea? Eyes open, mind alert. Ferret out and exploit profit ideas. Make each plant walkthrough—or office walk-through, or warehouse walkthrough—the educational experience it should be. Keep those blinders off.

The Telephone Self-Audit

A chief stumbling block in the way of success is success itself. The moment a manager decides he is successful enough or smart enough to "rest on his laurels" he shifts into reverse. The choice is clear. You either plod forward, or you slide backwards. Savvy companies and savvy managers know this well. They're never satisfied. They never stop trailing perfection.

The story is told of the New York agency that dreamed up a famous ad for a famous car. It read: "At 60 m.p.h. the loudest noise in the new Rolls-Royce comes from the electric clock." With great pride an agency adman showed this creation to a visiting Rolls-Royce executive. Instead of elation, the executive displayed a worried frown. "We'll have to do something about that clock," he replied.

Amusing story. But it makes a potent point. Dissatisfaction. The savvy manager's constant quest for self-improvement.

I don't think you can go too far overboard on this business of self-criticism.

Example: Whenever we have a meeting with a customer or supplier, we make it our business to review and evaluate the session. It's strictly a negative review. We always ask ourselves: "What went wrong? What could have been improved?" We search our own minds. We invite criticism from the staff. We try our best to ferret out the minus factors. The strategy seems to work. From year to year we find fewer minus factors, fewer things that we are doing wrong. Admittedly, we are still a long, long way from perfection. But who knows? Maybe we are slowly getting there.

We've already discussed other techniques to help achieve our self-improvement goal. Here's one more. We call it the Telephone Self-Audit. It has helped us immensely. It may help you too.

The procedure is simple. It's merely a matter of tape recording your telephone conversation. (If you record the other fellow's too, you're supposed to let him know you're doing it, according to the phone company.) But the important thing to get down on tape is your own part of the dialogue. Do this, and if your case is typical, you will be amazed at the results.

One of our supervisors tried it just recently. "How did it work?" I asked him. The fellow winced. "Listening to the replay of the conversation, I could see how disjointed my thoughts were. I repeat myself constantly. My speech is laced with "ahs" and "uhs." Brother, do I need improvement. When I think that with some people the telephone-me is the only me they know, it makes me shudder."

Question: Why shudder? The telephone is a key communications medium. Recording your conversation at regular intervals will pinpoint your weaknesses and help sharpen your telephone technique. Chances are that the Telephone Self-Audit will be as revealing to you as it has been to many others. Give it a try.

Make Knowhow Your Ulterior Motive

Sound sneaky? It is. But you hurt no one. You help yourself.

Back to the firing line. The other day I flew to Pittsburgh. On the plane I met a professional economist. Fascinating man. I struck up a conversation with him on the subject of—what else?—economics. Well, you could call it a conversation, I suppose. Mostly, I listened. From time to time I dropped in a question.

Now this man had a fine personality, an interesting way of expressing himself. He was friendly, likable. All good reasons for conversing with him. But for me there was an overriding reason more important than the rest. *Knowhow!* I was talking economics with an economist. I was learning. And the exchange was mutually beneficial. The man was fervid on the subject. His eyes glowed as he spoke. He enjoyed himself thoroughly. So did I. And I was learning at the same time. *Knowhow was my ulterior motive.*

Make knowhow *your* ulterior motive too. It's a powerful way to learn. Scout for sources of information. Learn to pump the experts. Most people love to talk about what they know best. You'll be doing your informants a favor. And yourself too. You'll be building your knowhow, boosting your savvy.

Track down trouble. Tackle it with zest

It has been said that in the presence of trouble, some people grow wings; others buy crutches. Well, here's news. Savvy managers grow wings.

To the ordinary person a tough troublesome problem is an ordeal. To the savvy manager it's a challenge and opportunity. And with good reason. You can become a hero overnight! Doing battle with a thorny problem and cutting it down to size is like waving a colorful banner before your boss' eyes. It's the best way known to win recognition, to add to your storehouse of knowledge, to boost your savvy rating.

Now, this doesn't mean you should get into a jam intentionally to see how well you can wriggle your way out of it. That would be self-defeating. But the truth of the matter is this: Jams are as inevitable to business as taxes and forms. And they do represent opportunities for advancement and development. One corporation's board chairman, in fact, was asked how he made it to the top. "It was a tough laborious climb," he replied, "up a rock pile of troubles." And he added, "It was also a ball."

It's strictly a matter of attitude and outlook. If you learn to relish trouble, you'll learn to like it. That's right, actually *like it*. Because expert trouble shooting can be fun.

Want proof? One of our engineers can give it to you. He's a fellow with real talent, a veritable whiz in his field. But talk about introverts! I think he coined the word. This presented management—and our engineer—with a problem. He was a valued employee, and we wanted him to grow. But the next step in his growth would necessarily have to draw him out of his shell. This I decided to do in "one fell swoop," as the saying goes.

I'll never forget the time I called him into my office. "You've been elected," I told him bluntly.

His worried eyes were wary. "Elected to what?"

I told him. One of our executives was slated to make a speech in Cleveland. "You're the best man for the job," I said simply. "Nobody else knows the subject as well."

Quite clearly, his worry turned to panic.

"Me!" he blubbered. "I never. . . ."

"There's always a first time," I said. And to cut the story short, he hemmed and hawed, but I finally goaded him—or shamed him—into responding to the challenge. Now I can sum it up in four words—*there's no stopping him!* The experience transformed him, virtually doubled his savvy rating overnight. You can do the same for yourself. By *forcing* yourself to respond without hesitation to rough, tough, unpleasant experiences. And that's the key word, experiences.

J. R. Miller puts it this way: "If you will call your 'troubles' 'experiences,' and remember that every experience develops some latent force within you, you will grow vigorous and happy, however adverse your circumstances may seem to be."

And that's as true a word as was ever spoken. Now for a recap.

Checklist summary of knowhow boosters

- Construct your "Personal Knowhow Profile" today. Parade your strengths and weaknesses in review. Shore up your weaknesses. Reinforce your strengths to make them overpowering, to change from "mere-expert" to "super-expert."
- Track down new ways to break the accustomed, well-ordered, specialist-oriented routine of your business life. Your personal life, too.
- Expose your people to as many different jobs and situations as you can. Observe how they react and adapt to each new assignment. Learn where they waver and where they shine. Uncover hidden talents and put them to profitable use.
- Use the "Auditor's Query Technique" to soul-search knowhow weaknesses. Be your own hardest critic. Build your savvy rating with an action-prodding barrage of toughminded questions.
- Don't back away from participating in experiments or from speaking your mind openly and honestly. Remember that "me-too managers" are a dime a dozen or cheaper. The savvy manager is above all else his own man, a pioneer, a thinker, an innovator. And he inspires his people to be the same.
- Don't take your quest for knowledge for granted. Become a compulsive knowhow seeker, an addict. Get yourself "hooked."
- Make each "plant walkthrough" an educational experience. Study your people, your systems, your operation. Spot for potential profit ideas.
- Tape your telephone conversations to sharpen your communicating skills.
- Make the quest for knowhow your ulterior motive. Pump the experts for information, advice, profit ideas.
- Convert your troubles into business assets. Treat each problem as a savvy building opportunity and as a chance to boost your reputation as an expert.
- Finally—and in a nutshell—*be the man they come to for help and advice.*

4

Act Like the Owner to Invest

in Your Future

"Born to be a man—died a grocery clerk."

So goes the simple epitaph inscribed on a Paris tombstone. The grave's occupant, an unfortunate named Arséne, hanged himself in a fit of depression.

Makes you think, doesn't it? The desire to get ahead torments most of us to varying degrees. Rarely to the extent that it did poor Arséne, fortunately. Still, when you face up to the hard reality of the matter, there *is* a lot at stake. Those who stand still in life miss out on so much. Not just the things that money can buy. Much, much more. They miss the feeling of elation that comes with success. The challenge. The zest. And most of all, the supreme self-respect.

Well, Arséne is gone. We can't help *him. But we can help you!* Or, more accurately, we can help you to help yourself. We can help you make sure that you don't wind up in the role of "grocery clerk." How?

By hammering across to you this potent savvy tip: If you want to run an important part of the show, maybe even in time the main part of the show; if you want eventually to become *the* owner of the business, or stand up right there alongside him, the trick is to *ACT LIKE THE OWNER*. This is a savvy tip that can propel you right to the top. And now for the "How-To."

How do you act like the owner? You begin by *thinking like the owner*. You learn what goes on in an owner's mind. You learn his desires and how to satisfy them. You learn by understanding what he is, what makes him tick. *By training yourself to see beyond the BENEFITS of ownership and appreciating the PROBLEMS of ownership, and taking positive, self-motivated action to help get them solved.*

Understanding ownership. How does it come about? Listen to this sardonic piece of advice offered by one businessman. "Be alert," he said, "work hard, do a good job every day, and who knows? Some day you may own the company, work in a big private office, and have the privilege of worrying about staying in the black, the pleasure of meeting the payroll, and the happy task of beating competition."

The point is clear. The owner's route is anything but rose-strewn. It's tough. It's thorny. But I've yet to have one owner tell me that the road's not worth the trip. On the other hand, show him a way to smooth the path and he's eternally grateful.

"The soundest way to progress in any organization," a top business leader once said, "is to help the man ahead of you to get promoted."

The man may be your boss, or your company's boss. It makes no difference. When you boil it down, it's just another way of saying:

Act like the owner!

Identify with the owner

One thing about the savvy manager. He's strictly a WE-man. *He identifies with the owner.* It's not "the" company, or "their" company. It's *our* company.

In the savvy manager's eyes *his* company is the greatest in the world. So are its people, its progress, its products, its achievements, its goals.

The savvy manager knows when he gives his company a boost, he gives himself a boost at the same time. That's the WE-approach. *It's acting like the owner.*

Is this just rah-rah talk? Or is it get-ahead talk?

Here's how one student of business answers the question: "If you work for a man, in heaven's name work for him; speak well of him and stand by the institution he represents." If you don't, he adds, "the first high wind that comes along will blow you away and probably you will never know why."

The decision is strictly yours. Do you want to be "blown away?" Or catapulted to the top?

Firing line proof? Here's a good example. A new Steelcraft distributor came to our plant in Cincinnati for the first time. Steve, one of our young employees, drove to the airport to meet him. An hour or so later he brought the distributor in to meet me and my brother Charles, who run the company.

Well, what can I say? It's hard to define. But from the moment the distributor entered the room, we knew that Steve had done his spade work well. We didn't have to *define* it. We could *feel* it.

It was a nameless something about the way the distributor grasped our hands. It was the look on his face, the glow in his eyes. They told us more eloquently than words that Steve had managed to spark the distributor with his own enthusiasm for his job and his company.

I don't know exactly what Steve said to that man. I don't care what he said. More important was the way he said it, the way he felt it, the way he hammered through his feeling to an individual who meant a great deal to all of us. I hope you get the point, because it's a mighty important one, I think.

Who is Steve? Top management? Key man? Well, yes, in a way you might say that Steve is a key man; at least he is as far as we're concerned. Actually he's hardly past his teens, not a year out of school. But in our eyes he's a key man of the utmost importance because we know that he's got the magic touch. Steve's savvy build-up has been well started. He's on his way up, and up, and up. Why?

Because he acts like the owner!

Invest in your future

Invest what? Money. No, not money. What I'm talking about is far more valuable than money. I'm talking about you. Your time, your effort, your think power.

The fact is this. Growing with a company is a kind of unspoken mutual-agreement pact. Your part is to contribute everything you can to your company's success and to have faith that your company will keep its part of the bargain and contribute in fair measure to your success.

What does your contribution consist of? The truth is that if you want to get ahead, *really get ahead*— and I'm not talking about a five dollar token raise, or a fancy title; I'm talking about the real thing, that trip to the top—you must be prepared to *SACRIFICE.* That's what your contribution consists of.

Why? Because *the owner* is prepared to sacrifice. And in order to act like an owner, you have to emulate an owner.

Sound rough? Maybe it is, depending on your point of view. Depending on *what* you want to achieve, and on what you're willing to pay to achieve it. I promised to level with you. Now I'm leveling, and if you want out, this is the time to leave. But I can tell you one thing. If you think there is any comfortable, plush-lined road to Owner-land, forget it. The road is rough and ragged. It's lined with sacrifices. But there's one overriding grand and glorious consolation—big as the sacrifices must be, the payoff is even bigger. Again, I'm not talking about money alone. I'm talking about personal satisfaction, personal gratification. "In the end," says one sage, "men love better that for which they have made sacrifices than that through which they have enjoyed pleasure."

Sacrifices? What kind of sacrifices? All kinds. For example:

This happened last winter. The event was a big Miami convention, a trip our people look forward to with relish. A week before the convention, I asked one of our managers: "Well, Jack, all set for the trip?" His response was a shade sour. "Can't make it this year. I'm working on a contract I don't want to delay. Besides, I expect a guy in from Albuquerque. Been trying to close a deal with him for months."

That's just one small example. We all knew how badly Jack wanted to go to Miami. And he could have gone. The only thing that stopped him was himself. Because it would never occur to him to permit his personal preferences to stand in the way of the company's goals.

Maybe as a sacrifice that wasn't exactly earth-shattering. But it's the kind of action that hits me, as an owner, where I live. Because, in Jack's position, I know I would have made the same decision.

What about you? What would you have done?

Here's another case. We had some work to give out, a profitable piece of business for someone. One of our people, I knew, had a close friend with the unique facilities to do the job. I asked him about it. "What do you think? Would your friend like to handle this job for us?" "He'd love it," our man replied. "But there's another outfit I heard about that will give us better service for a lower price." I gave him the green light and he contacted the other outfit.

Do you get the picture? Faced with an opportunity to throw a close friend a lush job, our man turned it down. Why? Because he acted like the owner. The company came first.

Or take one of our managers who holds down an administrative post and is especially knowledgeable on the subject of fringe benefits. One day I had an idea for a new benefit for our people. I went to this manager for his reaction. "Do you think they'll like it?" I asked. "They'd love it," he replied. "But it's a rough benefit to administer." He discussed some of the problems. "I think the headaches would outweigh the values. Much as I hate to say so, I'd advise against it."

See where the sacrifice comes in? This man has a big family. He would have profited greatly from that benefit. Still, he was instrumental in killing it. Because, just like an owner, he couldn't find it in his heart to recommend a move that would be bad for the company.

But there's another factor, too. And that's where the faith comes to play. This manager knew—without a word being said—exactly what was involved in the sacrifice he made. And he knew that I knew it, too, and that somehow or other I'll make it up to him in the end, and that eventually he'll wind up ahead of the game.

Don't Over-Socialize

Here's another kind of sacrifice, and this one separates the managers from the managed.

Example: This friend of mine has a key executive job in a

company not far from our own. A couple of years ago he developed a very close friendship with a fellow executive. The two men and their wives became inseparable. Parties, bridge, golf, the whole bit. Very nice. Very pleasant.

Until one day things started happening in the company. Major changes. Old policies revised, product lines switched, new goals established. In the end, my friend was made executive vice president. *His friend,* because of product changes and other factors, was released by the company. The reasons for his release were pretty obvious. His special skills just did not fit into the new setup. A terrible scene ensued. The other fellow felt my friend could have saved his job. And maybe he could have kept him on in a non-productive capacity. But he was too fine an executive to do this, and friendship or not, his dedication to his employer and his company's goals would not permit him to do it. The windup was that the friendship erupted into the ugliest kind of enmity. It left a scar which my friend knows he will never be able to completely erase.

The conclusion is clear. It's risky for men in management positions to over-fraternize with their associates and subordinates. The vicissitudes of business are too unpredictable. All too often, what has to be done has to be done. This, too, is a sacrifice that the savvy manager must make and sometimes it is the most difficult one of all.

Reluctantly, but realistically, what I'd recommend is this. Keep that friendship and good will with your associates warm and glowing. Keep that mutual feeling of respect and admiration actively alive. But take care not to extend the relationship too far beyond the confines of the job into your social and personal life.

You Again

It is time now to get *you* in on the act. *Fact one:* Management savvy in its purest form is simply human savvy applied to business. It is doing *unto* others instead of *to* them. It is what I like to refer to as *people-izing. Fact two:* At some point in his career the savvy manager wakes up to a strange and wondrous revelation. He realizes that the boss is human just like everybody else, and that, being human, if you make sacrifices for him, he'll show his gratitude by giving you the kind of boost you are after.

So get ready now to indulge in a bit of soul-searching. QUES-
TION: How badly do you want to get ahead? How important is it
for you to wind up owning that "grocery store"—or managing the
grocery store—instead of just clerking in it? If I've guessed your
answer right, and I think I have, the next step is to put on that
sacrificial cape. Sound hazardous? It's not. In fact, it won't even
hurt. You may even grow to like it. Most savvy managers do. As
one philosopher said: "It is what we give up, not what we lay up
that adds to our lasting store."

So let's get that store in order.

OBJECTIVE: To convince the boss that his goals are your goals,
his problems your problems. QUESTION: (And you're the only one
who can answer it.) What action can you take—I'm talking about
sacrifices now—*that you are not compelled to take,* to prove your
loyalty, devotion and allegiance to the company?

Think. For some the answer may be extra time volunteered for
a project. Or extra thought given to improve an operation or solve
a special problem. Or creating harmony in the shop where friction formerly existed.

Think, first of the action, then how your boss would react to the
action, what it would mean to him. Ask yourself what he, as the
owner, or the owner's representative, would like most to achieve
or unsnarl.

Now get out a pencil and pad. Jot down three, five, eight
actions to take—as many as come to mind. Actions made as
sacrifice, *above and beyond the call of duty,* if you will. Then get
cracking on them tomorrow or sooner, and watch with amaze-
ment the boss' response.

Career Investment Appraisal Technique

Suppose you make your sacrifices and the boss does not respond? What then? How long do you wait for the payoff to
occur?

All right. We're being blunt. We're being realistic. Let us
continue in this vein. How long do you wait? A reasonable length
of time. How long is reasonable? That's hard to say. It varies from
owner to owner, company to company. But that doesn't mean you
invest of yourself wholeheartedly and with dedication entirely in
the blind.

For one thing, there are signs to read. Others in the organization. Watch them closely. Observe. Ask yourself, who else has been pouring his heart and gut into the operation and for how long? And what has been his reward? One thing you can almost surely count on. If others are being rewarded you too will be taken care of in time—unless you're making the mistake of grossly overrating your efforts and abilities.

So, first and foremost, give of yourself. Never stop doing this because it is the only way to build and sustain your growth. Then wait patiently. Six months, a year, maybe longer. See how the wind is blowing. If you feel it's not blowing right for you, sit down and have a talk with your boss. Find out where you stand, where you're heading. Don't push or complain. Rather put your cards on the table. Ask for advice and suggestions that will improve your effectiveness.

Then—and you're the only one who can do it—make your final judgment. But try to be objective; try to gauge your *true* value to your company, your *true* potential. Realistically. Without wishful thinking or blue-sky speculation. Then face the issue squarely. Does it look like it's going to be all give, with little or no take? If so, this may be the time to move. The investment of yourself is too big, too overwhelmingly important, to be treated lightly or brushed aside.

And here's a tip. Once you decide to move, move fast. Don't lower the quality of your performance. This can only hurt you. The trick is to boost the level of appreciation you receive.

Agitate for profits

Somebody once said, and he must have owned a business: "No statue was ever erected to the memory of a man or woman who thought it was best to leave well enough alone." This swings the subject back to our main theme, ACT LIKE THE OWNER.

QUESTION: What does the owner do most of his working time? *Answer:* Directly or indirectly, he tracks down money-making and money-saving opportunities. He sharpens, he tightens, he improves. *He agitates for profits!* And he does so on his own. Nobody pushes or prods him.

Profits! Here's a tip. Bite into that word. Chew on it a while. It's the most important word in the owner's lexicon.

All right, back to the firing line. Scene I. It concerns Manager No. 1. I'm an owner. So I snoop, I pry, I agitate. A couple of weeks ago I was walking through the plant—one of my favorite pastimes. I entered a department and spotted trouble at once. Things were too chaotic, too piled up. Obviously, a bottleneck. You can sense these things after a while. I scanned the floor for Manager No. 1 and found him checking a shipment. We discussed the bottleneck and tried to get to the root of it. I pointed out a few things, fired a few questions. Why this? Why that? I pushed; I prodded. Finally I got him to act. All right, Scene I, curtain.

Now, Scene II and Manager No. 2. He runs another department. The other day he came to me and called a problem to my attention. "Now here's what I think should be done about it . . ." He outlined a plan to solve the problem. *On his own!* Without pushing, without prodding.

Get the distinction between No. 1 and No. 2? One's okay; he works hard. He does his best. But he's not *owner-oriented*. He's average, ordinary. He needs that prod. Not No. 2. This man has savvy.

Here's another case. One of our men flew out west. The day he arrived he called me long distance to inform me that one of our distributors was planning to retire and turn the distributorship over to someone else. Now here's the point. This fellow's mission of the moment had nothing to do with this distributor. It had little direct relationship to his job. Still, he was interested. He thought it was important to keep us informed. He questioned the effect of the change on our profit picture. Get the idea? He didn't *have* to take this initiative. He took it upon himself to do so. He self-started. In his own way, he profit-agitated.

Circulate

There's another thing about the owner, about the way he agitates. If he's a true agitator, if he's not an ivory-tower manager, he circulates. He's here, he's there, he's everywhere. There's one employee in our shop I try to hit with this message. It's not easy. Somehow or other I always seem to find him glued to his desk. "For Pete's sake," I'll say to him, "if you're a manager, manage. Get around the shop. Start wheels turning; start balls rolling."

Here's what I mean.

Example: A meeting's in progress, and I sit in for a while, and I see that things are bogging down. All right, I'm an owner, a manager. So I toss in a comment or two, a thought-provoking idea. I get people thinking. I whip up interest. Then, I take off. How long did I spend there? Five minutes. Maybe ten.

Example: I've got a long letter to answer, several points to cover. What do I do? I sit down for ten minutes or so, outline the main points, turn the outline over to my secretary. She responds like a pro. Trained to complement my thinking, she glances at the notes, asks a question or two, and that's that. More wheels turning. What's next?

Example: A production problem awaits a solution. I sit down with my production man and his assistant. We discuss the problem. Or, more correctly, *they* discuss the problem. They're better qualified than I am to come up with the solution. I just steer the discussion. I start the analytical gears grinding. Once this is achieved, I disappear.

Do you get the point? In your profit agitation role you can do only one thing at a time, talk with one person at a time, write one letter at a time. The challenge then is to stretch your *achievement span.* Accomplish as many tasks as you can in the shortest possible time. How? By using *Managerial Shorthand!* Press buttons, flick switches. Be a starter, a launcher, *not a do-it-your-selfer.* Push where you must; prod where you must; *get people to act.* You're only as effective as your staff. If you get people moving both mentally and physically, they will run the machines, do the work, make the profits climb.

Start Now

It's *you*-time again. *Destination:* Top Executive Suite. *Success Strategy:* Profit Agitation.

Step one. Get out that pencil and pad and prepare for a mental excursion to your shop. It makes no difference where you work. Factory or foundry, warehouse or office. It's all the same. One thing is common to all job situations. I'm talking about *problems.* Wherever you work, you can be sure that problems exist. And problems are costly, worrisome, irritating. They eat into profits.

So start now to make that career of yours zoom. Concentrate on your company's problems and what *you* can do to help solve them. Shift from area to area of your plant or office. As ideas come to you, jot them down. And ideas *will* come to you if you ask yourself the right questions:

What does it cost? Can we eliminate that step, this part, that form? Can we use a standard item or lower cost material? Is there a less expensive process that will do the job as well? Should we automate here; de-automate there? Should we make this part, or buy it; print this form ourselves, or give it out to be done? Can we combine steps, components, information? Are we buying more quality than we need?

Questions, questions, and more questions. And for each question there's an answer. Can *you* come up with the answers? You most certainly can if you probe, challenge, snoop, and profit agitate. *But do it NOW!*

Build yourself an owner image

Here's some simple career-building logic. If you're going to act like an owner, you may as well give the appearance of an owner. This doesn't mean you should grow a moustache, buy horn-rim specs, or strut around as if everything in sight was your property. It does mean that your owner-oriented attitude and behavior should shine through for all and sundry, and especially the boss, to see.

Now for objective number one. How do you get that owner-oriented, profit-slanted image of yours to come booming through? Talk it up around the shop about what a big brainy hero you are? Well, in a way, yes. But talk it up with ACTION, not words. *And never by politicking!*

Somebody once said, "People may doubt what you say, but they will never doubt what you do." As true as any words spoken.

It reminds me of a ball team, consisting of youngsters in their pre-teens, I once coached. No match for the Cincinnati Reds, perhaps. But it was a club to be proud of. Even today, people come to me and say, "Bob, I remember that club, it was a great organization, you did an outstanding job." Now I'll come right out and admit it. I like to believe that I'm as human as they come. I enjoy a pat on the back as much as the next fellow, maybe more than some. But I can tell you this. I didn't send any press clips to these people about that ball club. The organization—and what I helped do for the organization—spoke for itself. Not because of what I *said*. Because of what I *did!*

Give Your Horn a Subtle Toot

Does that mean you should keep your achievements a secret? Not at all. If you make a profit contribution it should be called to the boss' attention. But subtly, discreetly. Not by crowing about it. Not by being pushy about it. Not by saying, or implying, how great you are and how small the next guy is in comparison.

How then will the boss come to know about your irreplaceable merits? You can help him to know in 101 subtle ways. I told you about our man who tracked down a bottleneck, came up with a remedy, and brought it to me for my okay. That's one way. Another good way is to go to the boss with an idea, a plan, a profit suggestion. This will make your image soar.

Here's another key pointer. Every owner, of necessity, is interested in the total picture. If you're going to act like the owner, you too should be interested in the total picture. Take one of our purchasing people. He came to me and asked: "How can I find out more about the sales operation? It would help me to do a better job. And it would give me a more complete view of the business." P.S., that's *my* business he was talking about. Any wonder I was impressed by his interest?

As I've said, there are 101 ways you can build your image subtly and discreetly, but the most important way of all is action. *Profit action!* As Emerson said, "The thing done avails, and not what is said about it."

So talk less. Do more.

Surround yourself with potential owners

How can you get your people to act like owners? One: act like an owner yourself. Two: treat your people in a way that will inspire them to share your business views, your problems, your hopes. In short—and we're back to that favorite word of mine—*people-ize!*

That's what we try to do at Steelcraft. We try to establish a kind of closeness and rapport. For one thing, we're all on a first name basis, and I like to think it is more than just lip service. Our top management team stresses accessibility. Any man in our plant knows, for example, that he can walk up to me at any time and say, "Bob, here's my problem. . . ." And I'll listen to his problem, and care about his problem, and try to help him if I can. I will mention it to the department head and urge that consideration be given to the problem. At least the man knows action is being taken.

Another thing. In getting your people to respond like owners, *don't expect too much*. Don't expect them to be superhuman. Don't force them to put on an act. Let me show you what I mean.

There was a special profit bonus arrangement we once tried that applied under certain conditions. I felt it wasn't working out too well, and I wanted the reaction of one of my managers. So I approached him about it. Now, desirable or not, the man's income was determined in part by this bonus. How could I expect him to be totally objective on the subject? I couldn't, and didn't. So first I outlined the problem. Then I assured him, "Joe, don't worry about yourself. Whatever arrangement is made, your income won't be affected." Then we discussed the details and I found out what I wanted to find out.

Then there's the problem of imitation, emulation, call it what you will. "We are in truth," Lord Chesterfield said, "more than half of what we are by imitation. The great point is to choose good models, and to study them with care."

The trick, Mr. Manager, is for *you* to provide this good model for your people. Voluntarily or not, they're going to imitate you. Your chore is to assure that "imitation" is not preceded by the letter "L."

It's no easy road to hoe. You have to play a role. You have to hide your major weaknesses, keep them a secret. But whatever you do, don't try to convey the impression that you're above making mistakes.

I'm talking about the kind of weaknesses that undermine your owner-image, your leader-image. If you want to get high, for example, do it in the privacy of your own room, not in the presence of associates or subordinates *in or out of the shop*. If you have a job-related fear, keep it to yourself. Same thing if you feel indecisive about an important action. Don't forget, you're the man in the driver's seat and you have to pay the price. You're not *expected* to lose control, or show undue anxiety or indecision. If you do, the weaknesses will be picked up and reflected by your people in their attitudes, in their performance, in their appraisal of you.

Another thing. Getting your people to act and think like the owner takes much time, much training, much trial and error, and much patience. I have one manager in particular in mind. He arranged a deal to do some work for a customer for a set price of $20,000. The customer said fine, go ahead with the job. Then the customer came in and started making all kinds of changes in the materials and specs. The manager did not notify the customer of the corresponding price increases. When the job was done a bill was presented for $27,500.

The customer was flabbergasted. He refused to pay, and the whole thing was pretty embarrassing. But the point is this. In making that arrangement the manager had done anything but act like an owner. An owner would never have entered an agreement of that kind without working up the necessary forms and contracts in advance, getting complete approval on extras.

Okay, so the manager acted without good judgment, without savvy, not like the owner. Does this spell utter disaster? Not at all. This is where the *boss'* savvy comes into play, the training, the patience. *The really savvy manager milks every unfortunate experience for all the asset value he can get out of it.*

So first we reviewed the problem and I helped solve it. Next, I used the incident to ensure against haphazard contract negotiations in the future. *And all this time the manager, through exposure, was learning to act like the owner.*

Also, did you notice those three points: problem-solving, training, systems? Does it ring an old familiar bell? It should. It's just one further example of getting *multiple value from a single action.*

Roundup summary—proprietor's checklist

We discussed a number of techniques that will help you to act more like the owner, and that will help you to help your people act more like the owner. Now here they are in review.

1. Latch onto owner problems and aggressively track down solutions.
2. Always think, act, and talk *our* company; never *their* company.
3. Boost your company's people, products, policies every chance you get.
4. Invest *yourself* in the company with every fibre of your being.
5. Stand ready to make owner-type sacrifices to help achieve company goals.
6. Don't over-socialize with associates and subordinates.
7. Track down money-making and money-saving ideas every chance you get. It's the owner's favorite pastime. *Agitate for profits!* Start composing and acting on your profit agitation DO-list today.
8. Move, snoop, circulate! Shift from place to place. Don't wait for profit opportunities to come your way. Ferret them out. Get others moving, acting, thinking—then take off.
9. Boost your personal owner-image, first and foremost, with productive profit actions. When necessary, throw in a bit of tactful, subtle horn-blowing to call your achievements and actions to the boss' attention.
10. Inspire your people to emulate your ownership actions and attitude by playing the proprietor's role that is expected of you. Hide your major weaknesses. Don't tip off your fears, your feelings of indecision. And never take any action that will diminish your sense of dignity.

5

Spur People to Make Your

Goals Their Goals

What is a career? Isn't it simply an endless succession of goals? You get a task to do. Do it well, and you get another task. And another, and another. As you continue to achieve, your goals get tougher, more challenging. The more challenging they get, the more valuable and high-priced you become. The faster you grow; the higher you go.

Your success, therefore, depends on the skill you use to achieve your goals. True?

No, not quite.

There's one small flaw. The word "you" is singular.

However bright you may be, as every savvy manager knows, you would find it immensely difficult to make any truly significant career-building headway *without the wholehearted cooperation and support of your people*. Here's the way Sam Johnson put it almost two centuries ago: "No degree of knowledge attainable by man is able to set him above the need of hourly assistance." It's just as true today.

You can't go it alone. You're going to need help. The trick is to spur your people to adopt your goals as their very own, and to drive towards their fulfillment with the same vigor and zest that you yourself apply.

Do this and you will capture the very essence of management savvy.

Here's an interesting thought. The car you drive and the people you supervise have a great deal in common. Sound crazy? It's not. In a very real sense the people who work for you are your transportation. *You depend on them to get you where you want to go in your company and in your field,* just as you depend on your car to get you from one place to another.

Now let's expand on our parallel. For a car to travel smoothly, without stalling, without breaking down, you keep it maintained and in good repair, well oiled, properly fueled. Same thing with your people. You maintain them with training, oil them with information and guidance, fuel them with the kind of motivation that will inspire them to do what you want them to do in the way you would like them to do it.

Shoot for the same target

Arthur Sulzberger once wrote: "They said of Queen Victoria that she never looked to see where the chair was before she seated herself. She *knew* it would be in its proper place. On a team there is no substitute for confidence in one's teammates."

On the management team especially. The skilled savvy manager is an expert "confidence man." He sharply defines profit goals. He sees to it that his people all shoot for the same target.

In short, what the savvy manager scouts for are business skills and business instincts that complement—and compliment—his own.

How does it work? Back to the shop for an eye-witness account.

One key factor in our business is the distributor organization that handles our products. For us, the right distributor means profits; the wrong distributor means trouble. Problem: How do you pinpoint the right distributor? Roughly, he might be profiled as containing a certain level of competence, certain facilities for service, and certain intangibles—a kind of attitude, enthusiasm and ethical sense that blends with our own way of doing business.

It's hard to put into words. It's something you observe, you learn, you feel. There's a young manager in our company, for example—Fred, a real comer. He visits distributors now, shows our product. Fred knows our product line completely. He's been on trips with us, knows how we think, feel and act.

In Pennsylvania a few weeks ago Fred called on a distributorship where a father and son run the business. Good location, highly productive in the past, and they want our line. So far, so good. Fred spends time with these people. He observes the operation and is impressed that the father is a great businessman. But he's getting on in years, and is planning to spend half his time in Florida. The son is relatively new in the business, and he's weak. Not green-weak, but attitude-weak, with a dish-rag spirit.

The outfit, Fred concludes, is good for today, but shaky for tomorrow, in danger of sliding. It's not for us. Fred comes back and discusses the situation with us. We agree. Our confidence in his judgment is complete. Why? *Because his thinking complements our own.* The way Fred singled out the signs and read them is the same thing I would have done. He's 100 per cent with it, strictly on target.

That's why he's a comer. That's why he's headed no place but up.

No Carbon Copies

Caution. Don't interpret "complementary thinking" to mean carbon copy or "yes man" response from your people. *What the truly savvy manager wants is goal agreement, not methods agreement.* Profit builders, not ego soothers.

Take our financial director. We're both zeroed in on the same profit objectives. No squabble there. But in the "how to" department, it's another matter. I may become intrigued by a new system, for example, or a new piece of equipment. My financial executive? He may wince at the thought of it.

Why? Simply because we both have the same profit goal in mind, but his idea of how to achieve the goal doesn't always agree with my idea of how to achieve the goal. And this makes him one of the most valuable sounding boards at my disposal. To be perfectly blunt, I can think of more than one occasion when he has applied a much needed brake to my runaway enthusiasm.

All right. Now let's draw a capsule profile of the kind of man we're after. (1) His goals mesh with your goals. (2) His thinking and "feel" for the business complements your own. (3) He's a gutsy, independent self-starter, with imagination, initiative, enthusiasm and drive.

QUESTION: Where do you find such a phenomenon? Admittedly, we're talking about a rare bird. And rare birds are hard to track down. So why try? Why not develop your own species? And don't forget the key word—DEVELOP!

Be a TD Man

TD for *Talent Development*. A sage once said, "To encourage talent is to create it." Here's news for you. To encourage talent is to create profits, too. And supreme self-gratification. And genuine enjoyment and fun.

That's right—FUN! Some people say fun and business don't mix. They're wrong. I can tell you from long personal experience that *the surest way to get fun out of your business life is to develop the talents of your people.*

There's a company I know, a funless, sunless outfit. This company doesn't grow; it just stands still. Mention the word "talent" to the president and a puzzled frown would crease his brow. Year after year the company shows a moderate profit, and the stockholders are apparently satisfied because it never occurred to them that with a little excitement and imagination the profits could be doubled. Still, profits or not, stockholder satisfaction or not, the company is ailing. Why?

Because the people who work there are bored to death!

They're stifled, frustrated, unhappy. And that goes for almost every employee from the president down. The point is this. It's not enough merely to exist. You have to grow. Your company has to grow. Your *people* have to grow. They're *entitled* to grow. After all, their investment is bigger than any stockholder's. *They're investing their lives!*

So here's a savvy tip to take with you and cherish. Become a super-TD man. Pay your corporate dues—and reap your corporate reward—with your TD contribution. Give your people the chance to develop and grow. The philosopher La Rochefoucauld once said, "Nature has concealed at the bottom of our minds talents and abilities of which we are not aware." It's your responsibility to exploit these hidden talents of your people. Encourage them to spill out of their shells. Then sit back and bask in the joyful inner glow while you cash in on one of the most meaningful and exciting experiences of your life. And there's a bonus payoff to boot.

You will prove to your people that you are 100 per cent behind them and their goals. You will inspire your people to get 100 per cent behind *you* and *your* goals.

Check Your Personal TD Rating

Are your Talent Development skills sharply honed? Here's your chance to find out. First, get a pencil and pad. Then, do the following:

- List the name of each person reporting to you, one name to a sheet.
- On another sheet, make a Skills Inventory listing—the major areas of understanding needed by your people to most effectively achieve their goals and help you achieve your goals.
- Now make a list of all the goals and subgoals of your department or division that come to mind.

Once this is done, your next step is to evaluate your people one at a time. Do this by asking yourself the following five questions. Rate yourself on each question from "5" for *excellent* to "O" for *unsatisfactory*.

1. Are the goals—and the part he must play in achieving the goals—as clear to your subordinate as they are to you?
2. Is your subordinate motivated by an intense personal interest to help achieve these goals with a maximum degree of excellence?
3. Are the items on the Skills Inventory listing which pertain to him—about the product line, the operation, the customers, etc.—solidly understood and strongly rooted in his mind?
4. How much do you know about this person that extends beyond the scope of his routine daily job? When did you last give him a new and challenging task with an unknown factor tied to it, to excite his interest and exploit his unsuspected talents?
5. The savvy manager should spend from 60 to 80 per cent of his time training his people. How much time do you

spend? This refers to all training, not just formalized training. It takes in shop discussion, training by example, and savvy-oriented talk on a train or plane, during meetings, and on the job. But whether directly or indirectly applied, the kind of training I'm talking about is *conscious* training—*training with a definite, preplanned purpose in mind.*

Now, with your conscience as your guide, tally your TD rating. Be fair, objective, self-critical. Then, in all honesty, answer this question. *Does your score total 25?*

If not, your work is cut out for you.

If so, you can come to work for me.

Use Management Theatrics to Prod Profit Action

"All the world's a stage." Shakespeare said it, of course. And here's a savvy tip. "*All* the world" takes in the *business* world as well.

The savvy manager wears many hats, including the hat of the actor. With good reason, too. The dramatic blasts the humdrum. It gets noticed. It strikes with impact, provokes action.

Want to trigger a whirl of interest in an idea, a system, a product, an action you'd like to see taken? Try this approach. Get yourself worked up about it. Whip up excitement. Explode it into a big deal. Get emotionally involved.

Recently, one of my people stomped into my office. He had a salesman in the conference room, and just like June, he was "busting out all over." The man could scarcely contain himself. "*Bob, you've got to see this product!*" To hear him rave, this new product, whatever it was, would triple our business in two weeks. Did I go with him to see the product?

You can bet your shoes I did!

I saw the salesman too. Charged and sizzling, bubbling with energy and enthusiasm. He was acting a part. Like Barrymore, like Gielgud. And before he was through, he was writing an order.

Excitement! The rush of vigor! It moves mountains. It moves people.

Now for another brand of excitement: *anger.* Uncontrolled, it's just one letter short of *danger*, as somebody once said. Used with the histrionic wisdom and timing of the Shakespearean tradition, it can be a powerful management tool.

"Anybody can become angry," Aristotle said, "that is easy; but to be angry with the right person, and to the right degree, and at the right time, and for the right purpose, and in the right way—that is not within everybody's power and is not easy."

True, it's not easy. But with practice and patience you can develop this very special art to help spur people to make your goals their goals. How does it work? We'll soon see. Curtain coming up. It is time to get on stage.

Memory Booster Shots

It happened a year ago. I received a letter of complaint from an important customer. I don't like letters of complaints from important customers. This one involved caps that get screwed to the bottoms of certain doors. This customer's caps were loose, the screws not tightened properly. Simple carelessness. Easy to correct? You'd think so. I did. But this wasn't a new complaint. We'd had it before on two or three occasions. And each time I'd attended to it, I assumed it was attended to. Apparently I was wrong. Because here it was again.

Problem: *once and for all,* how could I take care of this ridiculous situation and make sure this would be the end of it? You guessed it. "The world's a stage." So, polishing up my best dramatic form, I boiled up to the supervisor in charge with fire in my eyes. And, plain and simple, *I blew my stack.* As I said, that was a year ago, and I can tell you this. I can't recall one complaint since that time about caps coming loose.

Another example. Passing through the plant one day after hours, I noticed that a gas tank we use to fuel our mobile equipment was left unlocked at night. Bad business. I talked to the supervisor in charge, explained how much easier it is to keep people honest if you remove temptation from their sight. He promised to set up a control which would assure that the tank was kept locked after regular plant hours. It must have slipped his mind.

But it didn't slip mine. A couple of nights later I passed the tank again, and tried the nozzle trigger. Gas gushed out. So once again I warmed up for the Barrymore bit and let loose. And here's one thing you can believe. Come around any night at all and check that tank. You won't find it open.

It's a funny thing. You hear a great deal about the importance of keeping calm, quiet, level-headed. And don't get me wrong. I'd be the last one to sell level-headedness short. But there's another side to the picture. It's just not *human* to be level-headed *all* the time. When there's a special point to be made, a special cause to espouse, if you have some good old-fashioned emotion and excitement working for you, it can go a long way. *Carefully administered, infrequently used.* Too much management theatrics will blunt the effect, give you a reputation as a hothead or erratic in the bargain. Moreover, it will turn you into a ham.

Another point. When you employ anger as a tool, *never personalize it.* Target your emotion against the incident, not the individual. And once you release it, forget it. Don't carry a grudge. In the case of those loose screws, for example, ten minutes after blowing my stack, the supervisor and I were knee deep in another discussion. The incident with the caps? I acted as if it had never occurred.

Recruit Allies To Keep Your Ideas Alive

Ever watch a fire in its last throes? Mostly ashes. And a couple of embers glowing, first faintly, then more faintly, until finally you can neither feel the warmth nor perceive the light of the glow. And that's it. The fire dies.

But suppose, while the embers still have life, that instead of just *watching,* you stoke the ashes and add new fuel. What happens? The glow gets brighter. Tongues of flame dart hungrily. The blaze stirs and crackles and leaps to life.

Know something? Ideas work the same way. All too often a good idea just wanes and dies because it was poked at feebly or not at all. Because no one took the initiative to stoke the fire.

Do you know what I'm talking about? I'm talking about one of the prime ingredients of management savvy—taking the initiative to snatch up that poker and stoke the fire. How? The answer is simple.

To keep a fire burning, you stir up the embers. To keep your ideas burning, you recruit allies to the cause. You whip up interest. You fuel enthusiasm.

Once, in a speech, I heard something I never forgot. "Enthusi-asm," the speaker said, "is the only thing that defies mathematics, because when you divide it, it multiplies."

Want to rekindle a good idea and hammer it home to achieve your goals and advance your career? Multiply enthusiasm! Re-cruit allies to the cause. Get everyone into the act. Why fly solo when you can rally a formation behind you? Get people involved and committed. Turn that one-man campaign into a united cru-sade. Now for a view of how this works on the firing line.

Last Rites?

It happened at a meeting. Twelve supervisors were around the big table, and the idea was to come up with some new ways to reduce our operating costs.

Steve, one of our tool engineers, had brought a list with him. Ten ways to save time in the plant. He passed out copies and made a presentation, reviewing the items one by one. Some of them looked promising.

But Steve just read off the items. He didn't get excited about them. He did nothing special to whip up interest. He just read them off.

When he was through, he sat down. Nobody yawned. Nobody did handsprings either. "Good stuff there," one man commented. "Yeah," another agreed. Others nodded. And that was that.

Next on the agenda? Last rites for Steve's list of ten?

Not on your life. I had no intention of watching this one die. I saw, too, an excellent training opportunity in this session. (*Multiple benefits, remember?*)

So I started passing the ball around.

"Pete, those storage bins in your department . . ."

"Sam, on that inventory suggestion . . ."

"Joe, those broken flats . . ."

Get the picture? I began to hit them one at a time. Rapid fire, machine gun stuff. Getting people involved. Stoking the fire. Stir-ring up the embers. Gradually, they began to respond. Joe had a comment to make. Then Pete, then Al, then everybody. All around the table people started stirring, their eyes sparked with new interest. So I fanned the fires.

"Marie, take that down in your notes . . ."

"Al, get Harry on the phone. Tell him to order the markers
. . ."

Pete, Sam, Al, George, Joe, Marie, Harry. Suddenly the meeting was buzzing, working up to a crescendo of excitement. Steve's
ho-hum list of ten, writhing on its deathbed at the outset, was
now *the* thing, the Big Ten.

Why? All because of that one magic word: *Enthusiasm!*

You Again

You've seen an idea kept alive in *my* company. Now let's see
one kept alive in *your* company. Step one. Make three separate
lists: (1) The people who are 100 per cent behind your idea. (2)
Those who oppose your idea. (3) Those who could be swayed in
either direction.

Now, those who are *for* your idea. Enlist their support as active
and aggressive campaigners. Get them to crusade among the
others in behalf of your idea. Don't trust to chance. Aggressively
sway them in your direction. Prove to them that, in helping you
to achieve your goal, they will benefit as well. Show them where.
Show them how.

Same thing for those *opposed*. Find out *why* they're opposed.
Then figure some important way in which they, too, will gain
from the success of your idea.

The trick is to get in there and sell. Punch your points across.
Get as many people as you can into the act. If there's a specific
individual you can't personally recruit, recruit him with the help
of an already-recruited ally who has better access to his ear.

The important thing is to stir up interest and excitement. Don't
count on your idea, however brilliant, to do it for you. Those
embers aren't going to whip up into a roaring, living blaze on
their own.

It's up to you to stoke the fire.

"Mr. Steelcraft" loyalist technique

Here's a hard fact of business life. You can have the brightest
subordinate in the world working for you, but if you question his
loyalty, take care.

Brains without loyalty is like ammunition without a pistol.

"All the scholastic scaffolding falls before one single word— faith." So said Napoleon.

Faith. Loyalty. Pick your own favorite word. The problem is, how do you win it? Not by trickery, that's for sure. And you can't buy it. But you can *earn* it. You can earn it on a fifty-fifty even exchange basis. And that's the only way you can earn it.

Emerson once said: "Trust men, and they will be true to you; treat them greatly, and they will show themselves great."

I'm talking about spurring people to make *your* goals *their* goals. Well, here's the simple truth of it. Only one kind of person will be motivated to make your goal his goal. A loyal person.

What about the other kind? Here's a case in point. A salesman friend recently told me he called on a manufacturing company's purchasing agent. Almost from the outset the purchasing agent started knocking his boss. Cheap, unfair, tyrannical. These are a few of the printable words.

My friend shook his head. "How can I have respect for that company, or confidence in their people, if a key employee can talk that way about his boss?"

The answer? You can't!

If your people aren't *for* you, you might as well assume that they're against you. And in the all-important game of Goalsmanship, that spells disaster.

The big career-oriented question, therefore, is how do you get them on your side? How do you win their loyalty?

First off, by acting like a human being yourself, and by treating your people like human beings, with all the honesty, decency and sensitivity that the word implies.

That's number one. After this you might try a powerful management technique which we have found especially effective in our business. How does it work? Back on the firing line for a first-hand look.

Ego Booster Shot

Jerry, one of our young employees, is an up-and-coming engineer. A few weeks ago I called him into my office. "Jerry, are you and Marge free tomorrow night?" They were.

I gave him the story. An important distributor was coming to

town to take advantage of our training program. His wife would
be with him. "I'd like for you and Marge to take them out on the
town, show them a good time. The company will pick up the
tab."

Was Jerry delighted and flattered? To say "yes" would be an
understatement.

Put yourself in Jerry's place. Most of your working life you're
just another engineer. But for one night you're Mr. Big before
your wife, your neighbors, your friends.

You are personally delegated to soften up and charm a key
company contact. To step out on the town in the style of an
executive earning three times your salary. That's why we call this
the "Mr. Steelcraft" technique.

For one grand and glorious night *you* are "Mr. Steelcraft."

Or Mr. "Acme." Or Mr. "National." Whatever the name of your
company happens to be.

All right, now let's evaluate. What does this do for a man like
Jerry? Don't forget, we're still trying to track down those multiple
benefits. Well, for one thing, it helps to build his confidence and
poise. It helps him to appreciate the problems of our distributors
who play so important a role in our profit growth. It gives the
distributor an insight into our manufacturing and engineering
problems. And it helps to woo Jerry's wife as an avid company
fan. Intangibly too, it gives our Mr. and Mrs. Big a taste of the
better life, sparks a new incentive and drive to press on toward
achievement and success.

Most important, it gives Jerry an ego booster shot that is worth
its weight in progress. And if you don't think this kind of treatment can fire a man with spirit and loyalty to the boss who made
it possible, then you've never been human. Because, let's be
honest. *Which one of us doesn't yearn inwardly to be Mr. Big in
our own eyes and in the eyes of others?*

Making up a bull's eye score, someone once said, "There are
two kinds of egotists. Those who admit it, and the rest of us."

Does the Mr. Steelcraft ego boosting technique work? We have
found that it does. We've been using it for years, and regard it as
one of our most successful development techniques. So, *in your
own way and within your own scope,* try this concept on your
own people. Make Harry, Sam or Fred Mr. Big for a day. Then

watch him burst with pride. Watch him glow with confidence. Watch him rally to your cause with the fervor of a loyal patriot.

Measured pressure

We've talked about putting screws on caps. Now let's talk about putting screws on people. Repugnant idea? Not necessarily.

Of course, pressure thoughtlessly applied can be dangerous and detrimental. It can undermine your people and trigger hostility.

But *measured pressure*, carefully metered, is another matter. This will spur achievement and provide a needed profit push.

The question is this: How can you tell when pressure is right and when it is wrong? Tough question at times. But a savvy manager can tell. He asks himself: "Is the man coasting, resting on his laurels? Are his goals too easily achieved? Is he starting to slide when he should be thrusting ahead?"

Take the case of Bill. He works in planning. A good man, he's been with the company for almost 20 years. Now I do not have to tell you what production planning means to a manufacturing operation. To do the right job, you must constantly be alert to capacities, supply of material, manpower, and the general business conditions of the company.

Bill has always been a prober, and he has grown accordingly. Then one day he suddenly stopped probing. He went through the superficial motions, but it became obvious to me that the man was starting to coast. Gaps in his knowledge started to blossom. He made mistakes, errors of judgment that could only have been caused by shallow consideration of vital data. He usually had one explanation or another, but the elements didn't jell.

One day he made a particularly expensive mistake. It was the kind of mistake he shouldn't have made. So we sat down for a heart-to-heart talk. Measured pressure; that's what I had in mind.

How did it go? No anger this time. No histrionics. Instead, sober, somber, dead serious persistence. Admittedly, I needled the man. One by one I paraded my grievances before him, mostly in the form of questions which left little doubt that improved performance was in order.

Then, apparently, I asked him one question too many. He couldn't take any more. He had had it. He was quitting.

This was more than I had bargained for. Bill was a good man. I wanted to keep him. I was sure I could straighten him out. Measured pressure—had I over-metered the dose?

"Don't be melodramatic," I admonished him. "Let's get back to work." But I couldn't talk him out of it. He had a streak of sensitivity I hadn't counted on. Right then and there he walked out of the office.

I don't mind telling you the incident gave me a bad time for a while. You don't just erase 20 years of a man's life at a single sitting. Then, I decided that whatever the consequences, it was an action that had to be taken. This too is the kind of decision a manager is forced to face from time to time.

In any event, this all happened on Friday. Monday morning, in walks Bill, worried, nervous. "I couldn't sleep all weekend," he admitted. "I did a darned fool thing on Friday. Is it too late to come back?"

I gazed up at him as if he was crazy. "I don't know what you're talking about. Come on, you're ten minutes late. There's work to be done."

Relief swept his face. "I don't know what to say," he stammered. "I . . . I'll have to call Mary. She's on pins and needles."

"So call her, for Pete's sake, and let's get some work done."

Well, that's the story. Most of it. There's one more thing, and this is it: *Make the most of every profit opportunity!* Remember that one? It's another vital savvy concept. And this was one opportunity I couldn't resist. I knew one thing for certain: *Bill would never be as pliable and as manageable as he was at this moment.* And there were a couple of things about his modus operandi I wanted to get squared away. So I started squaring. Not at length. Not in great detail. I didn't want to tear down what I had built up. Just enough to get the vital changes into the works. I was concerned at the time about Bill's toeing the line. That's all past history. You should see him today.

He's burning up the track.

Don't burn your bridges

Ready for another trip to *your* shop, *your* department? Your eye is on a better job, has been for months. But two, three or five competitors are eyeing the same job. Take one in particular. We'll dub him Tracy. He's not your supervisor; you're not his supervisor. You both work for the same boss. But being totally realistic, you're as much in competition with Tracy as your company that makes nails is in competition with the outfit down the street that makes nails.

Then one day your ship comes in. That spot you've been eyeing for an eternity is yours. It's not Tracy's. *It's yours!*

So what happens now? You're a Big Man. But *how* big? Big enough to step up to Tracy and say, "What a surprise! I never expected it. *You're* the guy I had pegged for this job. *You're* the one who deserves it."

Ponder this. Ponder it from Tracy's point of view. He too has been shooting for that star. But *you're* the one who hit the mark. Maybe Tracy's a good guy. Maybe he's a great guy. But he's human, too. And being human, maybe he's going to resent the fact that it was you and not he who did the scoring. And maybe, consciously or not, he's going to set you up as Number One on his dog list. *Maybe!* Unless you're savvy enough to consider the other fellow's feeling and help him to save face— *savvy enough not to burn your bridges.*

Bridge burning. It's an old Egyptian custom, and it's murder on careers. It makes no difference how you burn them: with a gloating peacock's strut instead of a humble and friendly word of understanding; with angry words instead of patience and tact; with a refusal to cooperate, or a refusal to consider the other person's point of view.

What's the main point? There's an ancient Italian proverb that sums it up to a "T." *Have you fifty friends?—it is not enough. Have you one enemy?—it is too many.*

Now Do This

Sit down with a pencil and pad. Call to mind every individual in your company who is not solidly on your team, whose attitude toward you ranges from lukewarm to ice cold.

What's next? One of the most important projects of your career. *It's bridge reconstruction time!* Mend those cracks. Cement those fissures. The personal satisfaction you derive will be priceless. The two legged roadblocks in your way will be removed.

Summing up

1. Search out and develop the business skills and instincts of your people that complement your own.
2. Don't confuse "Complementary Thinking" with "Yes-Man" response. Shoot for goal agreement, not methods agreement; profit building, not ego soothing.
3. Become a super-TD (Talent Development) Man. Exploit the hidden potential of your people. Expand their scope of activity beyond the humdrum everyday routine.
4. Blast employee apathy with Management Theatrics. When you have a special project to push, a special point to hammer home, use histrionics to explode ordinary sounding incidents into Big Deal events. Don't settle for mild interest or "maybe" action. Fire the imagination with anger, elation, super-charged enthusiasm.
5. Recruit allies to your cause to keep ideas alive. Whip up a turmoil; stir up a storm. Get Pete, Ella, Charley, Sue—*everybody*—into the act. Talk up your idea, and get others to talk it up for you. Invite suggestions; press for participation. *Stoke that fire!*
6. Double the loyalty of your people with an Ego Booster Shot. Use the "Mr. Steelcraft" motivation technique. Give your subordinate a coveted assignment or special responsibility beyond his normal scope. Make him feel Big and Important, Number One for a day. Then watch him respond.
7. Guide your people; train them; develop them. Then let them fly high on their own steam. Prove your faith in their judgment and ability. Trust them, and multiply their loyalty to you.
8. Use measured pressure to unsettle the laurel rester, to spur that extra plus in goal achievement, to brake the downward slide of a subordinate. Study your man carefully. Learn what he can do and what he can take. When you apply the screws, take a small turn at a time. Just enough to fan new life into tired attitudes and freshen interest with new challenge.

9. Don't burn your bridges. Today's enemy could be to-morrow's roadblock in your trip to the top.

10. Resolve today—*and start today*—to convert any person in your company whose attitude toward you is cool and distant into a warm and ardent fan. The path to the top is lined, not with roses, not with thorns, not with gold. It's lined with PEOPLE! Woo them. Cultivate them. Develop and motivate them. It's the surest, safest, most enjoyable way to get ahead.

6

Spark Interest and Enthusiasm

with Job Variety

How important is it for a man to do the work he is cut out to do?

Ask this of a savvy manager and he will answer: "It's just as important as satisfying the basic needs of existence. Without it other needs of existence are not enjoyed."

"Work," says David Sarnoff, "is all important, because that is the only visible and intelligible excuse for our existence. Man expresses the forces with which he is endowed. Work is the most satisfying experience of the day."

True. *If it's the right kind of work,* the job that matches your make-up and personality. Otherwise, the work you do can be boring, frustrating, expressive of nothing much. Take away the interest, the challenge, the excitement, and what do you have? Desolation, unhappiness, and a basic element to cause family problems.

In the case of our young people today this is a major problem. To hold their interest, confront them with challenging and meaningful work. Douglas W. Bray, a Columbia University psychologist, pointed up the importance of this in a special study conducted for A.T. & T. Its purpose, to draw a bead on the ingredients of success, to answer the eternally nagging question: "Why do some men succeed where others fail?"

The findings were revealing. One in particular was reported by *Business Week*. It deals with the relationship of a man's first job to his later performance. "The research group (says *Business Week*) postulated that a college graduate's first contact with an industrial organization would create the most lasting impression —that a challenging first job would be followed by a high level of performance even in relatively dull jobs later on, and that the unchallenged young manager would be severely handicapped throughout his career."

This then is the problem. It applies to a man who is halfway through his career. It applies doubly to a young man who is just starting out.

The trick is to trigger interest, spark enthusiasm, whip up excitement!

Where is the answer? It lies in two of the most potent words in the savvy manager's lexicon.

Job Variety!

What is it? How does it work?

A sage once said, "The wisdom of experience is incommunicable." It's a fact. You can tell a man and tell him. But only when he does it himself, and does it successfully, can you be sure that he has mastered the technique.

What is Job Variety all about? It's a program to keep people continually interested in their job, to keep them continually charged with enthusiasm for the company and, finally, a savvy way to find hidden talents.

How does it work? Quite simply. You take a man, and when he least expects it, you hit him with a spot assignment in an area that is unfamiliar to him. You send a draftsman on a sales call, a typist to the transportation clerical pool. You fly a factory man out of town on a trouble-shooting stint.

Well, perhaps this is a small exaggeration. You don't just *send* him. First you *select* him. You've been observing him, let us say, over the past weeks or months. You see that he's ambitious, willing, eager to learn. You're *fairly* confident that within him is a magic combination which will one day jell and mark him as a doer of deeds and possibly a leader of men. You can almost feel that budding savvy potential straining to burst its shell.

This, then, is the kind of man or woman we're talking about. Now you sit down with your man and brief him. Take that trouble-shooting assignment, for example. You give him a brief idea of what it's all about. You don't go into every detail, purposely. You throw in some tips to shore up his own knowledge—which is usually more than he himself suspects. You brace him further with your 100 per cent faith and if-anyone-can-do-it-you-can backing. You give him a hint that while he is on the selected mission he can feel free to check into any other items that he thinks are worthwhile. This, by the way, is the "bait" you are hoping he will take. Then you let go, and, sink or swim, he's on his own. Oh, he'll go in green, all right. But you hope not dumb green.

Scratching your head at this point? Do you want to know why? What will this do for the man? What will it do for the company? What will it do for *you* as a savvy manager? Four questions; one answer.

Plenty! (And now is as good a time as any to spot again for those multiple benefits from your single profit action.) Here they are.

• You can observe a man for months at his regular routine job and never really know for sure how much he's got on the ball. But throw him for one, two, or three days into an emergency situation, a pressure situation, a sink-or-swim situation, and bingo, suddenly you see him as you never have before. As one businessman put it: "There is no merit where there is no trial; and till experience stamps the mark of strength, cowards may pass for heroes, and faith for falsehood." Here's the simple truth. It takes "heroes" to win your battles. It takes Job Variety to spot heroes, and to milk a man's hidden potential in full.

• Training. To repeat, you can tell a man, and tell him. But throw him into the breach and his learning rate will be multiplied by twenty; his retention rate by a hundred. *He did it,* and he will become the expert on the problem.

• Benefit number three. You build back-up knowledge and flexibility in people to keep on tap for emergencies. Or to take the load off your key people—and yourself—freeing them, or you, for other important responsibilities. You begin to develop a new breed of specialist, a "generalist."

• Finally, and most important, you stir your people and keep them stirred. What can be more challenging and exciting than the prospect of pitting yourself against the unknown? Does apathy concern you? With Job Variety, forget it. Job Variety keeps a man on his toes. Expectancy keeps him alert. He never knows when you'll call upon him; or for what. As author Graham Greene once said: "When we are not sure, we are alive."

That's it. That's the essence of it, and what do we have? Four questions. Four benefits. A single profit action.

The "First-Time Shakes"

"The great man," a philosopher once said, "is the man who does a thing for the first time." With good reason. The first time is the toughest time of all. Whether it's driving a car, making a speech, or kissing a girl.

How do you steady the "First-Time Shakes?" Simple. Get 'em over and done with.

I mentioned a trouble-shooting assignment. The shaker in this case was Jerry, a young man from our engineering department. I handed him the assignment with a twinkle. He responded with a quake, and a worry-ridden, "Who, me!"

"Yes, you," I told him. The job was in Chicago. Jerry started to protest. I shrugged and gave him a chance to turn it down. I also pointed out he would be sidestepping a worthwhile experience if he did so and I gave him an hour to make up his mind. He didn't need an hour. The fact is, I knew my man, or I wouldn't have selected him.

We sat down for 30 minutes in my office. The Chicago distributor had a complaint or two, needed clarification on certain operating procedures, and on a particular product use. Jerry knew the product line. But he was light on procedures. I filled him in on the problem, gave him some pointers, and that was that.

"Your tickets will be waiting at the airport," I said.

Two days later Jerry was back. Talk about windbags. Talk about excitement. I couldn't shut him up.

Did I say "excitement?" It's an understatement. The experiment had pumped him full of enthusiasm; it had made him feel like a big operator. Jerry had fielded most of the questions well and had helped solve most of the problems. Where his knowledge was light, he had made notes. And he made it his business to fill in the gaps and get back to the distributor on the telephone.

Obviously, Job Variety works for Steelcraft. The question is, will it work for somebody else? Somebody else? *Anybody else!* Here's proof. I have a friend in the machine tool business, and I convinced him to try J-V in his shop.

He did. One of his customers had an order he wanted filled. It was a key account and a very special order. To provide extra service, my friend decided to send one of his people to pick up the order. He checked with the Chief Engineer and selected a young man who was an excellent draftsman, but had never been out of the office.

The young man was sent to visit the customer. He was told to pick up the order, review the details of the job, and, at the same time, look over the rest of the operation.

The draftsman made the trip and came back with the order. My friend asked how things worked out and how the customer was doing. The young man frowned. They were doing all right, he said, but he was convinced that they could be doing more business.

My friend laughed and told him not to be greedy, that they had already increased their business by 50 per cent.

The draftsman refused to buy this. With a little more effort, he felt, it could be increased 100 per cent.

My friend checked into the situation for himself and came to the same conclusion.

At the moment, my friend tells me, the young man is still a draftsman. But he gets out of the shop more and is being groomed for bigger things.

Build generalist skills

You hear much talk these days about adjustment. Throughout industry a vast manhunt is in progress for the self-adjusted, well-adjusted job candidate. We interview, test, check, and do as much as we can to see if Mr. Candidate will do job X. First of all, do we really know what we want? Are we more interested in the immediate prospect of getting job X done? Or are we willing to use the candidate's talent to its full potential by adjusting the job?

Most of the people who knock on my door for employment these days have neat little niches all set up for themselves, for example, accounting, production, or data processing.

Only rarely does a young fellow say outrightly and forthrightly, "I want to learn your business so that I can grow with your business. I'd like to have a crack at a *variety* of jobs so that I can learn what I can do best, and develop an understanding of the total business picture."

The young people are not to blame. They're bombarded from all sides—from schools, advisers, want ads, personnel offices—with specialization, specialization and more specialization. Maybe this is a one-man crusade. But I see the problem repeated again and again. *Business today is in critical need of generalists.* Why can't we think of a generalist as a "specialist " And just off the top of my head I can call to mind at least a dozen businessmen friends who feel the same way that I do about this. They'd lay out a plush red carpet for the young man who would come out and say frankly and honestly: "I want to learn this business. I'd like to switch from job to job. I'm willing to work any place, or do anything."

What is called for, I think, is a reshaping, or at least a partial reshaping of personnel policy in many companies. Too many personnel men view a specific job opening as consisting solely of skills one, two, three, four and five. So what happens? A man applies for this job, and maybe he's a bit light on numbers two and five. But he's ambitious, intelligent, eager to learn. He's light, but bright. And he has a plus to offer with skills six and seven. He's in a position to add new dimensions to the job.

Do you see what I'm driving at? There's too much rounding of men to get them to slide effortlessly into the round little holes that have been prepared for them. What I'd like to know is this. What's wrong with shaping the job to fit the man? Why not add *his* talents—those sixth and seventh dimensions—to expand and alter the duties and responsibilities involved? This kind of thinking can help expand your business. And the scope of your staff. It can improve decision making.

That's what we do in our company, and it works out fine. We forage greedily for new talent wherever and whenever we can. And we exploit it however we can, conventions be hanged. We have an engineer, for example, who can turn a phrase like a pro. He loves engineering too, and would never think of giving it up. But you should see the lift he gets when we consult him on a sales promotion problem, or seek his opinion on some advertising copy. Not only does he come up with interesting ideas, but his approach is fresh and new. He brings the technologist's point of view to the problem. This adds up to more profits for the company. It also fulfills a basic need for him, and it helps to spice his life with variety.

Your Future

So much for your people. Now, what about *you?* How can you be sure that *your* best talents and abilities are being uncovered and put to the most profitable use for your company and yourself?

One thing you can do is study the decision makers in your company. Make a list of the men who have it in their power to guide and shape your career. Be an opportunist; there's a vast amount at stake. Can you participate in the job variety program? Have you volunteered to tackle a tough or unusual assignment? Are you willing to respond to a challenge? Are you *eager* for the challenge? Are you prepared to meet a business situation head-on without knowing in advance just how you are going to handle the situation?

Get into the minds of the decision makers in your company. Analyze their actions. Then ask yourself these searching questions:

1. In your company, are employees at all levels urged and encouraged to express their ideas?
2. If a man wants to learn, does he get the opportunity to learn?
3. Can you point to specific instances where new talent was uncovered?
4. Does your company have a program—formal or informal—which in one way or other provides for job variety and *planned diversification?*

In short, are your company's decision makers *slotsmen*—or *spotsmen*?

Track down hidden talent

No pun intended, but the savvy manager is a dogged blood-hound. Take President Kennedy. He was a renowned snooper. He'd drop in on low-ranking civil servants or kibitz minor planning meetings with his ears open, his eyes alert.

The savvy manager tracks down the same trail. Reason: *To sniff out talent that might otherwise go unnoticed.*

Take my word for it. The talent trackdown is one of the most fascinating and rewarding of all management pursuits. You nose around the office or shop. You flush out people with spunk, with ideas, with imagination, who are buried in low-level jobs. When you spot a winner—Hallelujah!—that's when the real management kicks start. You feel the thrill of building people, the joy of molding pros.

Now, more than ever, your savvy perceptivity will pay off. You keep a sharp eye on your "quarry." You take note of his actions, observe his method of thinking and planning. You get to know him as a worker and as a person.

Ready for a live example? Young Jim K. will fill the bill perfectly. I "discovered" Jim a few months back at a production meeting. Plagiarizing the Kennedy technique, I had just happened to drop in, snooping, sniffing. The meeting was on the line and supervisory level. A discussion was in progress, and Jim, a production man, was giving forth. I nodded to him to continue, and sat down quietly. I watched. I listened. Adding two and two I saw that he had come up with a solution to a complex problem that had baffled his supervisor and others. There was something about this young man that appealed to me. I liked the way he put across his ideas. I liked the way he listened and reflected when an opposing view was presented.

I sat there five or ten minutes. Then, as quietly as I had entered, I left. Not one word said, but I had the feeling that my small investment in time would reap a handsome dividend.

Jim doesn't know it yet, but he's under close scrutiny. I mentioned his name to our manufacturing manager and he agreed that this man had exceptional talent potential. One day soon we'll earmark him for some special project. And when that happens, he'll be on his way. In the meantime we'll be informally developing his talents, fortifying his strengths, shoring up his weaknesses.

Sharpen That Pencil

It's *you-time* again. Operation Talent Hunt! More exciting than a fox chase; more fun than a scavenger hunt. And the payoff's magnificent. You help your people. You help yourself. You can't miss! Believe it or not, some so-called leaders are actually afraid of building other people. Perhaps they feel that the other person will outshine them or even advance further than they. To me this is ridiculous and is proof of a poor leader. In fact, I know of one manager in a large insurance company who is constanly developing outstanding supervisors. After he has developed them, they are usually pulled from his department and placed in strategic jobs in other departments. He could object, but doesn't. He puts the company interests ahead of his personal departmental interests. As a result, in the overall picture this manager has grown impressively in position, pay and station with his company.

Now, to really start the program, here's what you do.

The question is this: Which of your people are most likely to possess the hidden talent potential that can mean so much to them and to you? There's no positive and clearcut answer. But here are some of the key clues to spot for; they'll make your talent scouting a good deal easier.

- Your talented employee is probably a prober, a searcher. He asks questions. He's hungry for knowledge.
- It's against his nature to settle blindly for existing methods. He challenges the status quo; is chock-full of ideas of his own.
- He rebels against accepting orders routinely and thoughtlessly. He wants to know *why*. Yet he doesn't argue, or isn't belligerent.
- He turns restless and dissatisfied when idle. He wants to learn. He wants to do. If he's done with his own job, he'll volunteer to help others.

Are the clues foolproof? No. They're simply indicators, talent pointers. The man who quite definitely fills the bill is one to be watched. Handle him with care. Give him an added plus of training and development.

What about the man who doesn't fill the bill? What do you do, just write him off? Well, if you're really savvy, this employee will present a special challenge to you. He may be timid, unsure of himself. His hidden potential may be so deeply hidden it would take a derrick to uproot it. And that's where you come in. The derrick is *you!*

You motivate the man. You inspire and encourage him. You explore his interests, invite his opinions, build his ego and self-confidence. And I can tell you this. It won't happen often, but once in every long, long while you'll get a timid bud to bloom. And when you do, you can pat yourself on the back and strut around like the proudest of peacocks. Because you will have just chalked up the supreme achievement of the savvy manager.

So now is the time to take that pad of yours and start to write some names. List each and every subordinate who works for you. Then, using the clues above as a guide, run each one through the capsule talent test. The fact is this. There is a reserve of untapped talent hidden within every one of us. Your job is to learn how deeply the reserve is hidden within each of your people.

Then there's only one thing left to do. Start tapping.

When the Wings Are Strong, Release the Bird

What's the difference between management and life? No difference. Management *is* life. Or a vital chunk of life. Here's what I mean. To teach a boy to hit a ball, you stand him up at bat. To teach an 18-year-old to drive a car, you put him behind the wheel. In management you do the same thing. To teach a man to manage, you let him manage.

Back to the griddle for a case in point. His name is John; his job is in the order department. What kind of person is he? He's the kind who is never satisfied. He was stapling some promotional material, for example, a staple on each side. After 30 minutes or so he walked up to his supervisor. "I've been thinking," he said, "why can't we weld two staplers together, run a bar across the top, and do the job in one operation instead of two?"

See what I mean? The young man is a thinker. His thought is profit directed, savvy directed.

Well, one day recently, John received a call from a customer in the east who was hopping mad. He had problems, and one of our managers had promised to fly down there, but still hadn't made it. John had a worried look on his face. "The customer's really upset," he said. "I think somebody better get to him in a hurry."

"I agree," I said. "When can you leave?"

John didn't exactly gulp. But his, "Who me!" was a gulp in itself.

"Why not?" I said. "You know the problem. You know the product line. You talked to him on the telephone. Why not you?"

John looked miserable, but that afternoon he left. He took off with apprehension and misgivings; he returned with a light in his eyes.

And what's more, John waved a fat order before my eyes.

Apparently John made a big hit with the customer. Every time he calls on the phone, there's only one man he wants to talk with. That's right, you guessed it. It's John.

The point is clear. A boy with a bat; an 18-year-old with a car; a young fellow in the order department. It makes no difference.

When the wings are strong, release the bird.

Roll the Dice and Take Your Chances

It has been said, "Who bravely dares must sometimes risk a fall."

One problem today is that too many managers are afraid to risk that fall. They worry. They frown. The subordinate may lose the order. He may be unable to fix the trouble. He may fall on his face. So instead of sending a green climber to scale a new peak, they chicken out. They keep him rooted to the same dull desk, the same old routine ho-hum grind. When a peak needs scaling, they set out on their own.

There's an advantage to this approach. Give the seasoned manager a problem to solve, a trouble to shoot, he'll naturally get the job done faster and better. He's been there before. He's sure of himself. He knows the way.

But what about the other side of the coin? While the play-it-safer is out there scaling all the peaks himself, what happens to his people? Nothing happens. That's the problem. His people keep sitting out dance after dance. Day after day and week after week, they know what to expect from minute to minute and hour to hour.

They're bored.

Even if their mouths are closed and their eyes open, inside they're fast asleep. They're zestless and restless. Their interest fades. They yawn from within. Unless they're *really* smart. Then they quit.

I'll grant you this. It's not easy for a manager to risk that fall. But unless he does, he'll have the responsibility—whether he likes it or not—of stunting his people's growth, creating "mental neuters," instead of inspired producers.

Here's how Ronald E. Osborn expresses the thought in *Do a Good Job of Living:* "Undertake something that is difficult; it will do you good. Unless you try to do something beyond what you have already mastered, you will never grow."

This applies to you. It applies to your people.

So what's your personal decision? Are you after that "sure thing?" Or are you willing to take a chance and swing over to the savvy side? How does the swing work? Simple. You train and guide your people; you inspire them to scale those peaks—and you *equip* them to scale those peaks. You work with a man and put all that you've got into his development. Then at some point you come to the decision that, by George, I believe the man has got it now, and if I give him the chance I think he will make it.

And when you reach that point, you throw the dice.

Most of the time they'll come up seven or eleven. But on rare occasions, you may throw a deuce, or hit those box cars. Your man may fall on his face, make a mistake, blow an order, embarrass you. So what happens then? One thing only—if you've got the gumption and the guts, if you're really savvy.

You start all over again.

Because here's the gist of it. The people who will really go to bat for you are the good men that you've made good, and whom you've backed up with your confidence and your faith—and that roll of the dice.

How It Works

How does the system work? Take Bernie. He is a sharp accountant. He has been with us for years. He knows our products and methods backwards and forward. But in our outfit, traditional, chart-centered departmental lines don't count for much. We believe that if a man keeps balancing the same ledgers, writing the same releases, welding the same pieces, day after day, he's going to get bored. And if he gets bored, his growth is apt to stop.

Thoreau once put it this way: "What is the use of going over the old track again? You must make tracks into the unknown."

Bill's chance to start tracking came one day when I received a call from a customer. It was a request for one of our people to deliver a speech before an audience of 100 or so architects and contractors. It was the perfect opportunity to give our Job Variety program an energizing shot. Bernie was the target selected. I told him about the invitation. "Bernie," I said, "you have a great personality. At our staff meetings you give forth like a pro. You know all about our products. And here's a speech that's all written out in advance. I can't think of a more qualified man to represent us."

Bernie has a sense of humor. "It's a challenge, all right," he groused, "Like sending a man into a tiger's cage armed with a feather."

Feather or not, Bernie responded to the challenge. How did he do? Sensational? A second Oliver Wendell Holmes? Not quite. He was fair, perhaps, maybe even mediocre. But that was a year ago, don't forget. You should have heard him the other day. He brought the house down.

When You Bet and Lose

Here's another firing line case for you, a man by the name of Bob. We talked about Bernie just now. A year ago we shoved Bernie in front of an audience; today he's an accomplished speaker. Well, Bob got pretty much the same treatment.

How does the saying go? "You can't win 'em all!" Bob's a living example. I mentioned the "rare occasion" when the dice come up two or twelve instead of a "natural." Well, meet "Rare Occasion" Bob, the man we bet on and lost. *And then bet on again.*

The time of the first bet was during a series of meetings with distributors from all over the United States and Canada. Our chief engineer was slated to handle the technical part of the program. But a few of the meetings overlapped. The chief couldn't attend all of them at the same time. So we took some of our young inside men to sub for the chief at some of the meetings.

There was one man we really counted on. He was sharp, knowledgeable, and could talk up a storm. Back in the shop he could make the wildest idea sound logical. This was Bob. The other two we weren't too sure about.

So what happened? You guessed it. The other two men? Surpassed themselves, did an A plus job. Bob? Blah minus. It's hard to explain. At home Bob was virtually a silver-tongued orator. Before an audience of strangers he responded like a shy twelve-year-old reciting a lesson he had neglected to study. Oh well, these things happen. We chalked it up to initial stage fright and threw him into another meeting; to sink or swim. He sank. That was the clincher. As a public speaker Bob would never be anything to speak about.

He was a pretty fair inside man. Still, with his love for person-to-person contact and his ability to persuade, I couldn't shake the feeling that for him there was a sweeter cup of tea to be found. The chance to test my hunch came a few weeks later. We needed a man to work with a distributor on a new product line. It was a tough selling assignment. It meant stumping a territory, ringing doorbells, calling on architects, convincing them that this new product was just about what they had been waiting for all these years.

"Bob," I told him, "You're a natural for this job. You know how the product is made and how it's used. And you have more sell in your little finger than most people have in their whole body."

He didn't look convinced. But Bob is a gutsy kind of person. So he went off stumping. Eight days later he returned. He had called on 42 architects, got 15 acceptances of our product.

"How did you like selling, Bob?"

He shifted his feet, then came out with it. "I've been thinking, Bob. Maybe I'm not cut out for inside work. If it's all right with you . . ."

It was all right with me. Today Bob's in the field, working with distributors, shooting customer problems, selling doors, and selling good will. He's happier and richer than he ever was before.

What does it all prove? A potent savvy point. When you feel that one of your people has the right kind of stuff in him, he merits *training* and *trying* and *betting*. Again and again and again. Until that "natural" is thrown.

What about you?

Let's assume first that *you* do have the right kind of stuff. You must have, or you wouldn't be here now trying to improve yourself. All right, you are ready to *train* and *try* and *bet* on *your* people. But what about your boss? Will he do the same for you? If you're lucky, yes. If he's a savvy manager, yes.

But here's a super-savvy tip. *Don't count on it!* Don't hinge *your* career on another man's action.

Remember this. Planned diversification is meant for you as well as your people. If your boss doesn't apply it, it's up to you to apply it yourself. And this is going to take self-discipline. It means you force yourself to begin. You force yourself to continue.

And this is how you do it. You greedily absorb experience outside your own particular bailiwick. Osmosis. Remember? You keep the old maxim in mind that you're never too smart to learn. A sage once said: "However learned or eloquent, man knows nothing truly that he has not learned from experience."

That's the trick. You learn from experience. If the experience isn't thrown at you, you make it yourself. You question. You snoop. You read, not only what you're *expected* to read, but a little bit more.

You keep perpetually on the scent of thought starters, new ideas, and you don't restrict your thinking to conventional habits and systems. There are times, of course, when you can take an idea and virtually superimpose it on your own operation. But more often it's a matter of taking the idea, mulling it over, and dreaming up a profitable ramification to suit your own purpose.

All right, here's another savvy example for you. A manager I know works for a Kansas manufacturing company. His plant borders on an unused overgrown field. The high weeds and grass constitute a distinct fire hazard, especially during the dry season. One day, tracking down ideas in an issue of *Profit Improvement News,* he read that the Aerojet Corporation in Downey, California, had a similar problem. To solve it, Aerojet made a deal with a local stockman to have his sheep graze on the land. This mowed down the weeds at a fraction of the cost of the bulldozers and chemicals that were formerly used. It also set this man to thinking. There were no sheep nearby, but a farmer down the road bred cows. Cows, as it turned out, were even more hungry than sheep. Get the idea?

The magic key is awareness and alertness. Get to know your company's problems in a variety of areas. Don't limit your thinking to your own department. Actually, this Kansas manager is a production man. What does grazing have to do with a production man? Plenty, if he has the savvy. *He feeds on ideas.*

What about you? Are you constantly on the prowl, foraging for ideas in all areas of the company? Do you ask yourself over and over again, one day after another: "What can I improve today? What new aspect of the business can I master today?" If so, do you follow through with a definite plan? And definite action?

Time to Plan

Pencil and pad time again. Ever hear of the youngster who wanted more than anything to march in the big circus parade? Hearing that trombonists were needed, the boy signed up, and when the parade started he was in it. But almost at once the horrendous sound of his horn caused two old ladies to faint and a horse to go berserk. The redfaced bandmaster raved at the boy, "Why didn't you say you couldn't play the trombone?" The boy gazed up at him. "I didn't know. I never tried before."

He didn't know. But that didn't stop him. He was ready and willing to explore the unknown.

Are you prepared to do the same? If so, your best bet is to start today to plan for tomorrow. *Think!* What *new and unfamiliar* problem or learning assignment has your boss given you for tomorrow? If your answer is "None," don't settle for this. Come up with one of your own. Investigate an unfamiliar technique. Pioneer a new strategy, even if you must invest your own time to do it. Remember, solving problems is your job.

Repeat this procedure the day after tomorrow, and every day thereafter. Track down thought starters. Find new ways to improve the business, and improve your understanding of the business.

Resolve now that your sideline days are over.
March in that parade!

Variety roundup

1. Do your people enjoy job satisfaction, or suffer from job frustration? Your answer could well be a clue to your savvy achievement to date.
2. Bombard your people with the unexpected, spice their lives with surprise. "The more we look forward to anything," said Schopenhauer, "the less we enjoy it when it comes."
3. If a man's first job is challenging, the experts find, it will boost his performance in all jobs to come. In a very real sense the level of balance between the happiness and frustration of your people is under *your* control. Are there any career freshmen on your team? It's a thought to mull over.
4. You can't *talk* a man into becoming a thoroughbred. But you can work him into one by saturating him with experience. And don't get discouraged if progress is slow. Says Homer: "After the event, even a fool is wise."
5. Keep the multiple benefits of Job Variety in mind to spark and sustain your program. (1) J-V stimulates job interest, challenge, and excitement. (2) It gives you the chance to watch a man under fire, determine his real potential as a worker, as a person. (3) Under J-V men learn faster and retain what they learn longer. (4) You build job flexibility, more people equipped to handle more tasks. (5) You build ego, develop self-confidence.
6. Don't tailor people to fit job slots. Instead, shape slots to fit your people. Take advantage of every opportunity to add a new dimension of talent and achievement to each and every job.
7. Test the J-V climate in your company. Analyze those decision makers who wield the greatest amount of influence on your career. Are they interested in exploring and using *your* talents? Or, in their eyes, are you simply a peg that fills a slot? If there is no opportunity to.branch your knowledge and expand your growth, you may be rowing with the wrong crew.

8. Nose out hidden talent in your office or shop. Pop in on meetings; drop in on people at work; observe rank-and-filers in action. Spot for ideamen and potential leaders who are buried in low-level jobs.

9. Don't yield to the temptation to always do the job yourself because you can do it faster and better. After developing an employee, and imbuing him with your knowledge and savvy, it's time to let go. Roll those dice. Give him a chance to take off on his own.

10. Organize a planned diversification program for yourself as well as your people. Don't count on the boss to do this for you. Resolve—and *plan*—each day to learn something new and to do something new.

7

Squeeze 70 Minutes Out

of Every Hour

I have always said this. The savvy manager leads a well-rounded life. He is a first-rate businessman, a successful husband and father, a prime contributor to the community.

Who has time for all this? YOU have. *If you organize your time properly.* As Goethe said: "We always have time enough, if we will but use it aright."

Each day I run into managers whose lives are hectic and hollow. They have not yet mastered the art of using their time "aright." Instead of getting the clock to work for them, they are slaves to the clock.

Rarely do I work more than nine or ten hours a day. Some managers tell me they *have to work* 11, 12, even 13 hours a day, just to keep up. Do they really have to do this? I doubt it. I think that if they use their time in a sensible, SAVVY, well-planned way they will be able to do in eight hours what most men do in 12.

There's a way to use time imaginatively and productively. And there's a way to just "use it up," like a plow horse on a farm. As the saying goes, "There is no better way to kill time than by working it to death."

It is the purpose of this chapter to help you to become a "clockwatcher" in the most positive sense of the word. To impose practical and productive deadlines on yourself. To evaluate each task and allocate your time accordingly. To help you, in short, to squeeze 70 minutes of value out of every hour you work.

Make time for must-do functions only

There are five basic areas of time use that a savvy manager should concern himself with each and every working day. If you plan on these five, and stick to plan, the subfunctions will fall into place on their own.

1. START BY PLANNING YOUR DAY IN ADVANCE. A well-organized time plan is a flexible time plan. You can get a head start at planning your daily priorities from the moment you rise in the morning. It's a matter of opening your mind to the sequence of events in the day ahead of you, sorting out essentials in the order of their importance. You don't have to wait till you arrive at the office to start this. You can do it while shaving, while dressing, while riding to work.

Once this is done, your day's basic format will be set. But not rigidly set. The keyword is still *flexibility*. Strategy number two goes into being when you arrive at work. I refer to this as the "Circulation Phase." Here's how it works on the firing line.

The first thing I do each morning is to circulate among my key people.

This is the time my people know they can call my attention to anything on their minds that is important to them. It is also the time I begin to finalize my plan for the day.

Get the idea? First the master plan—before arriving at work. Then the modifications. Put it all together and your day is organized. Not only that, but it's a good application of training in action. As you organize *your* day, your people learn to organize theirs. And in the process *it forces you to force your people to diversify their talents and shoulder new responsibilities.*

2. GIVE PEOPLE DEVELOPMENT YOUR SUPER-AAA TIME PRIORITY. We all have to cut time corners to get essential tasks completed. The problem is in knowing which corners to cut. Well, I can tell you this. *The one corner you positively should NOT cut is in the area of people development!*

Training and development is the key to management savvy. Don't give up on training or development until you are reasonably sure that it's hopeless. Don't be afraid to use intuition in your judgment. The Alexander Hamilton Institute's desk dictionary of business terms defines management as, ". . . the judicious use or skilled application of people to accomplish an objective." The day you find yourself without time for that "judicious use," my advice is to take a hard second look at your operation, because it means that something is wrong.

3. MOVE AT LEAST ONE IMPROVEMENT STEP FORWARD EACH DAY. What happens when a manager gets himself snowed in by day-to-day operations? That's right, *he forgets to manage.* He forgets to IMPROVE, which is the most vital part of management. How can you make sure that *you* improve yourself and your operation? *By pushing up your personal IQ (Improvement Quota) each and every working day.* The trick is not to let one day pass by without making some change for the better. Here's the way I work it in my own shop. Each day I select a different improvement target. I ask myself: "How can I cut the budget?" "What can I do to sharpen the selling effort?" "How can I boost production of a particular product?" "What can I do to cut down scrap?" Each day something else. I make sure that the target is not so big that I can't accomplish it within my time schedule.

Where does the payoff come in? Simple. There's no better way to flag top management attention. *Because when you think improvement, you think like an owner.* And when you think like an owner, the owner sits up and takes notice.

4. GIVE YOUR OPERATION A DAILY ONCE-OVER. Here's a fact of business life. Your people need your leadership. It's one of their basic requirements. They need to know you're around, that you're interested in what they are doing. *That you care!* I make it my business to go through my operation at least once a day. I would suggest, in your savvy-building effort, that you do the same.

I'll ask one man how his wife is doing after the operation. I'll ask another how a particular machine is working or a system is operating. What does this do for me? It keeps me in the midst of things, alert to problems. I remain a vital part of the operation. In my book, absentee management does not work. You have to be there, on the scene, participating, probing, checking and managing.

What does it do for my people? It gives them reassurance. It lets them know I'm concerned about their jobs, their lives, their problems.

But now we get back to time. A savvy manager is a busy manager. Granted. But if you resolve to do it, you can *make* time for the operational walkthrough each day. As I said, the best time plan is the most flexible time plan. In almost any working day you can steal a few spare minutes if you are really determined to. You finish a particular task ahead of schedule. A visitor you had an appointment with doesn't show up. You sneak out of a meeting early, leaving your subordinates to carry the ball in your absence.

Little bits of time, wherever you can snatch them. To the savvy manager they're more precious than diamonds.

5. RETAIN TASKMASTER CONTROL OVER EVERYDAY ESSENTIALS. This includes an infinite number of tasks too numerous to cite in detail. Correspondence, scheduling, reports, fixing, arranging, putting out fires. They vary by occupation and responsibility. And they take up the bulk of a manager's day.

Most important, these are the time-eaters that cause so many non-savvy managers to mismanage their days. How do you beat the time-eaters down to size? It's easy. *You narrow your definition of "essentials" into the time slot allocated for essentials.* Sound like gobbledegook? It's not. You simply make positive provisions for your people, your improvement effort, your time planning and the rest. What's left over gets assigned to "essentials."

The obvious rejoinder is this. What happens if you wind up with five hours' worth of time balance and eight hours' worth of essentials?

No problem. You redefine your "essentials." You eliminate, you shortcut, you delegate. You turn over left-over tasks to the people you are *training and developing* to cope with them. You build your people's savvy and growth. At the same time you release yourself for broader duties and more important responsibilities.

Take Positive Steps to Plug Time Leaks

Your goal as a savvy manager is to expand your activities to achieve more on any given day. Some managers, it is said, are unable to see the forest for the trees. Others are unable to see the hours for the minutes.

I'm talking about time leaks, the kind that defeat that activity-expansion goal. Precious minutes drip away from day to day. Over days and weeks they add up to pails filled with hours. Priceless hours down the drain.

The question is this. How can you spot time leaks and plug them before the trickle becomes a stream? *The trick is to alert yourself to time-waste signals,* and trouble-shoot those leaks out of your system.

TIME-WASTE SIGNAL No. 1—COMPLAINTS. Premise: If you're a savvy manager you operate on the "exception" principle. You take action on a job or transaction only when trouble appears. The system is as practical as wheels on an automobile. The problem is to build the exception tip-off into your system and to respond to it as it occurs. And this means savvy tip-offs as well as job and transaction tip-offs.

Example: COMPLAINTS. Specifically, the presence of too many complaints. This is a tip-off to the savvy manager that something is wrong. Here is a firing line illustration.

A financial vice president I know uses a voucher system in his office. One day recently he noticed that one of his supervisors was spending a great deal of time messing around with the vouchers. He inquired about it. "Well," the supervisor began, "we've been getting a lot of complaints. . . ."

"That's all I had to hear," this savvy financial manager told me, "'. . . a lot of complaints.' That was the tip-off. 'Why are you getting a lot of complaints?' I wanted to know. The supervisor had no answer. He was too busy fiddling around with the trees," my friend said. "He never took a good hard look at the forest. As soon as he probed into the forest, the complaints cleared up."

Here's the point. When you get too many complaints about any aspect of your operation it's time to take some time to save some time. Take a look at the overall picture. Do some sherlocking. Get down to root causes and root effects. Because complaints can wade through a manager's time faster than a rat through cheese. When you handle complaints on an individual basis instead of tracking down the cause, it's like putting a pot under a leaky faucet to catch the drips. When what you should really do is change the washer.

TIME-WASTE SIGNAL No. 2—TONGUE TIME TWISTERS. You don't have to work time to death; you can talk it to death—

on the telephone; face-to-face; with visitors you shouldn't be seeing, or whose visits are over-extended. No truly savvy manager can afford to chatter his minutes away. They're too precious. Still, the temptation is great. Everyone enjoys the sound of his own voice. Too often we repeat ourselves in conversations. Learn to be more concise. One way to defeat this temptation is to take the words of the philosopher Seneca to heart: "A man who has taken your time recognizes no debt; yet it is the one he can never repay." And remember this. It works two ways.

TIME-WASTE SIGNAL NO. 3—PAPERWORK PILE-UPS. Show me a desk piled high, and I'll show you time laid low. I've seen it in my own shop. We have two supervisors on our sales staff. Both have similar jobs, similar territory responsibilities. One day I passed through the office. Al's desk was clear; Fred's was loaded.

"Fred," I asked, "what is that big pile of papers?" He was out of town a few days, he explained, and the work was backed up. The papers? Mostly copies of orders. He liked to go through them himself; it gave him a feel for what was going on in the field. But now he looked nervous and harassed, far more than usual.

I advised him to get rid of the stuff, and you should have seen the relief on his face.

He had never thought of this, the simplest of all solutions, for himself. The reason, he was *habit-ridden!* In his view, going through the orders was an essential. And it was—*when time permitted it to be an essential.* That's the distinction. When time does not permit, that's the best time for a re-evaluation of essentials. And one of the best tip-offs to this is when paper piles high on your desk.

Sometimes I think every manager should have a scale on his desk. When his paper pile-up weighs more than a pound, he should start thinking of ways to cut down, to delegate, or, as in this case, eliminate.

TIME-WASTE SIGNAL NO. 4—IDLE TIME. To repeat, your main achievement as a savvy manager will be, not on a do-it-yourself basis, but with and through your people. It stands to reason, therefore, that you should never be too busy to keep your people busy. When they are idle, it indicates a double leak in your system. Because idle time of your people could always be better spent taking over tasks that you are doing yourself. As I said, there's nothing wrong with being a clockwatcher if you watch it constructively. As one wag said, "The thing you can learn by watching the clock is that it passes the time by keeping its hands busy." Where people are concerned, it applies to minds as well.

TIME-WASTE SIGNAL No. 5—EFFICIENCY DRAIN. When a subordinate does not fulfill a responsibility, it generates inefficiency. This is probably the worst kind of waste because of its pyramiding effect. How can you control and suppress efficiency drain? By sharp management follow-through. This doesn't mean you peer constantly over a man's shoulder. And you don't breathe down his neck. But you do keep a savvy eye peeled for *results*. When results don't live up to expectations, you probe, you investigate, you find out why.

You on Stage

It's time for you to get into the act again. Now, presumably, everything you do you consider essential or you wouldn't be doing it. But chances are, unless your savvy rating is close to the top mark, there are many things you classify as essential—possibly out of habit—that would show up under close scrutiny as not really essential at all. Savvy action number one, therefore, is to review as many of the tasks that you can call to mind, and see how many you can redefine OUT of the essential category. Your target, in short, is to come up with:

Your own personal checklist of unessential essentials

You can do this by writing each task that comes to mind on a sheet of paper. (Or six sheets, depending on how busy you are.) Then pose the following questions for each item listed:

- Can it be eliminated altogether?
- Can it be time-shortened through simplification?
- Can it be turned over to your secretary or assistant?
- If it's a task for someone else, can you persuade him to do without it?
- Is the task paying its way? (The idea here is to use the Value Analysis approach. Make sure that the value derived from the task's achievement exceeds the cost of the time and effort you are putting into it.)

Boost Time Productivity by Sharpening Your Systems

Nothing can foul a time plan faster than a system shot through with flaws. A shaky system spawns problems, breeds complaints, generates extra correspondence and a multiplicity of chores. It makes the job long and tempers short.

When a system functions smoothly people derive a necessary feeling of achievement and self-satisfaction. Frustration and griping are kept at a low level.

How do you get a system organized so that it will run smoothly and efficiently with a maximum of production and a minimum of problems? By giving it your close and personal interest. By getting the person who will administer the system to help develop it. For example:

Work Side by Side with Your People

We put in a new system some months back to handle customer requests for literature. Ben, the savvy manager in charge, knew that all systems—*especially new systems*—bear close watching. Thus, it didn't take him long to note that the girl processing the requests was having her problems. He determined this by making the time and taking the time to sit down with her and analyze the operation on a firing line basis.

He made sure that the brochures and folders were set up logically and accessibly in the racks. That the customer's request form was properly designed. That the catalog numbers were sensibly assigned, the materials easily identified. In short, Ben saw to it that the girl could pick up a request, walk down the line of racks from beginning to end, and pull every piece of literature with a minimum of time, effort and confusion. And the payoff was worthwhile.

For one thing, as he sharpened the system, he trained the girl, developed her systems awareness. He got *her* into the act as well as getting in himself. This gave her a personal stake in the operation, made it *her* system as well as his own. This stimulated the girl's satisfaction in her job and boosted her productivity. And by keeping problems to a minimum, he kept his own time involvement in the future to a minimum. (Multiple Value, of course.)

Here's another case example for you. We've developed a form

that is highly unorthodox, yet has saved many hours over the past year or two. The form was created in response to our need for faster answers to the information requests we send to our distributors. What was happening was that the slow replies delayed our processing and generated extra correspondence and phone calls. Expensive and time consuming.

The solution? It would make you blink—*literally*—to see it. It's a sunny bright "Day Glo" form. It reads: URGENT—IMMEDIATE ACTION NECESSARY! It is on a dazzling red paper, and as I said, it makes the reader blink. It also triggers the immediate action called for. Why? Because people want to get it out of their sight as soon as possible!

The point is this. *To produce results, the savvy manager dares to be different.* He hacks out paths of his own.

Who says a form has to be a certain size or shape? Who says it has to conform to a specified layout or wording? If it will save you time and sharpen your systems, you can produce a round form, or a triangular form, and have it printed in purple, three-inch letters. Why not? There's no law against it. But there *is* a savvy law that fairly cries out: Experiment! Pioneer! Be unique!

Draw a Bead on Your Operation

Sharpshooting time again. Step one, have your staff members make a list of every job in your department, and make sure there is a clear and simple written procedure in the works to describe each one. This alone will do much to tighten the system. Putting it down on paper tends to pinpoint the flaws, and suggest improvements more readily. Next, schedule a personal systems review for each project and job within your scope. Examine each step of each procedure with your people on a side-by-side basis.

Looking for a special area in your department to improve each day? This is as good a place as any to start. It will boost your savvy rating, and one day soon you will wake up and wonder:

"Where did all that extra time come from?"

Trim Time-Consuming Fat With Management Shorthand

Elsewhere in this book I stress the powerful results you get when you communicate in shorthand. You can extend this vital concept into every management function. You will save hours each week if you work, act and think in shorthand.

SHORTHAND! The art of distillation. The art of boiling down a paragraph in a sentence. Trimming excess fat (non-essential details) when you talk, when you write, when you think—*and when you listen!*

As a sage once said, "The more ideas a man has the fewer words he takes to express them. Wise men do not talk to kill time, they talk to save it."

Too often a subordinate will waste precious time by embellishing his conversations with details which add nothing more than minutes and monotony to the exchange.

Well, at some point I'll cut in and say: "All right, what's the problem?"

That's when I find out what he really came to tell me about in the first place. And sometimes I realize that if I *didn't* apply this time saving and time shaving technique I'd often wind up spending as much time on trivia as on the business at hand.

Don't Slaughter Time and Kill Sales

A savvy manager simply cannot afford to listen in detail to every song and dance. I'll show you what I mean.

One of my managers came to me about a factory machine. He told me the price, told me why he needed it, and I told him to go ahead and buy it.

That should have been that. But the man kept on talking. He described the machine in more detail; he elaborated on its functions. To what avail? He had already made his sale.

Now I could have continued listening, wasting his time and mine. Instead, I asked him if he wanted the machine. He said he did.

"Okay, then. Adios." He got the message.

It's the old story. Every good salesman knows enough to shut up after the sale is made.

Shorthand and People

Your goal as a savvy manager is to spread yourself as thin as you can in order to cover as much ground as you can. *The trick is to do this and still retain the assurance that all functions are being handled properly and in sufficient depth.* How successfully you do this will depend on how well you train and develop your people. You see, one way or another, it always gets back to PEOPLE.

If you have built a strong staff you can spread yourself thin and feel safe in doing it. You'll know instinctively that your mental shorthand is taking. Your people's thinking will supplement your own. They'll learn to grasp a situation quickly. They'll become extensions of yourself.

But there's danger, too, in spreading yourself thin. In applying the shorthand technique you'll do well to tread gingerly at first. If not, your people may misinterpret your motives. Take Joe, for example. I cut him short when he continued talking after getting my okay to buy that machine. But he understood exactly what I was doing and why.

A person unfamiliar with the technique might have taken it the wrong way. He might have construed my shorthand as brusqueness, considered me rude, disinterested in him and his ideas. The problem in applying shorthand is to achieve a balance of response. On the one hand, you want to save time and teach your people to save time. On the other, you don't want to produce misunderstanding or morale damage. How do you achieve this proper balance?

The following checklist will help you to answer this question.

• When using shorthand on the uninitiated, make them consciously aware of your strategy. Explain the technique and its value. Give practical demonstrations of how to boil down problems and trim unneeded details.

• In using shorthand, let the other fellow know you are acting in his best interests as well as your own. ("I know how busy you are, George, so I'd like to cut this session as short as possible.")

• In working with your boss, determine from experience how much shorthand he likes to receive. Some managers (mistakenly or not) insist on getting as much detail as they can. If this shoe fits your boss, it will probably be easier to join him than to fight him. It's tough enough to train your subordinates. Don't go overboard trying to train your boss as well.

• One way to determine your boss' shorthand preference is to be sensitive to his reactions. Spot for signs of impatience—which usually means he wants you to get on with it. Or boredom—

which means you're giving him too much detail. Try supplying key facts, for example. Then offer to fill him in on the details if he wants to hear them. Let *him* guide your actions.

• In selling an idea, or seeking a favorable decision, search the other person's face for signs of approval. If it looks like he's all for the idea—even if he hasn't actually said so—it may be time to wind up your pitch.

• Train your people to start by giving you the main gist of their problems and ideas. They can then expand from that point, giving you the chance to cut them short when you feel you have enough information for your judgment or decision.

• Bear in mind that management shorthand applies to business problems only, not personal PEOPLE problems. When a subordinate feels inclined to pour out his heart to you, your best bet is to sit back and listen—details and all.

Your Girl Friday can save you time each day of the week

I live by the clock, and so does my secretary. It's a way to count your minutes and to make your minutes count. Getting to the nuts and bolts of it, here is how the system works.

I have a customer on the phone. He's concerned about a special shipment. It is very important to him, and so to me. "Please follow it through personally," he requests. "Make sure no hitch develops."

Here's where my calendar comes into play. I jot down briefly, a week ahead, the name of the account. Check Blank-Blank order.

That's it for the moment. At this point my secretary takes over. It's what I call "Constructive Ball Passing." *Sarah works from my calendar.* She traces down the order to make sure the Shipping Department has the information. On the calendar date she checks to see if it is being shipped. If not, I then step in and handle the problem with the appropriate department. *No more of my time is taken.*

Management by Exception, this is the principle in action. Here's another important way my Girl Friday helps to shorten my work week. *I make it a point never to read a letter more than once.* When Sarah brings me the mail she sits down by my desk, notebook poised. Some executives prefer a dictaphone. For me the live steno is important. She forces me to tackle the mail and complete the job—or tie up a busy secretary. In practice, there's very little tying up.

Now I'll illustrate with a specific letter. A customer complains that he put through a backcharge and our people disallowed it. He felt he was entitled to the credit. I, of course, cannot know the right and wrong of the matter until it is investigated. Constructive ball passing again. I have Sarah check with the order department, dig out the correspondence, get to the root of the problem.

Next day Sarah comes back with the information. The customer had repaired a product on his own for fifty dollars. Had he checked with us, as he was supposed to, we would have shown him how to get it fixed for a fraction of the cost. We were right in disallowing the backcharge. So I dictate a letter, explaining our position and backing up the decision made by our credit department.

See how it works? One reading only, and a minimum of my time used.

I pick up another letter. There is a reply to be dictated. No problem. I reel it off, and that's the end of it. A third letter. This is one I feel Sarah can handle on her own. I turn it over to her. One reading. A fourth letter. This one should really be handled by accounting. "Sarah," I'll say, "turn this over to Bill. Tell him I'd like him to handle it on his own. He'll know what to do." One reading.

See how it all works together? Training, development, time-saving, sink-or-swimsmanship, the multiple value concept? You can wrap it all up into one neat little package, and paste on a label that says SAVVY MANAGEMENT.

Get YOUR secretary ino the time-saving act

Sit down now with that pencil and pad. Then write down five or more tasks that you are presently performing yourself that you can turn over in whole or in part to your secretary or assistant.

The big squeeze

Review this recap summary and roundup of time-saving tips. It will help you to wring a productive 70 minutes (at least) out of every working hour.

1. Plan flexibility into your time schedule. Be prepared to cope with new situations as they come up. Circulate among your key people to uncover pressing matters that warrant your time involvement.

2. In sorting out your time priorities, keep in mind that Priority No. 1 is always PEOPLE DEVELOPMENT.

3. Analyze the way you use your time. Eliminate tasks you shouldn't be doing. Or constructively "pass the ball." Train your people to do the same.

4. Train yourself and your people to think, talk, act and *listen* in shorthand. Teach them to boil down each problem and idea to its essence. Chop out unneeded detail. Apply the necessary self-discipline to achieve this vital goal. One executive, it is said, required employees having questions for him to write them down on a piece of paper. This forced them to express what they had to say concisely and precisely.

5. Give your operation the "once-over" at least once a day.

6. Manage on the "exception" principle. Plan your department so that your time will be spent only on situations warranting your special attention, and not on routine matters.

7. Track down root causes for excessive complaints and paper-piled desks.

8. Sharpen your systems to shorten tasks, minimize problems and complaints, and cut down your personal time involvement in everyday transactions.

9. Read your mail once only.

10. Always keep a pad and pencil handy. Write down things as they come to you. Then make it a habit to look at the notes you take. Don't spend time taking them only to forget that they exist.

11. Don't postpone the things you hate to do. Discipline yourself to dig in and tackle them at your earliest opportunity.

12. When you take a problem or idea to the boss, be prepared with the facts you will need. Anticipate questions and be ready for them.

13. Don't kill time with long-winded visitors, or with visitors you shouldn't see. Don't be afraid to cut a visit short.

14. Shorten your goodbyes. They can be great time wasters. One tactic: Stand up and say, "I know how busy you are and I don't want to keep you." Usually your visitor will end the discussion.

8

How to Trigger Ideas and

Keep Them Alive

An idea is born. Spawned by you, or conceived by one of your people; it's no matter. The fact is this. *An idea is born!* For the truly savvy manager there is no more blessed event.

The savvy manager is a realist too. He knows that a new idea, like any other newborn thing, is delicate and shaky. Nourished and protected, it will develop and grow. Neglected, it will die.

Ideas! Shakespeare refers to them as "the coinage of your brain." As a manager, they are your main stock in trade. *Question:* What, specifically, can you do to cause the ideas of your people to sprout into profit opportunities for you and your company? The answer is a clearcut and simple one.

Breed 'em and Feed 'em

Here it is—the care and feeding of a new idea. Right from the shop. The story I'm about to tell is still unfinished as these words are being written.

It happened just the other week. A visitor—I'll call him Conrad—called on me from a national company that makes products related to the doors we produce at Steelcraft.

Conrad's idea involved a way to use our product and his together. Now, right from the start I had Conrad pegged as a

113

savvy manager. *He knew our product well.* He talked flush bolts and panic devices. He talked with authority. Keep that in mind any time you want to impress a businessman. Get to know his product and his business.

As Conrad described his idea, my enthusiasm bubbled over.

Was I acting? Frankly, yes. But don't forget, *every savvy manager is one part actor.* And I was not acting to deceive or mislead. I was acting with a very definite and constructive purpose in mind.

At first blush, Conrad's idea actually did trigger a spark. Maybe at second blush I'd find something to fault the idea. But for now it was very much in my best interests and in Conrad's best interests to keep this idea aglow with life.

As we talked on I felt more and more that this idea was a live and lusty one. It was the kind that starts as a glint in your eye and winds up as a million in the bank. So we talked and talked and, as is my habit, I began to do some picture sketching in my mind. This is a powerful idea-generating and idea-building technique. *You visualize your thoughts in pictures rather than words.* You work up a mental image of the package, the system, the action. It expands your avenues of consideration. It broadens your perspective.

The discussion continued. We talked distribution, marketing, packaging. The ideas tumbled out one after another. Our enthusiasm was contagious. Conrad and I understood each other.

Conrad and I spent the rest of the day winding up the preliminaries. "Now what?" Conrad posed the question to me. One thing, for sure. Keep thrusting forward. Don't let the idea pall.

Well, let's see. Step one. Prepare an outline. There's another powerful management tool for your savvy file. Use the "Mental Outlining" technique. It serves me well.

How does it work? You visualize the entire project in your mind from beginning to end. You organize—actions, people, materials—headings and subheadings. (1) Get your technical people together to work out the nuts-and-bolts details. (2) Get your plan down on paper; frame up a preliminary agreement. (3) Arrange a meeting on the decision-making level. (4) Brief distributors on the arrangement; get their thinking. (5) Etc., etc., etc.

Do you get the idea? You don't wait for an idea to fade, for opportunity to pass you by. An important national company has expressed interest in our company, an outfit one-twelfth its size. Can we ride the coattails of a big organization like that? We can and we will.

That's the strategy. It's the profit motive in action. No hemming and hawing. No stalling around. Movement. Wheels in motion. An idea is born. Explode it into life!

And that's exactly what we are doing right at this moment. The final contracts? Hopefully, they should be ready within three or four weeks.

Multiply ideas by sharing them with others

Mining an idea is like prospecting for gold. The more veins you try, the better your chance for a strike. With an idea, the more minds you explore, the more thoughts you generate.

I know a businessman, a very small businessman. He belongs to no associations, attends no business conferences or conventions. Everything is hush-hush. "I keep what I know to myself," he boasts. Where others in his field have grown, he stands still or slides backwards.

I know another man who started life as a door-to-door canvasser. He makes it a special point to exchange ideas with other merchants and to disseminate information. Today he owns six stores. Some day soon he will own sixty. He attributes his growth to the exchange of ideas.

Here's the point I am trying to make. If you want your ideas to multiply, you've got to get others into the act. Collar them in the corridor. Call them on the telephone. Sit them down around a table. Spread the word. By getting others interested, excited, involved, you can enlarge on an idea. You can breathe new life into it and make it grow.

I can't overstress the importance of this idea-expansion process. You know the great value of surrounding yourself with people who are imaginative and smart. Well, that's step one. Step two is to put those minds to work, tap their full potential. How, on a step-by-step basis, can this be done?

Here is your day-by-day answer right from the shop.

Idea-Building on a Day-by-Day Basis

First Day—The idea is spawned. A problem arises in the plant, an inquiry poorly handled. The result: confusion, customer dissatisfaction. It points up a lack of departmental coordination in the handling of calls. A meeting is called. "What can we do to keep this kind of thing from recurring in the future?" Suggestions are thrown on the table, considered, rejected. But one comment, in particular, triggers the germ of an idea. *A centrally controlled communications system in the heart of the plant to improve service and reduce costs.* Gradually faces brighten as the idea takes hold. "It could just work!" "There'd be no need for call-backs!" Discussion enlargement. Period. Enough for now. Something to sleep on. Something to think about.

Second Day—The idea casually mentioned to two or three others, sounding them out, spreading the word. Then back to the originators, to get their views in light of a new day.

Third Day—"Frank, about that communications center (*it now has a name*). You thought it might be a good idea to have one man in charge of the controls. That makes sense. Talk to some of your people. I'd like to get their reaction, too." See how we're building now? Focus on *Frank's* idea, *Frank's* contribution. He's flattered now. He has a personal stake in the project.

Fourth Day—More building. More discussion. Frank's idea. Joe's idea.

Fifth Day—Meeting, semi-formal get-together. Ideas to date are recapped, thinking explored.

Sixth Day—"Paul, you were at that meeting yesterday, and your idea about the hold line has great possibilities. Now, why don't you get together with Frank and Bill and work out the details . . ."

Seventh Day—Another meeting. The staff brought up to date on the latest innovations and developments. Remaining "wrinkles" discussed. New refinements, elaborations and more suggestions.

Eighth Day—Project scheduled. Overall effort coordination. Specific target dates set.

Ninth Day—Personal recognition to Mike, Paul, Frank, Bill, Joe and others who contributed to the project. Special plaudits from the boss. Plant-wide publicity.

Tenth, Eleventh, Twelfth, Thirteenth Days—Explain program to employees, and the benefits to be derived. Solicit further suggestions. Expand interest and involvement. Meeting. Progress and development. Finalization of program. Scheduling. Finishing touches. Necessary construction planned and initiated. Authorization given: action started to order equipment and other necessities.

How do you give birth to an idea and make it work with people and through people? You play it up and talk it up. You generate interest and excitement and personal involvement. You make it *your people's* idea instead of your idea. And this is what you don't learn in school. It is savvy management.

Your Personal Idea Survival Score

How skilled are you at keeping ideas alive? Here's your chance to find out. First, think back. Recall as many ideas as you can that crossed your mind or your desk during the past few months. How many can you think of that might have turned into profit opportunities but which, for one reason or another, were permitted to expire?

Jot down briefly as many of these ideas as you can call to mind.

Now—and here's the big question: *How many of these ideas can you revive?*

You can do it by talking them up, exploring them further, proving your case more conclusively, sparking new interest, getting others involved and giving them a special personal stake in putting the ideas across.

Here is a challenge that no real pro could resist.

If you can succeed in reviving even ONE dead or dying idea it will be one of the most invaluable and unforgettable experiences of your career.

To spark ideas, respond with gusto

It has been said that the true test of a red hot idea is the amount of heat it loses when somebody throws cold water on it.

But throwing too much cold water on an idea can kill, not only the idea itself, but the proponent's incentive to produce more ideas.

I know a man in the real estate business. An employee will come to him with a suggestion. "I've heard that before," he'll reply. Or, "I've been thinking about that myself." Or, "It doesn't make much sense to me."

Instead of watering ideas to make them bloom, he smothers them and makes them wither.

Here's a management savvy tip that is worth a mint. *Show genuine interest, enthusiasm, and appreciation over each and every idea that is presented to you.* Why? A nationally prominent consultant I know offers these four important reasons:

1. Your positive response will provide a next-time promise to keep the idea mill churning and imaginations stirred up.
2. When you respond with gusto, you flatter the ideaman's ego and shore up his confidence.
3. You never know. There may be a hidden potential in the idea that is not apparent at first glance.
4. It means a great deal to a man to know, even if his idea is rejected, that it was given careful and serious consideration.

Milk Each Dud for All It's Worth

A subordinate comes to you with an idea. The possibilities? Nil. The impossibilities? Rampant. What happens now? How do you keep the man's spirits from sagging? What can you do to keep the think mill functioning?

Here's the way I coped with exactly this problem just a few short weeks before last Christmas.

The employee's name? I'll call him Charley. The idea? On first thought, not bad. On second thought, it fell apart.

"Why not get our employees to stop sending Christmas cards to one another?" Charlie wanted to know. "Instead, we'll have them chip in a quarter apiece, and donate it to some worthy cause."

Now, I'm all for worthy causes. But this one looked like a fat load of trouble. But if I tipped my reaction to Charley it would have deflated his ego.

Instead, I said, "That's an interesting idea. I like it. In fact, I think nine out of ten people would be all for it." At this point I frowned. "But what about that tenth person?"

Already Charley was flattered. The boss liked the idea. He was giving it careful and serious consideration. I continued with the soft approach. "I'm not sure, Charley. Do you think we should get involved in an area like this? Some people enjoy sending cards. They might insist on sending them. They might feel it's none of our business if they send cards or not."

Charley saw the point immediately and backed down.

Do you see how the strategy works? I squelched the idea without squelching Charley at the same time. I made it my business to sustain his enthusiasm so as not to put a damper on his next idea, which just might be the greatest idea in the world.

Try for "Go, go, go!" Instead of "No, no, no!"

We had a supervisor working for us, and one of the great imponderables of my career is, "How did this fellow ever get to be a supervisor?"

Any time an idea was presented, he found some reason to knock it down. Invariably, his reaction was: "Too expensive;" "Too difficult;" "It'll take too long."

"If it were as easy to arouse enthusiasm as it is to arouse suspicion," somebody once said, "just think what could be accomplished."

This employee was living proof. In his view, *nothing* would work. He was suspicious of everything.

Not so the savvy manager. His stress is on the "can-do" approach. His search is for the "how-to," for the technique to mow down the roadblock.

Now don't get me wrong. I don't believe in accepting an idea blindly. I welcome the questioning and challenging attitude.

But you can overdo this to the point where you create a negative image for yourself. You can give others the impression that you're anti-everything. And the fact is this. Too many die-hard rejections, too many doubts, too many "it-won't-work" frowns tend to sap enthusiasm. They discourage people from sharing their ideas with you.

Look for problems, by all means. Search out objections. Pinpoint flaws. But dwell with equal concentration on the strengths of an idea, on the values and profit potential to be derived. Chase down reasons why the idea *can* and *should* work.

I think too that there is another important, if somewhat subtle, point to be made. It is this. *There does not always have to be a carefully calculated 100 per cent mathematically clear and conclusive reason for launching a project or executing an idea.*

As you know, there are many people who say, "Don't just change for the sake of change." I don't wholly subscribe to this philosophy. I maintain that sometimes a person should make a change *just* for the sake of change. Day-to-day jobs grow boring; people lose interest; their attitudes droop.

Sometimes all that is needed is a change of system or procedure or environment to agitate interest anew and regenerate excitement.

Washington Irving, in a droll frame of mind, once put it this way: "There is a certain relief in change, even though it be from bad to worse. I have found, in traveling in a stagecoach, that it is often a comfort to shift one's position and be bruised in a new place."

You Again

Rate your idea receptivity. Think back once more to ideas presented to you in the past. Recall your initial spur-of-the-moment response. How many times did you react with enthusiasm and gusto? How often did you make the ideaman regret having come to you with his suggestion?

Next to each suggestion recalled, jot down an objective evaluation of your response: HOT—WARM—COOL—COLD.

Now, resolve for the future to give every appealing idea a hot reception. Resolve to give every mediocre or poor idea a warm reception.

Resolve never, *never*, NEVER to give *any* idea a cool or a cold reception.

A time to quit—a time to persist

You're the author of a brilliant idea—you think. To what degree do you persist in trying to hammer it across to your boss? There's no pat answer to this one. There's a time to press forward; there's a time to abandon the cause.

When the Boss Says No

Back to the shop. I know a savvy promotion manager in the soft goods business. Some time ago he went to his boss with an idea. It would be advantageous, he thought, to display in a certain trade show. His boss wasn't interested. They were in too many shows already, he felt. There were budget problems, manpower problems, conflict with other projects.

The manager was still sold on his idea. Three days later, he was back again.

"Look," the boss said, "I already explained. . . ."

The manager listened patiently, then cut in. "I'm only practicing your own philosophy," he told the boss. "You keep telling us not to be 'yes-men.' This is an idea I believe in, and I've been doing some probing since we last spoke."

The promotion man had explored the idea in depth with the sales manager. He had obtained facts and figures from the display people and others, and was sold more than ever on the idea. Now, here's where the tact and discretion come in. *The manager didn't argue with the boss; he reasoned with him.* He didn't push his attack to the point where the boss became angry or impatient. He carefully gauged his reaction, saw that he was still open to further persuasion, and cashed in on the opportunity to drive home his points. In short, the manager knew how to "stick to his guns" while they still had fire power. And he made the sale.

Too many sales are lost, too many deals collapse, too many potentially profitable ideas die on the vine because managers drop out of the race too soon. It's a thought to take with you.

When to Abandon the Cause

It has been said that a quitter never wins and a winner never quits. But sometimes it works the other way around. Sometimes you can stick with an idea or objective so long that you tend to lose your perspective. It crumbles all around you, and leaves you standing in the wreckage. *Case example:* Jim, a manager in one of our subsidiaries.

He had hired a young man ten or twelve months back. The man hadn't lived up to Jim's high expectations for him.

There were a number of incidents, a period of prolonged absence, friction with some of the other people. But Jim kept making excuses for him. We had worked him into our Job Variety program, presented him with plenty of challenges, new jobs, fresh opportunities. He simply hadn't responded.

Now, at salary review time, the man's name came up for consideration.

"Jim," I said, "do you think this man is going to make the grade?"

He frowned. "Well, no, but . . ."

"Then darn it, fire him! Get someone else."

You know, I think Jim was actually relieved. He must have been wrestling a long time with that decision.

The point is this. Not everything in business or in life can come up roses. When you see a weed appear, very often your best bet is to pluck it out before it can choke the rest of your lawn.

How to start a mental chain reaction

What good is brainstorming? Some people don't believe in it. They contend idea conception is a one-man job. Group sessions, they feel, are worthless.

I disagree with this concept. I think there is much to be gained through the skilled and careful use of brainstorming in business. What benefits, specifically? Here's a brief rundown:

- The explosion of ideas. Thoughts, like certain atoms, are fissionable. Most ideas sprout from their association with other ideas.
- Brainstorming is a powerful training vehicle; it develops new approaches, new techniques.
- It broadens your scope, exposes you to the other fellow's point of view.
- It encourages the shy employee to emerge from his shell.
- It sharpens your powers of expression and persuasion.
- It develops your ability to think on your feet, and to come up with ideas on an off-the-cuff basis.

Put them all together. What does it add up to? That's right: MULTIPLE BENEFITS. In our company, brainstorming is a prime savvy management tool. We use it for a variety of reasons.

For one thing, we try to get as many minds as possible into the act. We look for fresh approaches, different points of view. We get "inside-outsiders" in on our brainstorming sessions, men engaged in different areas of the company. What's wrong, for example, in getting your advertising manager to sit in on a production problem? Who knows, he may come up with something obvious.

Trouble is, few people know how to use brainstorming to its full advantage.

The trick, first, is to generate the right climate for free expression. It's a matter of giving everyone the chance to say what he wants to say—whatever happens to pop into his mind at the moment. To really motivate such expression—*and the only way to get it is to motivate it*—you must make it clearly understood that some ideas, maybe even the majority of ideas expressed, are going to be wild, improbable, off-track.

There should be no penalty or onus on such expression. *No man should ever be made to feel the fool!*

The idea is to stimulate, agitate, and inspire participation. It's the moderator's job to get the ball rolling and keep it rolling. To keep the dialogue lively and exciting. *Example:* Some snatches from a recent group session in our plant:

". . . now look, here's the problem; what can we do about it?"

". . . great idea! What about you, George, what do you think?"

". . . our customers wouldn't go for that. But if we modified your suggestion a bit to . . ."

Chain reaction. One thought leading to another thought. And finally, the harvest. Ninety-eight per cent chaff. Two per cent wheat.

But I can tell you this. That two per cent wheat is worth the effort!

Another example. We bought a new Xerox machine. It made beautiful copies. Everybody loved it. Only one thing was wrong. After one month, we almost doubled the number of copies turned out. People were using the machine to copy recipes, cartoons, whatnot.

Brainstorming session. How can we get this to stop?

First, frowns of concentration; then the ideas started grinding out. Make people sign a ticket each time they use the machine? Rejected. Put one girl in charge of the machine? Rejected. More ideas. Rejected.

Finally: Why not make up an official looking sheet? Attach it to the machine. Require anyone making a copy to initial the sheet and explain the purpose of the copy.

Hmmmm? Silence at first. Then, one or two minor objections, quickly disposed of. In the end, agreement. It's worth a try.

The idea was put into effect the next day. Immediately, production returned to normal and the problem was solved.

That sheet on the machine? We never gave it a second glance.

Take a Wild Idea and Tame It

Brainstorming. I recently discussed the subject with a friend of mine who is violently opposed to the technique. "Do you mean to tell me," he snorted, "that you have time to sit in on meetings and listen to a bunch of wild ideas?"

Are you kidding? I wouldn't miss it for the world. It's a lot of fun. And it leads to profits.

Wild ideas? Don't knock them. The airplane was once a wild idea. Television was once a wild idea.

Dazzling red memos? Why not?

Triangular sales letters? Why not? That's another wild one we've been playing around with. What would happen if you sent someone a triangular letter? He couldn't file it. What would he do with it? Maybe drop it in the round file. *Maybe act on it.* Is it worth a try? You never know.

That friend of mine? He's still not convinced. But maybe one of these days he will be.

When he gets a large triangular envelope in the mail.

Now, Try It for Yourself

Any problems facing you at the moment? Write them down. Then take two or three of them and try to brainstorm your way to a solution. Bring together a few of your people; four, five, six. Explain the technique, and YOU moderate the session. Present it as a challenging experiment; make a kind of game of it. Encourage wild ideas, improbable "brainstorms," stream-of-consciousness nonsense. *Free expression.* The freer, the better.

See if you can loosen up some mental springs and send those think wheels spinning. See if you can identify yourself with that special breed of savvy manager who knows how to make a brainstorming session work.

Above all, adopt a positive attitude, a "this-will-work" approach. You may find the payoff to be a really big one. We do. Others do. Why not you?

SUMMARY RECAP: Braindrops from an idea faucet

1. Enthusiasm multiplies enthusiasm. The best way to trigger the expansion of an idea is to show that you're excited about it.

2. Try visualizing your thoughts in pictures rather than words. Work up a mental image of the package, the system, the action.

3. Thrust enthusiastically and persistently forward on every potential profit idea. Don't permit it to drag or lag.

4. Use "Mental Outlining" to translate ideas into action. Visualize the action from beginning to end. Then organize your plan into headings and subheadings as you would a composition or report.

5. Expose ideas to as many minds as possible. There's no better way to make them grow.

6. Encourage your people to expand your ideas by contributing to them. Win allies to your cause by sharing pride of ownership with others.

7. Praise ideamen and publicize their contributions. Keep the old saw in mind: "There are two kinds of egotists— the kind that admit it, and the rest of us."

8. Follow through on each accepted idea with the necessary steps to "get the show on the air." Schedule deadlines. Obtain commitments. Keep wheels turning.

9. Show genuine interest and appreciation over each and every idea that is presented to you, *regardless of the merit of the suggestion proposed.*

10. Use special caution and tact when confronted with an idea "dud." *Never make an ideaman feel ridiculous.*

11. Take care not to build a "no-man" image for yourself. Look for weak points and flaws when an idea is presented to you. But, equally important, search out reasons why it *can* and *will* work.

12. When the everyday routine grows dull, dreary, and too ho-hum, think in terms of change—even if it is simple change for the sake of change alone.

13. Persist in selling your idea as long as the climate is favorable for persistence. Gauge the buyer's response to your appeal. When he begins to show impatience and irritation, be wary. It may be time for you to "stop beating a dead horse." Or time to put your idea in cold storage for another sales shot at a later date.

14. Don't sell brainstorming short. Give it a chance. Ideas often sprout from their association with other ideas.

9

People-izing and Developing

the Team

Winston Churchill achieved world renown as one of the greatest leaders of modern times. But without the British people and the British military behind him, we might never have heard his name.

Lovable, rambunctious Casey Stengel won immortality for himself in Baseball's Hall of Fame as pilot of the first team in history to take five pennants in a row. But without the scintillating performance of the New York Yankees of the forties and fifties, Casey might be a comparative unknown today.

David Merrick's skill and sensitivity as a gifted director have made his name a byword in the theatrical world. But without the talent and drive of the men and women who work under him, no outlet for his genius would exist.

In business, in government, in politics, in sports—or anywhere else—*if you're a manager, you succeed through your people!*

The formula is clear-cut. First, *pick* the right people. Next, identify and *tap* their abilities. Finally, *build* their abilities and *channel* them towards the achievement of profit goals.

The point is this. No matter how smart you are, how well educated, ambitious, personable, enthusiastic, conscientious —YOU SUCCEED THROUGH YOUR PEOPLE.

Track down natural leaders and let them lead

How well your people on the line perform will depend largely on the quality of inspiration and guidance provided, not only by yourself, but by their close and immediate supervisors.

Your selection and development of these key people, more than any other single factor, will determine your personal reputation and growth.

I'm talking about your subleaders. There are two kinds of supervisors in business today:

(1) THE NATURAL LEADER—A pleasant individual, he is friendly, interesting, personable. You're warmed by his smile and provoked by his style. There's something about him. He exudes confidence. You get the feeling that he's in control of the situation. Was he born this way, or did he develop along these lines? You can argue this one at length. It's no matter. The stuff is there. The feeling is real.

(2) THE APPOINTED LEADER—He may be the most able person in the world. Or a ho-hum character. Cheerful and amiable. Or cranky and cantankerous. Exciting or dull. He may be holding down his job because of seniority, because of a special skill he possesses, because of a giant-sized mistake that somebody made. Whatever the reason, he's there. Appointed. In charge of a division, a department, a group.

Now, what is the ideal mix for *you*, as a savvy manager, to seek? Let me give you one example, a young fellow, Bill, who works for us. He's in his early thirties. Bill's eyes spark with personality. Sharp, easy to work with, he automatically inspires cooperation. Bill has plenty to crow about. But you never hear him crowing. His actions crow *for* him. Bill is a *natural leader*.

One thing more. Bill started as a rank-and-filer. Today he's a supervisor. Tomorrow he'll be a department head.

Not by Accident, but by Design

How come? Because Bill likes people and people like him. He motivates them. He inspires them. He gets them to respond.

He scores high on what Walter Lippmann refers to as "the final test of a leader." He "leaves behind him in other men the conviction and will to carry on."

Once again, what ideal should *you* shoot for? *You do your utmost to make the natural leader the appointed leader.* You tie the two together wherever you can.

The *appointed natural* leader will stimulate superior performance, excite interest, perpetuate high standards, and keep friction and resentment to a minimum.

How to pick a winner

Chemical Reactions

There's a service company in our area. Its management team works well together. The men understand and respect one another.

A few months ago a promotion manager was hired. He was capable and experienced, with an excellent background. No apparent reason why he shouldn't have made the grade.

But he didn't make the grade.

The new man wasn't a snob exactly. But the men sensed a too-patrician bearing about him, an almost imperceptible superciliousness of manner.

Or maybe it was their imagination?

In any case, he didn't last. The men were unable to accept him on comfortable terms. After four weeks he resigned.

The reason? It would be difficult to explain in concrete terms.

But here's what I always maintain. I believe that for people to work well together there must be a kind of chemistry between them. It may be forced to begin with. But after a certain period of association it must become natural.

I think it's important in selecting your people to keep sharply aware of this chemical reaction. In today's business organization people from all walks of life are thrown together. Their values, their hopes, and their aims may vary. Their family background, their upbringing, their accustomed economic levels may be different.

Still, to function efficiently as a smoothly operating, profit-minded team, an agreeable blend must be established, a common understanding and acceptance achieved. I call this "Chemical Response-ability." And I believe that as a savvy manager, you cannot do your compounding too carefully.

All it takes is a single wrong element to dilute and weaken the formula. And I want to make one thing abundantly clear. I am not talking about race or religion. I am not talking about nationality. I am not talking about ethnic background.

What I'm talking about deals essentially with the fabric of character and personality.

The trick in selecting a new employee is to project yourself into the minds of your people. Ask yourself:

- How will our people respond to the new man?
- How will the ingredients of his character and personality blend with the existing mix of our department or organization?
- Will he be comfortable in his association with the staff?
- Will his associates respect him and will he respect his associates?

Use the job interview as a powerful management tool

Time again to get into position on the firing line. This happened in Canada about two years ago. We needed a manager there, a truly critical post. We advertised in the Canadian papers and came up with a couple of hundred answers. We screened the replies and my brother and I narrowed the field to about 40 applicants. I scheduled interviews in Toronto and Montreal, each one a half hour apart.

Now to backtrack a moment. We were on the scent of that one man with the unique combination of talent, drive, intelligence, plus a compelling desire to develop his people and to be developed in turn by them, by us and by himself—the one applicant with the ideal mix of "Chemical Response-ability" that would be just right for us. My questions to the applicants were geared to produce this information. Not to tell him what *we* wanted or what *we* expected, but to learn from him just who *he* was, where *he* wanted to go, what *he* liked to do, what *he* would be capable of achieving.

The way to achieve this goal is to ask the right questions. Following is a brief list of "Truth Prodders" designed to produce the kind of information I have in mind. It is by no means complete. But it will serve, I think, to give you a good idea of what I'm getting at.

Truth prodders—designed to stir the applicant

- What prompted you to apply to our company? (Or answer the particular ad in question?) Shoot for specifics here; avoid generalities.
- What, specifically, (always specifically) do you feel you could contribute to this company?
- About your last job—what were your specific functions and responsibilities? (Get him to spell them out.)
- What are the main factors in your previous (or present, if you still work there) company that produce the profits for your employer?
- What actions have you taken to help contribute to the profit objective?
- What are some of the problems you ran into? How did you go about solving them?
- What did you like best about your former job? Why?
- Were you satisfied with the way you were treated by the company? By your boss? (If, "Yes," then why did you leave? If, "No," in what ways were you treated unfairly?)
- Now here's a situation that came up in our plant a few weeks ago. (Spell it out.) What would you have done in this case?
- What are some of the techniques you use to train and develop your people?
- Where would you like to be five or ten years from today? What kind of income are you shooting for?

Get the idea? Be concise. Be specific. Get down to cases.

Use a Camera as a Memory Booster

Now for a broad picture of how the interview process worked. As I said, I saw each man on the hour or half hour. I spoke with him. I made notes. I *listened*. And one thing more.

Forty men. Draw up a mind's eye picture. Seen one after the other in rapid succession. That's a lot of men. Easy to confuse? Easy to forget vital facts or lose sight of key impressions? Not if you use the camera as an aid to memory recall. I had a Polaroid land camera at my side. As I interviewed each man, I snapped a picture of him. Later, in reviewing the interviews, shaping my decision, I had in front of me my notes, each man's résumé, and the photo. You'd be amazed how this can help to bring a man back into focus after a series of interviews. It's a good technique to keep in mind.

Here's another point. "Forty men!" you might say. "Why not have a subordinate or personnel assistant screen down the applicants to five or six? It would save much time, trouble, and effort."

Just the question I asked myself. But I also asked, "What might I gain by conducting the interviews myself?" I came up with five powerful pluses which fit under the familiar heading of Multiple Benefits.

1. The interviews would give me an unparalled opportunity to meet Canadian people and get a feel for the Canadian market.
2. I would be personally assured that in filling this vital management position, no potentially capable candidate would slip by unrecognized.
3. It would give me a feel for the salary situation in Canada.
4. From discussions with applicants, I would get good insights into Canadian business, learn what other companies are doing, how they are operating.
5. It would make each applicant feel like someone special—knowing that a top man in the company considered it worth his while to see him personally.

As the Mounties say, we finally "got our man." He is with us today and doing a topnotch job. The extra time and effort in this case really paid off.

How to Shake the Cart Without Spilling the Apples

We needed a supervisor in our engineering department some time ago. Our normal policy is to bring people up from within to fill key jobs. But we were in a period of explosive growth. We had advanced as many people as we could at this particular time.

So we scouted the field and found a man who was interested in joining our organization. This man currently held down the top engineering post with a smaller company.

Now I don't have to tell you that when you bring in a key man to supervise other people you're treading on delicate ground. For one thing, you risk a serious morale flare-up. Some people will be upset that *they* didn't get the job. Another thing. *Any* employee in a new job is on trial, so to speak. A supervisor is doubly on trial. The supervisor who is also an outsider has *all* the chips stacked against him—unless you take positive steps to unstack them. That's exactly what we did in this case. Here's a step-by-step rundown of the unusual "reverse interview" strategy we used.

1. We permitted our man to be interviewed by some of the people who would be working under him. He was not interviewed in the usual sense. We did nothing to dilute his authority as a manager or to undermine our own management prerogatives. We simply told our people we were thinking of hiring this individual. We encouraged them to speak with him and let us know how they felt he would fit into our organization. This made them feel important and included. It offset the effect of having an unpopular management action thrust down their throats.

2. We had each of our people report his findings to us. Though most were guardedly cautious, it helped pave the way to ultimate acceptance.

3. When we made known the addition to our organization, we announced other changes at the same time. This helped to offset and minimize the major change.

4. We worked up some popular innovations for the new man to initiate. By having him announce the innovations himself, he was regarded as either the author of—or at least a strong campaigner for—the moves.

5. We played up his image of professional achievement. We publicized his former top engineering post, his awards and published work.

6. Most important, we went out of our way to give him our fullest cooperation. We made every effort to implement his ideas without delay.

Why all this rigmarole over one man? The reason is clear.

We could easily have announced the mandate: "This is our man. He will be your boss. You will carry out his orders, or else!"

But that's not the way we do things at Steelcraft. My theory is, you don't command when you can convince.

Result: This man's career with us has been distinguished by outstanding success. His department is one of the most productive in the company.

Find Your People and Help Them Find Themselves

I sometimes have a job applicant come to me and say, "I'd like to work for a company where you don't get lost in the crowd."

This brings up a good question for you to ask yourself. *"Do your people feel that they're lost in the crowd?"*

If you're a big company manager it's a dangerous pitfall to guard against.

If you're a small company manager your task may be simpler. It's easier for a man to sink out of view in a big lake than in a shallow pond.

But the truly savvy manager—big company or small—takes positive action to make sure that his people won't feel lost or neglected. This is extremely important in any company, large or small. In a small company, especially, the man who gets to feeling lost is apt to grow restless.

What can you do to combat misguided wanderlust and keep your key people happily at their posts? One thing you can do is let them know what your company has to offer (assuming you're a small company manager) that might be hard to come by in that giant operation on the other side of town.

Like what? Like getting in on the ground floor of things. Like working side by side with top management men. Like having the opportunity to grow with the company, not a baby step at a time, but in leaps and strides.

This is a real live fact and more and more job hunters are becoming aware of it. An increasing number of business schools, moreover, are taking special note of the situation in their attempts to place graduate students.

According to *Business Week*: ". . . for the aggressive B-school student, nothing offers so great a chance for rapid success as the small company big enough to have a management team. Here the ambitious man can find more responsibility, faster promotion, broader experiences—and even ownership. Says one student: 'Small business puts us closer to the decision-making action, and gives us a chance to rub elbows with top management.' Richard Kotz, co-chairman of the small business placement group at Harvard, says: 'Everything is compressed in small business. You may step from trainee to vice president in one year.'" And a Stanford student adds: "It's where you'll be in a few years that counts!"

Compelling selling points for the savvy manager to make in the recruitment and retention of his key personnel.

Practice "people-ized talent exploitation"

As a savvy manager, your prime objective is to expand your *Span of Control,* to multiply the number of profit actions you take in a given period of time. That means you keep your fingers in more pies, but because of the reliance you place in your people, you keep in the tip of your finger only. In short, you double your time availability. You exercise management control with a ten-minute check instead of a two-hour probe. You take advantage of summary appraisals and shorthand reviews.

As the poet, Schlegel, says: "Every enterprise begins with and takes its first forward step in faith." But faith doesn't just happen. You work with and through people to develop it. The extent to which you succeed in having this blind faith in your people testifies to the effectiveness of your training ability, the skill with which you practice "People-ized Talent Exploitation."

Your Personal Trust Fund

How much faith do *you* have in your people? Write down the name of every person who works for you, using a separate sheet for each one. Then list each major job he performs. Now analyze the amount of time YOU spend on each job, and resolve to cut that time expenditure in half or better—*to spread yourself thinner without lowering the standards of performance.* How? By training your people to operate more independently of you. By imparting your savvy to them, and thus increasing their capability. This will enable you to expand your *span of control* and prepare yourself for more important responsibilities.

If at First They Don't Succeed—Teach, Teach Again

Directly or indirectly, a savvy manager spends 75 per cent of his time guiding and instructing people. This doesn't have to be a formalized procedure. Training is more often a matter of exposing people to right ways of doing things. They learn by osmosis.

If your people respect you, they will imitate you. They will follow in your footsteps much faster than they will follow your advice. Here's another live example to prove the point.

PREMISE: *The best way to solve a problem is to break it down into bits and pieces and analyze it in depth.*

In this case, we had an order handling problem. We had set up a scheduling system in the plant, and it wasn't working right. So I called a meeting. My MULTIPLE VALUE goal was to get this scheduling problem solved and to sharpen the problem-solving ability of my people.

The problem-solving objective was to meet a three or four week delivery schedule regardless of quantity ordered and other factors involved.

I kicked off the meeting by asking to have the system defined.

An order department supervisor took the floor. "Well," he began, "an order comes in and we process it. Then it goes to the . . ."

I interrupted. "What do you mean, it 'comes in'? Where does it come from? Which desk does it go to? How long does it stay there? What does the processing consist of?"

Step by step. Every detail accounted for. Depth analysis. But I didn't do it for him; I goaded him into doing it for himself.

That's what I mean by *training*. It's not preaching. It's not lecturing. It's guiding and goading. It's organizing and directing, individual therapy and group therapy.

I rode herd on those men. I chewed them out. I laced into them. What I really did was unite them. Six men all driven by the boss. They teamed together in their common misery—*and they loved it*. They also learned.

Detail by detail the system started shaping up. Just what I was waiting for. The group began to carry on by themselves. My job was done. Off I went to expand my span of control.

Training—There's Nothing Cut and Dried About It.

Training is a highly individual process. Each manager has his own way of teaching. Each trainee has his own way of learning. One man will respond to pressure, another to a well-presented challenge, a third to a carefully calculated vanity prod. The idea is to experiment. Vary your strategy until you find the one that works best for each person.

On one of my people, for example, I use this strategy. "Joe," I'll say, "the trade show mix-up is giving us a lot of trouble. What do you think would be the best way to handle it?" Joe, flattered that the boss wants his opinion, goes all out to study the problem. And he usually comes up with a good solution.

It's the old story. The effectiveness of your training program boils down to the question of how well you can *motivate* the participation of your people. As N. J. Berrill points out in *Man's Emerging Mind*,* "A great teacher is not simply one who imparts knowledge to his students, but one who awakens their interest in it and makes them eager to pursue it for themselves. He is a spark plug, not a fuel pipe."

Your job as a teacher is to start the engine running. Once this is done, the "distribution system" will usually take care of itself.

Compile Your Personal Checklist of "Response Factors"

As I pointed out, how a person will respond to a training motivator is unpredictable if you go about it on a guesswork basis. One man needs a shot in the arm, another a shot in the ego. That's why a reliable inventory of "Response Factors" will make your training job a great deal easier. Such a checklist is easy to compile. You start by writing down every training motivational strategy that comes to mind. Pressure. Challenge. Ego feeding. Promotion bait. Appeal to special talent or interest. Plus others of your own that you have tried or might try.

Next, write the names of all your people on a sheet of paper. Alongside each person's name enter the motivators that work best for him. Finally, experiment. Learn about your people. Try *all* your strategies on *all* your people. Then all you have to do is pinpoint the ones that work best.

"People-ize" your firing strategy

You might as well face one fact. All the management savvy in the world won't make you infallible. No matter how much skill

* Published by Apollo, 1961.

you apply in the selection and development of your people, you are going to make mistakes from time to time. Weaknesses will crop up in people that neither you nor they are able to overcome. Or the growth of an individual may not keep pace with the growth of his job.

Whatever the reason, at one time or other you are going to be faced with the miserably distressing job of having to fire one of your people.

Distasteful as this is—and I can think of no management task that is more onerous—firing one of your staff can have its positive side, too. If the job is done properly, it can be constructive and beneficial for your surbordinate and yourself. But it takes a special kind of skill and savvy to "people-ize" your firing strategy.

Positive Value from a Negative Task

It's difficult to fire any man. But take a man who's been 12 years with the company, who walks with a limp, and the task is one that can haunt you at night.

The situation was this, the man—we'll call him Jack—was a chronic attendance problem. He was often absent, more often late. We spoke to him about it repeatedly. He promised to change, but the promise was never fulfilled.

Attendance was Jack's biggest problem, but not his only problem. His attitude was worse than poor. He gave the impression that he didn't like people, and they responded in kind. Jack was the most unpopular man in the office. He admitted that he had no reason for being late. But because of his seniority and personal situation we were slow to take action.

We tried everything: warnings, discussion, Job Variety, special challenges. Nothing worked. Finally, we ran out of solutions, and there was only one solution left. We had to let him go.

All right. Here's where the "people-ized firing strategy" comes into the picture. Briefly, to set the framework, here are the seven key points that comprise the technique:

1. Clearly establish the reason for the firing action, and prove the fairness and justice of your decision.
2. Give the man a chance to have his say and present his side of the story.

3. Use your persuasive powers to help straighten the man out, so that he will have a greater chance to succeed at his next job.
4. Inject a positive note. Stress his abilities and strengths. Show the man how the change will benefit him in time to come. He might get a much better job.
5. Play up and dramatize his "bird-in-the-hand" severance benefits.
6. Wish him luck. Convince him of your genuine interest in his welfare and future.
7. Reinforce your show of concern by expressing your willingness to help him should he need it in the future.

No Textbook Solution for This One

I called Jack to my office, and he limped in, dour as ever. What do you tell a man after 12 years? How do you get through to him?

One thing I knew. As past president of a Community Chest agency in town, I had worked with many handicapped people. I remembered from long experience: *You don't treat a handicapped person like a handicapped person.* You treat him like the mature adult that he is.

I took a deep breath, and prepared to treat Jack in this manner. I pulled out a copy of the record and reviewed past performance, past promises repeatedly broken. There was nothing Jack could say in defense, no denials. I was completely in the right, he conceded.

But there's more to it than being in the right. I'm not just talking about firing a man. I'm talking about "people-ized" firing. The simple and painless way would have been to hand Jack his walking papers right then and there and get him out of the office as quickly as possible. But this wouldn't have helped Jack. And it might have hurt the company.

Why? First, Jack had been with us 12 years. Bitter by nature, had I fired him summarily at this point, his bitterness would have rocketed. He'd have complained to every available ear about the raw deal he received. Others might wonder, "If it can happen to Jack, why not me?"

Also, Jack is a member of the community. How many people

would he try to convince that we were the world's worst company? How many potential employment recruits would he turn against us?

All things to consider. In firing a man, the challenge is to kick him out of the company, yet retain him as a friend.

It's not easy, but you have one strong factor working for you. You know that at the windup of the session the man will be an ex-employee. That means you can lower the customary barriers. You can say things that you wouldn't say otherwise.

What things, specifically? That's where the savvy comes in. Apart from the seven points mentioned, I use no established guidelines. There's nothing spelled out in your Management Manual. You play it by ear.

"Jack," I said, "it's pretty obvious that you haven't been happy here."

His silence was confirmation enough.

Now to the constructive part of the interview. How could I help him? Now was the time to level with him, give it to him straight. I talked about his attitude. "You walk around with a chip on your shoulder. I don't think I've ever seen you smile. You're unfriendly, even rude at times. You act as if you hate the world. This gets through to customers and to the people you work with. It's bad for you. It's bad for the company."

Jack lowered his eyes. My remarks had hit home. "But I was passed over for promotion," he complained. "I figured I was getting a crummy deal."

"Sure you were passed over. But did you ever stop to figure why? We gave you every opportunity to improve. How did you respond? Did your attendance improve? Did your attitude change?"

He met my eyes squarely; I'll give him credit for that. "No," he admitted, "I guess not."

I had made my point, and I hoped it would do some good. That was that. I wasn't going to beat it to death.

Now for the positive note. I paraded Jack's qualifications in review. "You have a high IQ. You have years of good diversified experience. . . ." That and all the rest.

What I got across was this. Jack was an employable guy. However, we had no choice but to let him go—those words "let him go" were shocking to him. It was hard for him to realize that it was happening. He realized that it was too late, time had run out. He was an ex-employee at that point and he began to think in those terms.

Finally, the clincher. Jack had been with us 12 years. He knew he was entitled to some kind of separation pay. As I pointed out what we would do for him, his spirits brightened with each benefit and item.

"Look, Jack," I rose after a tough and lengthy meeting and shook his hand. "It's been a pleasure knowing you and working with you. My advice is to get back in harness as soon as you can. Find yourself a good company, and get off to a new start. You've got what it takes to climb *if* you put some effort into the job. And if I can ever help you in any way, my door is always open to you."

That was it. We parted friends, and you can never be sure, of course, but I felt that I did him some good. I *knew* I had done the company some good. There'd be no kicks about a raw deal, because there had been no raw deal.

And nobody knew this better than Jack.

People-ized team building—roundup tips

(1) Here's a thought to take with you and come back to at regular intervals. *You succeed through your people!* Any uncorrected weaknesses they possess, any undeveloped talent, is an obstacle in *your* path to success as well as theirs.

(2) Try where you can to appoint natural leaders to key spots in your department. The APPOINTED NATURAL inspires co-operation. People instinctively turn to him for direction and guidance.

(3) A tuba player and a piccolo player would render a weird duet. For people to play or work well together, the ingredients of their character and personality must blend. Orchestration! Or "Chemical Response-ability," if you prefer. Keep it in mind when you organize your department. Team piccolo players with flutists. Keep tuba players in the brass section.

(4) Try the "Snapshot Technique" when interviewing several applicants in succession. Snap a picture of each person you interview. Later the photo, plus the résumé, plus your notes, will

help bring the individual back into focus quickly and accurately.

(5) If you have to go outside your company to fill a key post, proceed with extreme caution. Don't drop the newcomer like a bomb among your people. Ease him in gradually. Take definite steps to encourage his acceptance and build respect for his professional competence.

(6) The small company employee often has an exceptional chance to grow. He "rubs elbows" with the boss, has top management attention called to his talents. He gets in on challenging tasks and decision-making responsibilities and achievements. If you're a small company manager, use this persuasive selling argument in the recruitment of key people. It will help offset big company benefits you may be unable to match. If you're a big company manager, battle the tendency for employees to feel lost in the crowd by "people-izing" your approach. Even if a man feels small in the company, you can make him feel big in the department.

(7) Expand your *span of control* by developing blind faith in your people. Use "people-ized" techniques to exploit their talents. Work with them and through them, build their strengths, shore up their weaknessess, tap their natural talents until you foster in them the ability to operate independently of your close surveillance and control.

(8) Take stock of your "Personal Trust Fund." Analyze the degree of reliance you are now placing on each of your people. Then take positive steps to strengthen their abilities, and as an automatic by-product, YOUR trust in their abilities.

(9) Use the "Follow the Leader" development strategy. Show a man what to do and how to do it. Then get him to DO what you've shown him. Repeat the process until it takes.

(10) MOTIVATION! It's the master key to people development. It's the launching pad of savvy management. Horace Mann puts it this way: "The teacher who attempts to teach without inspiring the pupil with a desire to learn is hammering on cold iron." So warm up that furnace. Stimulate. *Inspire*. MOTIVATE!

(11) Don't train your people in ho-hum routine fashion. Analyze their motivational "Response Factors." Find out what makes them WANT to learn.

(12) "People-ize" your firing strategy. When forced to let a

man go, keep three key questions in mind: (a) How can you help him? (b) How can you minimize the adverse morale effect of the firing on other employees and the community? (c) What reasonable steps can you take to assure that you and the discharged employee part as friends, not enemies?

10

Apply People-ized Objectivity to

Performance Appraisal

A manager manages with one key purpose in mind. He manages for profits. He sets profit goals for himself, or has them set by the boss. The end result is the same. A team of managers is like a firing squad. The target is PROFITS.

How good has *your* aim been of late?

More specifically:

1. How are *your people* doing?
2. How are *you* doing?

Your soul-searching response to these questions will reveal how well your goals are being set and met. But the key to your response lies not only in evaluating performance. It lies in evaluating your METHOD OF EVALUATION as well.

The trick is to: (1) Sharpen your evaluation techniques. (2) Get fuller and more meaningful insights into your people. (3) Alert yourself to a "man-slide" *before* it takes place. (4) If a slide does start, learn how to stem it quickly. (5) Make sure your profit goals are realistic, and that they are fully understood by your people and yourself.

Power Your Development Thrust With People-ized Appraisal Techniques

Joe Smith has been an employee in your department for six months, a year, five years. What do you know about him?

How good is he? Does he merit a pat on the back or a shot in the arm? Should you be priming him for growth, or stepping in to head off trouble? Key questions in the development of a man, the department, *your future.*

There are three main guideposts you can use to evaluate Joe Smith or any employee:

1. Smith's past performance.
2. The performance of others.
3. Yourself as Smith's boss.

The first two guideposts are useful. Number one indicates Smith's rate of improvement or decline. The second defines his standing in the group. The third?

That's where the pitfall lies.

A philosopher once said: "We do not judge men by what they are in themselves, but by what they are relatively to us." I think there's a great danger in evaluating your people against yourself, and it's a mistake that many managers make.

Take Joe Smith. He's a young man with years of development ahead of him. You are a seasoned pro. Still, in evaluating Smith against yourself, the tendency is to forget this. You tend to judge Smith's performance in a given situation against how *you* might have acted or reacted in the same situation.

The word MIGHT should be stressed. The pitfall has a false bottom; it's deceptively deep. Here's an example: I received a call from a customer who was pressing for delivery of his order. He had just spoken to a foreman. He knew his order was in the shear department waiting to be cut. If the order was that far advanced he saw no reason, and so forth. The outcome is not important, but my reaction when I hung up, is. I was burning.

"For Pete's sake!" I exploded, "Who talked to that customer?" It was Jim. I growled at him. "You should know better than to let a customer know the stage of production of his order."

Jim looked surprised. That's what made me catch myself.

But hold on a minute. We're talking about evaluation. What has this to do with evaluation? Everything! Evaluation is a continuing process. Evaluation doesn't mean sitting at a desk with a man's chart in front of you and making out a report card. When you decide that a man made a mistake, you're evaluating him. When you feel he acted with poor judgment, you're evaluating him.

In Jim's case, I was evaluating him in relation to myself. *I* would have known enough not to tell the customer too much. But was Jim trained to know this? How often was he called on to take such a call? In this case, actually, the call shouldn't even have gone to Jim. Yet here I was using my own knowhow and experience as a basis of judgment.

I hope the point is clear.

Set up mental evaluation guideposts

Let me stress a key point regarding this vital management process of people-ized evaluation. *Evaluation is a never-ending procedure!* Moreover, it is essentially a process of weighted value judgments.

The eight direct, hard-hitting questions that follow will make your mental evaluation course easier to chart. First, consider each question individually, then in total context, to draw up a COMPOS-ITE APPRAISAL of the man.

Finally, before starting, keep this savvy tip in mind. Give each of these questions a two-way application. First, pose it to yourself with your own people in mind. Next, ask the question with your boss in mind. Put yourself in his shoes. *Imagine him asking himself these questions about you.* Don't just do this once or twice or six times. Do it habitually.

The idea is to memorize the vitally important questions that follow. Make them a key part of your savvy inventory.

1. *What is the employee's relationship to others in the organization?*

How well does he get along with people? Do they respect him for his knowledge and ability? Do they like him because he's decent, friendly, personable, fair-minded? This is sometimes difficult to assess. It may take time before you can form a reliable reaction.

2. How much aggravation does he cause you?

Many managers underestimate the importance of this question, or never ask it. You work best with the man who is comfortable to work with. You can do more for him, and you can get him to do more for you.

3. Is he an "er-uh-umm" man?

We honestly do our best to foster independence of thought and action. But there's a limit to anything. Even independence. Sometimes you spell out how a job should be done, and that's the way you want it done as quickly as possible. But there's at least one man I know—an ex-employee—who just couldn't seem to say, "yes," or "sure," or "okay," or anything affirmative. His response was always, "er-uh-umm," or "I don't think I can do that," or "well, I don't know." The man was a hemmer-and-hawer. In the end he hemmed himself out of a job.

4. Does he respond willingly to a challenge?

How much of a prod does the man need to follow through on a challenge, a project, an idea? How well, in short, can you motivate him to motivate himself?

5. Is he well-tuned to the company, and to you as his boss?

This is one of the toughest points of all to evaluate. The man's outward actions may indicate that in his view the company is tops, and you are even topsier. But how accurately do his outward actions represent his inner feelings? Is he sincere? Or is he being political? Largely, I think, arriving at these answers is a matter of experience.

Somebody once said, "Good judgment comes from experience—and experience comes from poor judgment." There is much truth in this. In the beginning you tend to fumble a bit, but gradually you will find that your instincts will sharpen along with your experience.

6. *How well does he perform his specific job?*

I'm not talking about how many errors he makes, or how many times a faulty decision is called to your attention. What I have in mind is the Quick-Alert observation technique. How do *other people*—customers, suppliers, employees—react to the man's performance? *The idea is to extend your evaluation beyond your own personal dealings with him.* It's a matter of developing a sensitivity to the unvoiced evaluations of those who work with him. This will help supplement and confirm—or deny—your own findings.

But again, a note of caution. We're working with human factors, evasive and deceptive. You can't rely on the reaction of any one person. The trick is to assimilate and weigh ALL evidence. When an image is reinforced three times, eight times, ten times, it begins to take hold and have meaning.

To illustrate, I'll take one of our engineers. As part of the Job Variety program, we sent him to help a customer solve a problem. Later I had occasion to visit the customer. I tried to judge his reaction to the man. The rating: satisfactory, no complaints. Quickly-Alert translation: no great shakes, unimpressed. How could I tell? Easy. I knew the customer. He rarely complains. But when he's pleased, his eyes glow. He crows. He raves.

So what now? Does this evaluation condemn the employee? No, not of itself. But it's one piece of that total composite picture we're shooting for. Five or six similar responses will tell me, if nothing else, that the engineer is not cut out for field work. This Quick-Alert technique is a subtle piece of business. Sometimes, in gauging the reactions of others, what's left *unspoken* is as eloquent, or more so, as the reaction that is voiced.

7. *Is he an effective trouble-shooter?*

You'll find two kinds of people in business: (1) Those destined to fulfill routine functions—bill an order, ship a carton, type a report. (2) Those destined to plan, to manage, to lead—the *Why-Man Probers.*

The prober doesn't need a boss on his back to tell him to do this or do that. He makes work for himself. He tracks down problems and scouts new areas to improve. He digs in. He gets to the bottom of things. And he doesn't do it for show. He's sincere. He digs because he wants to dig. Because he'd be bored and restless otherwise.

Want an example? The other day one of our supervisors approached me with a sheet in his hand and a frown on his face. He didn't think a suggestion of his was going to pan out. But he wanted to give the system another week or so. If it still didn't work he had some other ideas in mind.

There's nothing I admire more than a man who will come to you and point out a weakness in his own plan or operation. This subordinate climbs way up in my estimation because it means he's aware of his own shortcomings. This man is a good example. He shoots trouble every chance he gets. He loads his gun with question marks, and usually his aim is pretty good. There's an old Chinese proverb: "He who asks a question is a fool for five minutes; he who does not ask a question remains a fool forever."

The "Why-Man Prober" is no fool. He does not shrink from inquiry. He shoots trouble. And he shoots in only one direction. Up!

8. How does he rate as an evaluator?

Finally, about the person you are evaluating—how good is *he* as an evaluator? How well does he rate *his* subordinates? How effectively does he rate himself? Also, and this is a subtle point, does he use your evaluation of him as a tool to strengthen his people and to strengthen himself?

The point is worth illustrating. Mike is a production supervisor, hard-working, intelligent, well liked.

There's only one trouble with Mike. He forgets things. Sometimes he forgets important things. Like the day I flew to Atlanta. Mike, I said, before leaving, don't forget to call so-and-so. It's very important. He nodded solemnly. He took a piece of paper and made a note. But note or not, Mike forgot. He's got notes all over the place. They don't help much. He forgets to look at the notes.

"Mike," I told him, "for Pete's sake, instead of writing all these notes on pieces of paper, why not carry a small notebook in your pocket, and write them all in the notebook. Then as you complete each task, you can check it off. And twice a day, you can check the notebook for open items." Mike tried the idea. It worked pretty well. He still forgets things, but not so often.

Now, here's the point I'm trying to make. There's a fellow named Joe who works for Mike. Joe has the same problem as his boss. There's no elephant blood in his veins either. The other day I noticed Joe taking a phone call in the plant. The party at the other end apparently had instructions to relay because Joe asked him to hold for a minute. Then he pulled a brand new notebook from his pocket and started to write. The notebook looked familiar. Suddenly I realized why.

It was just like Mike's.

Load Your Mental Computer

Evaluating an employee—or yourself—is like pulling data out of an electronic computer. Only there's one big plus working in your favor. The human mind, YOUR mind, is more complex and efficient than any computer ever contrived. If you use it efficiently.

Efficiency factor number one is storage. Input. In this matter of evaluation, what gets loaded into your mental computer? The answer's a simple one.

EXPERIENCE. What we've been talking about. It's all a question of programming and planning your input properly. What do you read into storage? You read: the way a man plays politics, blends with your personality, carries out instructions, responds to a challenge, reacts to your leadership, impresses or depresses a customer, tracks down trouble, evaluates *his* people—the eight magic guideposts.

Now, carry the process one step further. You have a decision to make, three people to consider for a key job opening. Tom, Dick, Harry. Step one, you press a mental console button labeled "Tom." Zingo, out pops the answer. Tom did this; Tom did that. Responds well to a challenge, good trouble-shooter, and so on. Same thing for Dick. Same thing for Harry.

Finally, that's it. End of program; the loop is closed. You branch now to "print-out," to decision. And you decide. That's all there is to it. Well, almost all, except for the one most important point we already mentioned.

To launch your program, you must first get those eight Mental

Evaluation Guideposts burned so well into "permanent storage" that they will never be erased.

Your Turn

GOAL: To establish a "permanent storage" file of mental evaluation guideposts. *Achievement Strategy:* Become so familiar with the eight "input" questions, they will never leave you. How can you do this? Simple.

First, provide a separate sheet of paper for each person in your department. Head up each sheet with the employee's name.

Next, leaving four or five lines between questions, write in all of the questions on each of the sheets. IMPORTANT—Write each series of questions individually each time. Don't use carbon paper or a copying machine. You may get a small case of writer's cramp, but after all writings are complete you'll be surprised how well entrenched in your mind the questions will be.

Next, taking one employee sheet at a time, start with Question One and jot down significant incidents and observations related to each question as they come to mind.

Finally, go through the same process one more time using a sheet headed up with your own name. The idea is to evaluate yourself from the boss' point of view. Put yourself in his shoes as honestly and objectively as you can.

How will YOU benefit from all of this? In three powerful ways:

1. You will get those eight Guidepost questions firmly planted in your mind.
2. You will be much further along the way than you are right now in the objective and scientific evaluation of your people.
3. You will have an enlightening new insight into the way YOU stack up as a person and employee from your boss' point of view.

Spot for telltale feedback signs

Thomas Carlyle once said, "What we have done is the only mirror by which we can see what we are."

Often, the best way to view that mirror is through other people's eyes. Management savvy implies management sensitivity. It's a matter of developing a well-honed reaction awareness, the ability to spot accurately for telltale feedback signs.

Where do you look? All around you. At your boss, subordinates, peers, customers, suppliers. The trick is to read between the lines. Only rarely do people walk up to you and say: "I don't like the way you act." "I don't like the way you treat me." "What you are doing is in bad taste." "I think you're being unfair." "You don't really know your stuff on this subject." They won't say it in *words*. But they will say it with their eyes, their mannerisms, their attitudes.

Telltale signs of response and evaluation—they indicate excitement or lack of excitement, contentment or dissatisfaction, respect or disdain. They exist in great abundance all about you. Your only job is to spot for them.

But one caution when you do. Don't lose sight of one key fact. YOU'RE THE BOSS. Under no conditions should you relinquish your position of control. Take care that you're not *over-defensive* in reacting to those signs. In pinpointing weaknesses in your make-up, the idea is to shore them up, *not reveal them*. Don't give subordinates the impression that you can be molded or shaped to convenience.

Use on-stage techniques to spot a man-slide and head it off

How do you rate as an evaluator? One test is your answer to this question: *How effectively can you spot a man-slide and head it off?*

In one form or another, you've seen this pap statement a hundred times or more: A good manager does not get involved in the day-to-day operations of his department.

Know what I say to this? Hogwash! I don't think that ivory tower management works. I'll *show* you what I mean. I'll show you how a man-slide can and should be averted.

The "slider" in this case was a supervisor in our customer service department. Walking through the department one day I had a feeling that wasn't new. Things looked too hectic. Desks were piled too high with papers. Something wasn't right. I could sense it.

I asked the supervisor how it was going.

"Okay," he replied. "Few problems. Nothing I can't handle."

"Good. But promise me this. You've been very busy lately. Maybe you're spending too much time at your own desk. I'd like you to double-check the operation on a first-hand basis."

He agreed to do this. But a week later things seemed more hectic than before. Faces looked strained. I caught drifts of conversations, edgy, sharp. I checked with the supervisor. He had done what I asked.

I pressed him a bit. "Did you *really* check? Did you get down to the nuts and bolts of things?" "Oh sure," he said. We talked about it. What he had done was to go from desk to desk asking about the work. Any problems? That kind of thing.

I laid it on the line. I told him I felt there were serious problems he didn't know about. I spelled out what I wanted him to do. I instructed him to sit down alongside each of his people as they opened the mail, processed papers, worked up reports, spoke with customers on the phone. I told him that I wanted him to live through every phase of the operation and become a part of it.

Two days later he came to me, shaking his head. He was flabbergasted at some of the things his people had been doing, he confessed, the way some of the customer complaints were being handled. He promised to make some major changes.

Did I say "man-slide"? In this case, an understatement. What I had succeeded in heading off was a *department* slide.

I don't want to belabor the point. But you can't properly evaluate a man, a department, or an operation by remote control methods. Ivory tower management may work for poets and painters. But not for managers. To manage people with savvy—and to rate the effectiveness of your management—you have to do it onstage. You can't settle for rose-colored explanations. You have to dig. You have to get into the act. *You have to spend an hour to save a day.*

Get group support behind your non-mechanical goals

In business you'll find that there are two kinds of goals. One is the mechanical kind: Complete a project on the 16th. Make 7.2 per cent profit on a product. Increase sales 5-1/2 per cent in the next six months. The mechanical goal is clear-cut and easy to understand.

Not so the non-mechanical goal: Institute a new employee

department strategy. Change a product concept from one kind to another. Revamp the research and development program with a broader perspective in mind. Change your method of marketing from direct selling to distribution by middlemen. This involves getting people to abandon old concepts and accept new ones.

You know, nothing is harder to change than a man's deeply rooted habits. Even an intelligent man's. Once George Bernard Shaw was invited to take lunch with Lady Randolph. "Certainly not!" Shaw telegraphed. "What have I done to provoke such an attack on my well-known habits?" "Know nothing of your habits," Lady Randolph wired back. "Hope they're not as bad as your manners."

Sometimes I think it's as tough to put across a development, a marketing, or a product idea as it was to get Shaw to alter his deep-rooted dining habits. And these are the goals that desperately need a concentrated selling effort behind them. In my opinion, too much emphasis is placed upon the mechanical goals, and not enough on the non-mechanical goals which, in many cases, lead to greater profits and greater growth.

What's the best way to hammer across a non-mechanical goal, to get people to open their minds, to break down resistance to change? *The strategy I find most useful is to rally group support behind your objective.* And the way to do this is not with pep talks, but with on-hand participation. The idea is to *get others to practice what you preach.*

Now for another firing line case history to prove my point. The target in question: *to build good will and rapport between our shop people and our distributors' shop people.* Here's what we did.

We invited our distributors' key warehousemen to participate in a training program in Cincinnati. These are sharp people I'm talking about, men with a practical knowhow and understanding of shop problems.

One objective was educational. The other was to get these men to understand and like us better. The question was, "How?" We could do what 99 out of 100 other companies might have done. Wine them and dine them. Give them the red carpet treatment. Let them shake hands with the chairman, the president and other top brass. But . . .

BUT . . . ! Take another look at that goal. *To build rapport between SHOP PEOPLE—our shop people and their shop people.* So we called a meeting and threw an idea on the boards: hospitality night in a downtown hotel, to be hosted, *not by top brass,* but by shop supervisors and shop workers.

We got 30 or 40 of our key people together and threw the idea open for discussion. See what I'm driving at? We were shooting for group support, and that's what we got. We got the men involved. The ideas came spilling out. And before that meeting was over it was as much *their* idea as it was management's idea.

The shindig started in a local motel, and it was run just like a house party. The distributor shop people were invited guests. And that's how they were treated.

The affair was a huge success because the goal was pre-sold on a group basis. The warmth and friendship generated was priceless. And the concept—the non-mechanical goal—was hammered across, not by preaching, but by group participation.

There's just one more thing that should be mentioned. MULTIPLE BENEFITS. Remember the phrase? At least four solid by-product benefits were reaped from this program: (1) Renewed interest and excitement from the outset. The idea took the men off the floor and into the conference room for a welcome change of pace. (2) An ego-boosting jolt. Being selected to teach and host the session made the men feel important. (3) Better in-plant teamwork and rapport from this total group effort. (4) Improved harmony and cooperation between plant and distributor shopmen.

Cash in on your mistakes

In evaluating others—*and yourself*—you're going to run into negative as well as positive factors. And this will involve mistakes. I'm not referring to clerical-type errors, transposing a figure, misfiling a paper. These are relatively simple to handle. You track them down. You analyze the cause. You take steps to prevent their recurrence.

What I'm talking about is the mistakes that stem from poor judgment or a failure to calculate all factors in making a decision. How you react to such errors will either encourage a free flow of ideas in your department, or it will make people afraid to open their minds and their mouths.

You're the boss. Your attitude makes all the difference.

I have said this repeatedly. In my book there is only one kind of mistake, the kind that does not increase your knowledge. "We learn wisdom from failure," the English writer, Smiles once said, "much more than from success; we often discover what will do, by finding out what will not do; and probably he who never made a mistake never made a discovery." I am a great believer in this philosophy.

Worrying about a mistake that you are liable to make can be more damaging than the consequences of the error itself. It can produce a kind of mental numbness or decision paralysis.

One of my key objectives as a manager is to determine to the best of my ability that this never happens in my company. How? The "Case of the Gaping Pit" will give you a good idea.

It happened some time ago. We had ordered a massive machine for the plant. It was so big, three car loadings were needed to deliver it. The pit built to contain the unit was larger than the average size swimming pool. On the day the machine was due in, the engineer who designed the pit came up to me with a blueprint in his hand. His face was white.

"I made a terrible mistake. We can't use the pit."

Well, my breath drew in and there it stayed. There was a great deal of money involved, and much more. Then I thought, what do you do with the man? Call out the firing squad?

He stood there waiting, like a prisoner braced for the executioner. The execution didn't come. I managed a weak grin.

"Let's get a cup of coffee," I said.

After that we talked. We went over the figures and drawings and salvaged what we could. In the end, it wasn't quite as bad as we had thought. It rarely is.

All right, here's the big question. What had I gained by failing to follow through with the execution? For one thing, we learned something about controls. We sharpened our specifications procedures. Another thing, in the past, this engineer had always made his decisions freely, imaginatively, and for the most part, wisely. He would continue to make them that way. Finally, I think the incident helped to convince my people of something that has always meant a great deal to me. And that is that, boss or not, I try to be a human being first.

You know, most of the mistakes you find in business are honest mistakes. The screwball kind, or those deriving from negligence, are uncommon. And people who make honest mistakes cause themselves more than an ample amount of worry over them. There's nothing to be gained by worrying them more.

Another thing. If a manager wants to establish a fear-free climate he must be a pace-setter himself. His own attitude toward his own personal errors will not go unnoticed. The biggest mistake a manager can make is not being big enough to admit a mistake when he makes it. Looking at it another way, as one French philosopher said: "An error gracefully acknowledged is a victory won."

I believe that when a manager makes a mistake his best chance of cashing in on it is to face the error squarely and promptly. Respond to it openly and matter-of-factly on a non-personal basis. Make your objective clear: *To track down the cause, to take anti-recurrence action, to rectify where possible.* Don't—and that is a big DON'T—treat your own mistake as a cause for shame, as an act to be concealed. Treat it rather as an integral part of the learning and growing process.

Test Your Personal Error Response

How do YOU respond to mistakes? Your own mistakes? Your people's mistakes? Think back. Call to mind as many mistakes as you can that were made in your department. Set each one down in writing. Then arrive at an objective evaluation of the aftermath. Are you cashing in on your errors? Or compounding them?

People-ized evaluation—roundup checkpoints

1. *A pitfall to sidestep:* Don't set yourself up as the standard against which to measure a subordinate's performance. You are probably smarter than he is, more experienced, and perhaps just a mite prejudiced in your own behalf.
2. Evaluation is a continuing mental process. You unconsciously judge your people every time you speak with them, work with them, or watch them in action. Keeping this in mind will help you to evaluate more *consciously and objectively*—hence, more accurately.

3. Make evaluation a two-way street. Use the eight mental evaluation guideposts cited in this chapter to appraise your people. Then reverse the procedure, and use the same guideposts to evaluate yourself—*from your boss' point of view.*

4. Keep zeroed in on your long-term objective—to sketch out a total *composite picture* of each employee's performance. Each guidepost, therefore, will serve as a single piece of the whole, to be weighed by its degree of importance. Don't permit yourself to be unduly influenced by any single action, incident, or outside opinion.

5. Turn back to those eight powerful Mental Evaluation Guideposts. Read them now. Then reread them. Review them again and again until they become an integral part of your permanent storage file.

6. Management savvy implies management sensitivity. Develop a well-honed reaction awareness. Learn to read mannerisms and facial expressions as well as words.

7. Don't try to spot and stop a man-slide from an ivory tower. It can't be done. The trick is to get on stage. Sit down with the man as he opens his mail, compiles his report, speaks on the telephone. Visualize his job through his eyes. Climb into his skin. Think with him and think of him. Live with his problems.

8. Drive doubly hard to achieve your *non-mechanical goals* —changing concepts, boosting cooperation, selling new ideas—the kind you can't spell out in numbers and percentages. Rally *group support* behind your objectives with action instead of pep talks. *Get others to practice what YOU preach.*

9. Failure, mistakes—they're inherent to the learning and growing process. Show your people that you believe this. Show them that you're big enough to act accordingly. *Resolve now that you, as a manager, in one way or another, will derive some positive gain from every mistake that is made in your department.* Back this resolve by responding with courage and forthrightness to your own errors.

11

Management Savvy Is
90 Per Cent Sell

As the title of this chapter states: *Management Savvy is 90 Per cent Sell.*

The "selling" referred to is all-encompassing. It includes product selling, idea selling, people selling. Most of all it includes selling YOURSELF—as a manager, as a person.

"Patience is power . . ."

A key ingredient of salesmanship—*and savvy management*—is patience. "Patience is power," says an old Chinese proverb. "With time and patience the mulberry leaf becomes silk."

With patience an idea bud blossoms into full-blown profit action; a "maybe" becomes conviction; a prospect's "not interested" becomes his name on a dotted line.

To some degree, patience is a by-product of your environment. But one thing is certain. Whatever patience you already possess can be developed and expanded. How? By applying the following Four-Step formula to your daily pattern of life—both on and off the job.

1. *Conduct a CONSCIOUS campaign to combat IM-patience*

"It's easy finding reasons why other folks should be patient," George Eliot once said.

Developing patience in yourself is far more difficult. Mostly it's a matter of self-discipline. It's a matter of *regarding an impatience-provoking situation as a patience-developing opportunity.* The technique itself is simple. The idea, when you encounter a situation that edges you toward impatience, is to CONSCIOUSLY force yourself to remain logical and calm. "Consciously" is the key word. The human inclination toward impatience takes years to ripen. You won't send it packing by either stating your good intentions or relying on your subconscious to do the job. You have to make a concerted, wholehearted effort to keep yourself alerted to the irritational tip-off signals of impatience as they occur in your day-to-day functioning as a human being. Case in point:

It was a Friday. My wife and I had an engagement that evening and on the way home I was caught in a traffic tie-up. I started to simmer, the irritation creeping up on me. I'm sure you know the feeling. Then, suddenly and decisively, I caught myself. Impatience-provoking situation; patience-developing opportunity.

All right, I reasoned, how can I use this time constructively? The answer came quickly. I could concentrate—not on my irritation, but on something worthwhile, a problem, for example.

What manager doesn't have a whole inventory of problems on tap? I selected a good one, to resolve a difference that existed between two supervisors in the plant. I was soon engrossed in this challenging situation, considering it calmly, *patiently*, and with one by-product benefit—no interruptions.

Before traffic started to move again, I had the answer I was looking for. It took me 20 minutes to resolve the problem in my mind—20 minutes I would not have to spend the following day. Thus, what might have been a 20-minute vacuum spent scowling at traffic had been converted to a profitable think session. And when I arrived home, I was in the best of moods.

Another by-product benefit when patience takes the helm.

2. *Follow the leaders*

Many famous statesmen, writers, businessmen, scientists and others of great repute are particularly well-known for their patience. Patience helped these people to conceive their ideas and to put them across.

Bernard Baruch is a good example. He would sit for long periods on a park bench immersed in thought. While thousands all around him were victimized by their own impatience, he patiently gave way to reflection. While impatient men generated problems, men like Baruch came up with solutions.

There were many great persisters. Schweitzer, Einstein, Churchill. Jascha Heifetz, the violinist. Henry Thoreau, who would stroll and think for hours. Aristotle, who said that "patience is so like fortitude that she seems either her sister or her daughter."

Here's what I'm getting at. Pick your own favorite hero. Read his biography. Find out how he lived. Learn what he did differently.

You'll be surprised how much this will help. Some of *his* patience may even rub off on you. By osmosis. Or inspiration.

3. *Build a little "BEND" into your makeup*

You're the boss. Basically speaking, there are two ways to get a job done. You can roll over your people, thrusting mandates down their throats.

Or you can reason, *persuade*, SELL.

As you well know, the impatient manager bulls his way through; the patient manager *sells* his way through.

What does it add up to? One thing. *Build a little "bend" into your managerial makeup*. Patience breeds understanding. Understanding is the magic ingredient that hammers enthusiasm, inspiration and SELL into goals and ideas.

Firing line case example? Here's a good one.

It happened in a paper products company. About ten people were assembled in the conference room. Development of a new product was under discussion. The general manager was hot on the trail of this project, eager to get the preliminary aspects wrapped up and the production stages under way.

"Gentlemen," he announced, "I want that model by tomorrow."

A wave of protest hit him. "We don't have all the materials." "We need a new drawing." "We'll have to experiment with bending that part." "We're not sure we can work to the tolerance."

They were right. The boss had oversimplified the project. Focusing on *his own* desire and need, he had overlooked *their* problems. You can push people only just so far. It was time to bend.

But *the idea was to bend, without yielding control,* to make it *his* decision, not theirs.

"All right," he said. "Who can you get to help you, to expedite this project?" He knew this was no answer, but it was a way of giving in without giving in.

"Well, I don't think . . ." One of the men started talking. Others took it from there. They discussed the matter back and forth. Now the boss' role was one of patience and understanding. His mind was open. He reasoned with them. He listened to their point of view.

"All right," he said finally. "Get as much as you can get done by tomorrow; then show it to me. That will give me enough of an idea for the purpose I have in mind."

Get the picture? The boss had backtracked, but without abandoning control.

4. *Make your lucky number the "Magic Number Seven"*

You may have heard the story. A young insurance salesman was ushered into the presence of the chief executive of a major corporation. "You can feel pretty proud of yourself," the president said. "I've already refused to see seven insurance salesmen this week." "I know," the agent replied, "I'm them."

It's an old selling truism. About 80 per cent of the orders are brought home by about 20 per cent of the salesmen. These top producers are the men of patience and persistence who are willing to call back on a prospect again and again and again—five times, six times, *seven times*—until they wear the opposition down.

As the writer, DeMaistre, once said, "To know how to wait is the great secret of success."

This was hammered home forcefully not long ago by a "lobby-ist" from Cleveland who spelled the word NO with four letters, KNOW.

At the time we were talking about buying a half million dollars' worth of structural steel on a subcontract basis.

One day I got a call from Cleveland. "I'd like to write the order for that steel," the voice said. "When can I discuss the contract with you?"

We appreciated his interest, I told the man, but we're not ready to place the order as yet.

"Tell you what," Cleveland said. "I've got to be in Cincinnati anyhow. Do you mind if I stop in to see you?"

"You're welcome any time, but at the moment we're not interested."

Next day the man appeared at our offices. I received a call from the lobby.

"As I mentioned yesterday," I told him over the phone, "we're not interested right now, and I'm rather busy, so . . ."

He assured me he understood. "But do you mind if I sit in your lobby? I have some paperwork to go over, and I'd just as soon do it here. That way, if you should happen to have any questions during the course of the day, I'd be on hand to answer them."

Well, you can't throw a man out of your lobby. I went back to work and forgot about him.

An hour or so later my chief engineer came to see me. "That guy waiting in the lobby must be some kind of a nut. He knows we're not ready to move on that contract. But he says he doesn't mind. He'd just as soon sit there anyhow."

In the afternoon, the chief and I were discussing some aspects of the job. A couple of questions came up, and we remembered the man in the lobby. We called him and asked him the questions. He had ready answers. Later on, we had more questions to ask. And he had more answers.

What it boiled down to was that later in the day we decided to move ahead with the project and we gave the man the order.

"That's right," I said, "let's give him the order."

"Know something?" the chief said afterwards, "Maybe he wasn't such a nut after all."

Don't sell drills: sell holes

I know a veteran sales manager who gives young trainees this advice before sending them into the field: "Remember that customers are interested only in results. They're not so much concerned with the product as with what the product can do for them. Millions of drills are sold, not because customers want drills, but because they want holes."

A good point to keep in mind whatever or whomever you sell. Big man, medium man, small man—all men have one common motivating trigger: WHAT'S IN IT FOR ME?

And if there's any secret to the art of zeroing in on a TOP-MAN AUDIENCE, it's to come up with the right answer to that question.

I recall the time my production manager tried to get me to replace an existing machine with a unit costing $32,000. He had been after me for months to order the machine. He raved about its design, how the trouble caused by the aging machine now in operation would be eliminated, how much easier it would make his job.

I kept stalling him off. Finally, one day he came to me with a new pitch. "I figured it out," he said, "the new machine will save us $12,000 a year and pay for itself in less than three years." He had papers to prove his point.

I looked at him and I looked at his papers. That day the machine was ordered.

The production manager couldn't get over it. "After all this time! Why, all of a sudden, today—and just like that?"

The answer should have been clear, but I spelled it out.

"Until today you always told me what the machine would do for *you*. Today you showed me what the machine could do for the company."

I think we are all selfish to some extent. But well directed selfishness can be an essential savvy ingredient. As long as your personal goals tie in with the company's profit goals everyone will benefit.

And, in crusading for profits, one of the best ways to get your points across is to remember that old admonition: *Sell the holes; not the drills.*

Spot Your Personal "ME-FACTORS"

Do you have a tough selling job on your hands? A new system you would like the boss to approve? A person in your department you are trying to promote for a bigger and better job? An opportunity you yourself would like to step into—if only you could get the boss to see things your way?

All right, maybe the selling job isn't as tough as you think—if the "product" you have to sell is a good one. The idea is to arm yourself with the proper selling tools.

How? The steps are simple. First, write your selling objective on a sheet of paper. Next, concentrate on the "buyer"—the boss, an associate, your subordinates, or someone outside the company. Explore in your mind—with the help of others, if necessary—the buyer's ME-FACTORS, what he stands to gain by going along with you.

The rest is easy. Get in there and *sell*, keeping those ME-FACTORS in mind.

Make the buyer your star salesman

Launch an Idea-Sharing Plan

"Better bend than break," says an old Scottish proverb.

Sometimes, if you don't bend, your idea might break, and your profit objective along with it. I'm talking about knowing how and when to compromise in trying to put across an idea to your subordinates. To the savvy manager this kind of compromise is the art of giving a little to get a lot. This automatically implies keeping an open ear to the views of your people. But I can tell you this. Listening *alone* is not enough. Here's a case in point:

A manager I know was sensitive to the importance of shooting for cooperation rather than blind obedience. Before changing a system or making an innovation, he invariably encouraged his people to express their views and suggest modifications. To these he would listen attentively. But in the end he would set up the job exactly as he had proposed it in the first place.

His people soon caught on that he was not really consulting them, but just going through the motions. In time, they stopped taking his "open-mindedness" seriously. He's going to do it his way anyhow, they reasoned. Why bother to even think about it? The truth is that my friend was deluding himself. Whatever guise they appeared under, for all practical purposes his ideas were presented as management mandates. They were being imposed, not sold. Reluctant compliance was there, but the priceless ingredient of enthusiasm was missing.

Getting compliance—as any savvy manager will tell you—is a far cry from getting the kind of wholehearted cooperation it takes to make an idea, a project, a plan, a goal catch fire, move forward and succeed.

I've said this before, and it's worth repeating.

Your goal is to make the idea-generating act a partnership venture. This simple Three-Step procedure will show you how.

1. Present your idea as the starting base.
2. Weave the thread of your people's thinking into the fabric of your idea.
3. Come up with a NEW IDEA that is both yours and theirs.

This is the way to get your Idea-Sharing Plan across, not just because you're the boss, but because your people are excited about it and have a personal stake in its success.

Idea for Sale? It's the Follow-Through That Counts

"Ideas are funny things. They never work unless you do."

I don't know who first said that, but it's loaded with truth.

Last week, a supervisor came to me with an idea. "You know, I was thinking," he began. Good start, but he never got much past the introduction. He tossed at me the rough mass of an idea. Not too useful. Like a snowball before it's compacted. You throw it, and it falls apart.

I frowned. "Where would the idea apply?" I asked. "How would it work? How can we use it to make a profit?"

The supervisor scratched his head. He had no answer.

You know, I'm sometimes suspicious of the man who tosses an idea on the table like some kind of magnanimous gift from on high for his audience to ponder in depth, to organize and develop into something workable. I question his motives. Is he really trying to produce a constructive and profitable action? Or is he simply trying to get himself pegged as a thinker, without being willing to put forth the effort required to earn the reputation?

"The actions of men," said John Locke, the English philosopher, "are the best interpreters of their thoughts." How true! It's not so much the idea itself that counts. It's what can be done with the idea. Presenting an idea without carrying it through to its natural plan and conclusion is like offering a shiny new ax without providing the log to chop. What can you do with it? I don't know. Maybe this fellow was just trying to impress the boss. There's nothing wrong with this if it is done in a positive and constructive way. Here's a good example out of the plant.

This morning, Alex, one of my production people, came to my office with an unfinished jig. He told me about an idea he had heard of the previous evening. He spelled out the idea for me, and explained how he thought it might be adaptable by us. Then he offered to follow through and develop the concept. It was obvious he had given it a good deal of thought.

Do you get the point? Talk about impressing the boss! Alex certainly succeeded in impressing me. And if that's what he had in mind, I don't hold it against him. Because he invested the necessary think time and work time—and he did it on his own.

You know, it has been said that every time a man puts a new idea across—and what I'm talking about is *total follow-through*—he uncovers ten more men who had thought of the idea before he did.

But they only *thought* of it.

It's the action that pays off. ACTION—the supersalesman of them all.

Cash in on "Enthusiasm Feedback and Chain Stimulation"

Is this double talk? No, it's double action. It's the personalized Grapevine Strategy to gun excitement and *sell* your ideas; to cook up so strong a sizzle that the steak can't help but be tempting to the buyer.

How does it work?

The technique is simple. A new idea is like a flickering flame. It must be fanned to be kept alive.

Your goal is to recruit "fanners" to your selling team. The more people you involve, the more "fanners" you recruit.

Enthusiasm feeds on enthusiasm. Your role is like that of a machine tool builder. He makes a machine, then uses it to make a new machine.

It's a process of continuous regeneration. Enthusiasm feedback. Chain stimulation.

But the question is this. How can you best whip up excitement

to begin with? How can you promote PERSONAL INVOLVE-
MENT? The answer is clear.

What excites the average man most? *Himself*, of course! The
strategy, therefore, is to focus the spotlight where it will do the
most good. Be generous with recognition and praise. People feed
on it. Push your own contribution to the background. Give front
and center stage to your people.

Recognition! Praise! It's a natural extension of the idea-sharing
plan discussed earlier. Not *your* idea; your idea and *theirs*. And
give *their* participation the full publicity push.

Crazy? Not at all. *Not if your boss is truly a savvy manager*. If
your boss has savvy, he'll understand what you are doing and
why. He'll realize that you are trying to stimulate and build. He'll
appreciate the fact that you are *the man behind the man*.

As far as your own good job is concerned, don't worry about it.
Your personal talents will be hard to conceal. And with the savvy
boss, underselling rings more success bells than overselling.

Turn objections into profit opportunities

Your Number One Product Is YOU

Before you can hope to put across a product or idea, your first
problem is to sell yourself. Objective number one is to get the
prospect to listen. Until you can establish his confidence in you as
an individual, he won't be much interested in what you have to
say.

The fastest way to build confidence is by demonstrating your
integrity and sincerity. Don't attempt to be any more than you
are, and don't assign to your product or idea attributes they do
not possess.

No man, no plan, no product is perfect. Claim perfection and
you'll invite suspicion. Face up openly and honestly to imperfec-
tion and you'll invite confidence and trust. Here are some savvy
guidelines to follow:

- Flatter the buyer. The average person enjoys being "con-
  sulted." His ego gets a welcome boost when he is asked for his
  opinion or advice. ("I wonder if you could suggest a way to
  handle this situation?")
- Display your openmindedness. Respond to objections posi-

tively; always constructively, never defensively. (*"You've brought up an excellent point, and it's one that we missed. I'd like to go back and discuss this with our engineers."*)

- Convert liabilities into assets wherever possible. But take care not to make statements you can't back up. ("It's true that this set-up will cost more than the old system to install. But with labor cut in half you will profit in the long run.")
- Level with the buyer. Don't concentrate only on the roses, and ignore the thorns. If you hold back "bad news" that he'll find out later for himself, your concealment will double the adverse impact when it does occur. ("Yes, your man will have to go through an extensive training course to operate this equipment properly.")
- Encourage objections. Look for bad points as well as good points. Hammer across the idea that you realize possible flaws exist in your product or idea, that you are anxious to bring them to light in order to rectify them. (*"I'm glad you pointed that out. Are there any other features you think might cause difficulty?"*)
- Pave the way for "next-time receptivity." Even if you're unable to "close the sale" at the moment, show your interest. Keep the door open. Next time around you may ring up a sale. (*"I'd like to give your problem some more thought. May I call you again in a couple of weeks?"*)

Anticipate Your Personal "Cash Ring-up" Barriers

You can cope more effectively with a "buyer's" objections if you know what to expect and are prepared for it. With this in mind, it's time once more to get out your pencil and pad. Enter on a separate sheet of paper each selling objective you have in the works right now. All the major plans, programs, ideas and products you are trying to put across.

Now, call to mind every selling hurdle—every objection to your product or idea—that the prospect is likely to make. Probe deeply for adverse reactions. Put yourself in the shoes of the "buyer." Leave two blank spaces after each objection you list.

Finally, after each objection, in those two blank spaces, enter the strategy you will use to cope with it. You'll find that, in general, objections will fit into one of four categories.

1. *Invalid objection.* Based on buyer misinformation or mis-conception. Easiest kind of objection to overcome, but, CAUTION: handle tactfully. The aim is not to win the argument, but to sell the prospect. Set the record straight —but subtly, helpfully; not in an I-told-you-so manner.

2. *Valid objection—a clear and unalterable minus factor.* Admit openly to the problem or disadvantage. Don't try to minimize or deny. But stress compensating virtues where possible. ("Yes, that's why we can afford to make the product for so little and transfer the savings to you." Or, "True, but this permits us to. . . .")

3. *Valid objection—one you are trying to eliminate.* Again, admit openly to the objection. Explain the steps you are taking to make changes or improvements.

4. *Valid objection—the kind you can turn to advantage.* This is a minus factor that makes a more important plus factor possible. You goal is to get across this point. ("True, metal is less apt to break than plastic. But because the frame is made of plastic, your office girls will be able to lift the machine by themselves.")

With the above pointers in mind, compile your own list of sell-ing objectives and selling objections. Spell out how each objection will be met by you. It will help you to do a sharper and more effective selling job.

Get the Impact of Authority Behind Your Sales Pitch

Who are you? What qualifies you as an expert to talk about office systems, wage compensation programs, billboard posters, kitchen sinks?

The prospect may not ask you this point blank. But it's some-thing he wants to know. The more authority you can link to yourself in his eyes, the more weight your selling message will carry.

The trick is to establish your authority in a casual way.

The peacock is a beautiful bird, but an obnoxious person. The one way NOT to establish authority is by strutting it. Even if you succeed, the compensating resentment built up will work against you.

The other day I was talking to a contractor about our fire

doors. At one point he disagreed with something I had said. I didn't argue with him, but when I replied it went something like this: "Last week we were discussing this very point at a meeting of the Underwriters Laboratories where I happen to sit on the industry advisory board. I think you'll be interested to know. . . ."

Get the idea? I didn't strut my membership on the advisory board. I simply tossed it in as a piece of incidental information when the right opening presented itself. And the information carried more impact this way than if I had paraded it as a special issue designed to impress the contractor.

Casualness in itself bears with it a certain measure of authority. I find that most men who are "big shots" don't act like "big shots." They don't flaunt authority. Flaunting authority raises the hackles on people. It carries with it an implied superiority that breeds resentment.

What if you don't happen to possess the credentials of authority? You belong to no prestigious organization. You have no fancy title, no impressive background and experience to cite. The idea then, if possible, is to rally those who DO have the desired credentials to your selling team.

One of our young engineers did this just the other day. A new piece of equipment was expected, and we were discussing where to put the machine. The engineer had planned the location on a work flow basis, but I wasn't sure that I agreed with him. Then he let drop that he had confirmed his findings with our chief engineer and with one of our consultants.

At this point I cut him short. That was good enough for me. Those two silent partners in the background had been powerful allies in his behalf.

SALES BOOSTERS—summary roundup

1. Patience is a key selling tool. But it takes self-discipline to develop. The trick is to spot for situations conducive to IM-patience. Then *consciously* force yourself to remain logical and calm. Use the session for constructive thinking instead of corrosive irritation.

2. Take a cue from famous persons noted for their patience and persistence. Baruch, Schweitzer, Einstein, Edison, Thoreau, Franklin, Aristotle, many others. Use their ex-

perience to help you structure your own living pattern.

3. Don't be a victim of crusty rigidity. Inject flexibility into your decisions. Bend where you must, but without relinquishing your managerial control.

4. Latch on to the "Magic Number Seven." When making a sale, resolve to come back again and again—*seven times, if necessary*—in order to achieve your goal. The odds work heavily in favor of the man with the patience and zeal to excel at "The Waiting Game."

5. Step into the "buyer's" skin when you have a sale to make. *"What's in it for me?"* Pose this question from the buyer's point of view. Then come up with the most powerful arguments at your command to answer it.

6. Use the idea-sharing technique, with your own idea as a launching pad. Next, weave the thread of your people's thinking into the fabric of your own. Then, come up with a NEW IDEA that is both *yours and theirs*.

7. A fragmented, undeveloped idea often has about as much impact as a soggy firecracker. Getting the flash of inspiration is an all-important first step, but it's the action that pays off. ACTION is the supersalesman of them all.

8. Idea for sale? Trigger a chain reaction of excitement and enthusiasm. Shoot for personal involvement. Be generous with recognition and praise. Push your own contribution to the background.

9. Win confidence when you sell with integrity and sincerity. Level with the "buyer." Give him the straight facts and figures. *Don't try to sell perfection.* Perfection is a dream. It does not exist at the human level.

10. Take the "buyer" into your confidence. Treat him as a consultant. He'll be flattered by your respect for his judgment and advice.

11. Casually build your authority image to help shore up your selling effort. Take care not to adopt a role of superiority. Peacocks are appreciated only in zoos. If you're weak yourself on titles, memberships, awards and the like, recruit authoritative support from others. Quote the experts, Show how their views agree with yours.

12

How to Become an Ace

Trouble Shooter

I know of a small cosmetics company. The same man had been president for thirteen years. Each year the company showed a modest profit. Some time ago the firm was bought out by a large company. The president lasted nine months. Then he was fired.

Many people were surprised. After all, the outfit had been making money under his leadership. But the new owners had good reason for making the change. And in his heart the president knew the reason. The company had gone to fat over the years— padded payroll; weak morale; production methods, in many instances, antiquated and uneconomical; and customer relations left much to be desired. The company showed a profit, true. But only a fraction of what it would have been were the president a savvy trouble shooter instead of a complacent status quo advocate.

The point is this. Whether you're the president of your company, or the third assistant to the fifth vice president, you'll be much better off if *you* say, every week and every month, "What's wrong?" than if you wait for the boss to come around and say it to you.

There's another point to be made. Don't knock trouble. It's what keeps you in business and helps you to grow. Anyone can run a trouble-free department or company. It's the problem aspect of business that calls for savvy management. If you ever get to be president of your company, you'll have trouble to thank for it—or more specifically, your ability to cope with trouble and cut it down to size.

Personalize your trouble-shooting effort

Attempting to run a department from an "ivory tower" is like driving a car with the windshield blocked. The truly savvy manager is the man on the scene. He not only watches trouble approach, but takes aggressive action to ward it off. Though he delegates like a pro, he makes it his business to stay close to *the action, the transaction,* and *the reaction.*

The ivory tower manager burns his bridges. The savvy manager builds them up. He works with his people on a side-by-side, person-to-person basis. He trains them to tackle problems, formulate decisions, evaluate subordinates the way he would do it himself. In the end, he winds up secure in the knowledge that the job is being done in the savvy and profitable way. When troubles come, they rarely trouble him.

Prospect for Clues

The business of trouble shooting is pretty much like the business of doctoring. The object is to spot for symptoms. There's an old French proberb, "Follow the river and you will find the sea." That's how it is with tracking trouble. Follow the symptom and you'll find the malady.

The trick is to trek through your department like a Master Snoop. Make everything happening there your business. It IS your business. Because YOU'RE responsible. That doesn't mean, goad a man while he's working. Or cast an evil eye over his shoulder 26 times a day. But it does mean, *know the score.* Scout around for profit leaks. Don't lose touch with those *actions* and *transactions.*

Here's a tried and proven success tip. *Resolve each day to track down at least one item that is not being handled to your complete satisfaction.* What, specifically, should you spot for? Here are some thought starters to trigger your own profit ideas. How many more can you add to this list?

Trouble signs that call for action

1. Workers clustered around a desk, machine, water cooler —or in the john.
2. An obviously ho-hum work pace.
3. Evidences of waste, careless handling of material. (One company spot-checks waste baskets from time to time to uncover excessive waste of copier machine paper, reports rerun too often, and so on.) Look at scrap bins, check reject areas.
4. Angry, heated telephone conversations, obvious irritation.
5. Improper attention to safety; failure to use machine guards, wear safety shoes and goggles. Cluttered aisles, careless lift-truck handling.
6. Abundance of workers coupled with shortages of work. (A vice president of a leading national manufacturer said if he doesn't have a need for overtime for at least 5 per cent of his work force, he has too large a work force.)
7. Too much overtime on a fairly regular basis.
8. Bottlenecks and delays in any area of the department.
9. Desks piled high with backlogged paperwork.
10. Continuously confused or hectic operation in any area of the department.
11. Check your operation on days when absence is excessive. If the stay-aways aren't too noticeably missed, your payroll may be padded.
12. Spot for sloppy work habits and work areas.
13. Look for signs of horseplay, a prime indicator of loose control.
14. Check for machines idle too long, or too often out of commission.
15. Pay particular attention to the attitudes of your people. Make this a habit, and in time an impression about each person will emerge. You'll sense that one man is bored with his work, another indifferent, a third bitter, a fourth irritable—all sure trouble signs. (You'll also spot potential leaders, people who are bright, alert, conscientious, hard-

working, those you can count on to back you up in your
trouble-tracking crusade.)

16–25. These are items for *you* to add to this list, out of your
own experience, from your own meanderings and nosing
around.

Time to act

A good sleuth and his notebook are inseparable, and the same
thing applies to the savvy trouble shooter. So get yourself a
trouble-shooting "black book" and keep it with you at all times.
Don't trust to memory. Jot down those telltale signs as you spot
them—loopholes in systems, misuse of machines, tools, and materials. And devote a special section in your notebook to the
documenting of individual weaknesses, for it is here that trouble
is spawned. Then, once the trouble spots are identified and
recorded, the next step is to follow up to root out the causes and
cancel the problems. Troubles are like weeds. They stop growing
when you root them out.

The payoff is a mansized one. It will help free you for bigger
tasks, bigger responsibilities and, you guessed it—BIGGER
TROUBLES.

But here's a fact to keep in mind. With bigger troubles go
bigger rewards.

Broaden your trouble-shooting scope

There's much to be gained from visiting other companies. For
one thing, you latch onto thought starters helpful in triggering
your own thoughts. Another plus is that it broadens your background and perspective in surveying the field. Your best bet is to
observe how a variety of companies handle the same job or
application. The idea is to expose yourself to as many points of
view as possible. Come prepared with a list of questions to ask. In
short, play the role of the trial attorney gathering evidence.

Finally, when your evidence is gathered, make your appraisal
on a step-by-step basis. You've just visited five companies, let us
assume, to observe and assess the shipping operation. Three of
the outfits do about the same volume of business. Yet one appears
hectic and confused. Why? Ask the right questions, and you'll
find out. Number two appears to be overstaffed. Why? The third,

which is highly automated, appears to be operating smoothly and efficiently. Does this mean automation is the answer? Not necessarily. What does the system cost? How much inefficiency lies hidden beneath the surface?

What does it all boil down to? More osmosis. Always osmosis. After the osmosis comes the trouble-shooting action. That's when all the tips and pointers you've picked up are paraded in review, and applied to your own operation on a hand-picked, custom-tailored basis.

Steer Clear of Commercial Ax Grinders

A company in our area was advised by its accounting firm to install a data processing system. Here is how the general manager followed through. Note the method closely. It's a prime illustration of how NOT to make a significant investment.

1. Representatives of three different equipment suppliers were contacted.
2. The company's operation was described, requirements defined, price range specified. This eliminated two of the three suppliers.
3. The remaining salesman worked out a system and specified the equipment that would be needed. The general manager and controller were impressed by the presentation, but they wanted assurance that the system would live up to the salesman's claims for it. To provide this assurance, the salesman arranged for the manager and controller to visit a nearby installation that was somewhat comparable.
4. The host company's obliging data processing manager cheerfully showed his guests through the machine room. They watched reports snaking off accounting machines, key punchers machine-gunning holes into cards, sorters whirring away at super-high speeds. They asked questions, received glowing answers, and were much impressed.
5. Shortly after the visit, an equipment order was placed. A supervisor was hired, the system planned, the necessary advance preparations made. Finally the equipment ar-

rived. It was at this point that disenchantment began to set in.

The installation as set up turned out to be wholly inadequate to the need. The equipment was excellent. There just was not enough of it. The actual cost, it was found, would run about 35 per cent in excess of the estimated cost.

Why this gross and serious error? Four good reasons:

1. Neither the general manager nor the controller had been properly indoctrinated. Their knowledge of data processing was not sufficient to qualify them for the decision that was made. Nor had they employed the services of an impartial expert in the field to compensate for this lack.

2. The installation visited was selected by the supplier's rep. No salesman in his right mind is going to take a prospect to a customer who is likely to come up with adverse reactions to his product.

3. The executives visited the installation accompanied by the salesman. Even if the host had been willing to divulge negative aspects, it's not likely that he would have done so in the presence of the salesman.

4. The installation was discussed with the data processing manager, the one man with the biggest personal stake in its success. Few men, however straightforward, would be willing to admit that the operation they fought for, planned, and set up is anything less than satisfactory.

When Field-Checking Equipment, the Trick Is To Lead— Not Follow

Firing line case history. We make door panels. Some time ago someone in our company got the idea of rolling the edges of these panels. There are special machines designed for this purpose. The idea appealed to my brother and me. We decided to explore it. First, we spoke with the rolling people, the ones who make the machines. They checked our plant, studied our problems, told us that their machine was ideally suited to our need.

The machine maker's rep graciously offered to take us to one of his customers. We declined the offer. Instead we contacted a company on our own. We made an appointment, and visited the plant. But instead of meeting with the production man responsible for the operation, my brother and I met with the president of the company.

He escorted us through the plant. The rolling machine appeared to be working smoothly. The production supervisor told us he was pleased with its performance.

But in the privacy of his office the president said, "Want my advice? Don't get it. We've had nothing but headaches. The darn thing is down as often as it's running."

Checking further, we found the advice to be well-founded. Result, we never ordered the machine. But had we spoken to the factory man alone, we might have ordered the machine. Or, had we spoken to the president in the presence of the supplier's representative, we might have ordered the machine.

The point is clear. In evaluating a significant investment:

- Investigate the experience of other companies on your own. Select for yourself the company you visit, and do so on your own.
- Get the view of the man whose job it is to assess the situation with *the profit* result in mind. Not the fellow with the career ax to grind.

Saddle your key people with responsibility

"Responsibility educates," the orator, Wendell Phillips, once said. Coupled with accountability, it spurs a man's desire and ability to grow. My policy is to saddle my key people with responsibility from the day they start a new job, whether it's a man I've groomed and developed for the spot, or a man I've brought in from the outside.

Stimulate the Managerial Art of "Self Defense"

Back to the firing line. A few weeks ago we put on a new man as head of a department. "It is only error, and not truth, that shrinks from inquiry," Thomas Paine once said, and this is the point I wanted to get across. "You're coming in here with a fresh perspective," I told the man. "I want you to challenge everything you see. I want you to get at the profit reason behind every action that's taken. If there's no profit purpose, eliminate the action. If you see something you don't like, change it. Or at least question it. Stick with the status quo and I'll assume that you subscribe to the action."

I also let him know that I'd be back from time to time. I'd ask questions, and I'd want reasonable answers. It was the managerial art of "self defense"; I was training him to practice it.

Now, Follow Through

Part two of your defense strategy is equally important. Your goal is now established: To build the profit awareness of your people to the point where they consider each action they take in light of the profit consequences involved. Your task now is to follow through to make sure they are carrying out this objective.

Keep in mind, though, that this is only one aspect of your training and development effort. You don't play the tyrant. There's nothing unreasonable about your demands. You are shooting towards a profit goal, and you're training your people to react like money makers. Admittedly, this is a hard line to take, but it is a practical and sensible line if properly balanced by the other aspects of savvy management—the knowhow building, career building, savvy building, ego building, the job variety and self-motivation.

Finally, how do you get your subordinates to defend *their* actions? In 101 different ways. They're not necessarily planned. They evolve. Opportunities arise constantly. You pick up a letter. "Why did you handle it in this way?" You stand by during a telephone call. "Why did you tell the customer you couldn't see him before the end of the month?" You pick up a memo. "What purpose did this accomplish?" You question. You probe. You become a darned nuisance of a snoop. But each pesky interference has a purpose. It's a method of training and a method of leading. You perpetually stimulate thought.

A Case in Point

It happened several weeks ago. The customer service department was getting a rash of complaints. Up popped my troubleshooting flag. Step one, track down the reason for the complaints. Customers were getting a lot of wrong merchandise. I asked my shipping man, "What's wrong? Why are so many shipments going out wrong?"

He frowned. "We're studying the situation. Every time a complaint is called to our attention, we make a record of it."

Fine, I pointed out. At this rate, in three or six months you'll have the answer. But that's not good enough. I want the answer now, today.

You know, in some companies statistics are kept on everything. They're record-happy. They can trace back events and transactions to the Year One. You get the impression sometimes that the outfit is running a history class instead of a business. But the big question is this. What do they do with all the history? How do they use it? Some companies use it effectively. They get results based on past experience. Other companies hardly use it at all. They just keep records.

"Record-keeping is fine," I insisted, "but in the meantime the customers are getting the wrong merchandise. Why?"

He had no answer, so we found one together. I picked up a shop order and looked at it. There were strange markings on the face of the document, instructions, directives. "Who puts on this stuff?" I asked. "Some of it looks pretty confusing to me."

"It's copied from the original order," the supervisor replied.

"Who copies it? Let's go talk to him." We visited the man who did the copying. "Show me the original order that this was developed from." He dug into a file and pulled out the order. It contained two long paragraphs of instructions. The markings consisted of a condensation of these paragraphs. Here was the root of the problem; without the records, without the history.

This was important. Then and there we called a meeting and set up uniform rules of procedure for transcribing instructions from original orders to shop orders.

Once I saw that the meeting was on the right track, I left the men to work out the details on their own. But the point is this. The root of the trouble had been unearthed by constructive meddling. Not in six months. In six hours.

Build your personal inventory of "Leading Lines"

What really counts in management is the action you take. A businessman I know puts it this way: "To *look* is one thing. To *see* what you look at is another. To *understand* what you see is a third. To *learn* from what you understand is still something else. But to *act* on what you learn is all that really matters."

Horace Mann said, "I have never heard anything about the resolutions of the apostles, but a great deal about their acts."

Our aim now is to turn those resolutions into profit-producing actions.

You'll need two tools to do the job. One is that trouble-shooting "black book" of yours. The other is your Personalized Inventory of "Leading Lines."

LEADING LINES. Inquiries sparked by those black book entries. Here in a nutshell is the formula for trouble-shooting success. John W. Hannon, executive vice president of the prestigious Maynard Research Council, told me recently, "I have yet to run into a business problem that can't be licked by firing the right questions at the right people."

That black book of yours is your trouble-shooting rifle. But you won't hit a thing until you load the gun. Which brings us right back to those "Leading Lines." Questions are your trouble-shooting ammunition.

So start today to build your own personal questionnaire based on your own experiences and observations recorded in your own section or department. In working up your list, dig down deep and dig down dirty. Get to the source of the action, the conflict, the document, or whatever. Personalize your snoop shots. Individualize them, keeping in mind the special characteristics, weaknesses, strengths and motivations of your people. First, pinpoint the problem. Then pinpoint the questions that are most pertinent to the problem. And fire them at the people most directly responsible for the functions involved.

Finally, you'll have but one step left. Sit back and relax. Watch those trouble spots evaporate like specks of water sprinkled on a blotter.

To make troubles scoot, make customers smile

A trouble-free company—if one could conceive of such an organization—would be the company where all customers were fully satisfied with every product and every service.

In my opinion, the man who can point to such an organization is either mistaken or an out-and-out liar.

In any case, more and more companies today are going to considerable extremes to woo the customer and keep him won. At

Gates Rubber Company, for example, "quality auditors" periodically visit key jobbers. The trouble-shooting objective is to uncover product and operating deficiencies before customer irritation—REAL TROUBLE—can set in. The auditors track down product defects. They check adherence to delivery schedules, condition of merchandise on arrival, quality of service, paperwork errors, attention to adjustments.

Westinghouse Electric has its own effective technique for trouble shooting customer complaints. New products are pretested in the homes of quality engineers. The objective—to spotlight flaws before they develop into customer dissatisfactions.

This trouble-shooting philosophy pays off in boosted reputations and the development of a definite competitive edge. In many cases, when trouble erupts, it is too late to repair the damage done. As one sage wryly expresses it: "Hindsight explains the injury that foresight would have prevented."

The key word, of course, is prevention. Preventive management works in the care of equipment. It works equally well in the care and feeding of customers.

Climb into the Customer's Skin

The first rate trouble shooter possesses the savvy and acuity to climb into the customer's skin and assess the product, the service, the operation, from *his* point of view. This is the manager with the capacity to lock horns with trouble and pin it down in record time.

Let me cite an example. Recently I had occasion to visit a customer's place of business. Usually this man was happy to see me. This time his greeting was a scowl. His complaint was a late shipment.

"Let me see the bill of lading," I asked. He couldn't find it. All he had was a shipping notice. I inspected the sheet of paper, and found a date. But it was the date typed, not the date of shipment. The notice of shipment was always stapled to the bill of lading. Without the bill we were unable to actually pin down the date we shipped the order.

Back at headquarters I made the rounds. I fired a battery of questions at different individuals. What happened to the shipment? How long had it taken to pass through Engineering?

Where was it delayed? Why was it delayed? Why should a shipping notice be sent to a customer with no date of shipment included?

As I explored the situation I kept one person in the foreground of my mind all the time—that disgruntled customer. Each person I talked to had his own story, his own point of view, his own justification or rationalization for what had taken place. But I kept only one point of view—the customer's.

That was all that mattered. I assessed the situation from the *customer's point of view*, gauging his reaction at every step. And when corrective action was taken it was with King Customer in mind. And it's this that brought results. The system was refined so that a similar situation could not occur again.

Extend This Objectivity to Others

The customer is number one on your profit parade. But you can multiply this skin-climbing technique to encompass every individual with whom you deal. In dealing with suppliers, competitors, associates, superiors, subordinates, develop the ability to assess *their* answers to *your* questions from *their* points of view. It will give you a penetrating new insight into the actions and reactions of others. To illustrate:

• You gave a subordinate an instruction. He didn't carry it out properly. Why not? Climb into his skin and find out. Was it due to some inherent weakness in his makeup? What did he stand to lose by obeying the order? What could he gain by ignoring it or changing the procedure? There's a purpose behind every deed and every response. The place to search for the purpose is in the other fellow's mind.

• A supplier promises delivery of a much needed item. The item doesn't arrive. Why not? Shift your locale via the wheels of your imagination and you may find out. Get into the supplier's plant, behind his desk. He's overloaded with orders, short of people. He's aware your shipment is past due and vitally needed. But so are other shipments. Maybe your competitors are breathing down his neck harder than you are. Maybe his operation isn't big enough to cope with your needs. Maybe *you're* not big enough, from his point of view, to warrant priority over other more important customers. Maybe a hundred things. Where are the answers? They're all in his mind. Project, and you'll find them.

• You're a sales executive. One of your men promised to send in a report from the field, but didn't comply. Why not? Start projecting again. The man's on the road all day. Get into that car with him. He's had a gruelling day; he's driven three or four hundred miles, fighting hard from morning to dusk to beat down sales resistance. He *meant* to write up that report when he got to his motel. But maybe he was too beat to tackle it. Or maybe, in his view, the only thing that really matters is calling on customers. Or maybe he's just too fed up to give a darn one way or the other. The answer? You know where it lies. The question? It depends on how well you can project.

The Payoff's in Spades—the Kind of Spades You Dig with

Skin-climbing is one of the most powerful techniques I know. The more advanced your skill in this art, the more perceptive your questions will become. The reward is clear. Uncover the right questions and the facts you want to know will come to light. For every question there's an answer. For every answer there's a process of logic and reasoning that takes place in the mind of the responder.

The skill may seem largely instinctive. But experience proves it's a skill that can be sharpened and developed. And you can encourage your people to work with you in the development. My secretary serves as a good example. We have come a long way, I think, in getting through to one another. I have learned to visualize problems and situations from her point of view. She does the same from her end. It has been a great boon for both of us.

One Thing That Has Helped Immensely Is Never to Let Misunderstandings Pass By

There was a time, I can recall, when dictation with Sarah was a totally mechanical process. I would speak; she would write. At times I thought that if, in the middle of a business letter I were to suddenly switch to the Declaration of Independence, she would hardly note the difference.

All this has changed. We now shoot for understanding—and we shoot trouble at the same time.

Convert subordinates into expert trouble shooters

A few weeks ago a credit supervisor came to me with an order in his hand.

"What do I do with this guy?" he wanted to know. "We've been doing business with him for almost five years. He owes us $10,000. His account is four months past due. Now I've got a new order for $2,200."

He filled in some more facts, the customer's D & B rating, his history, information about his operation. Then he stopped talking and waited for an answer.

No answer. I sat there gazing at him.

He shifted uneasily.

Finally I said, "You're waiting. So am I. I'm waiting for the rest of the story; the second half."

He frowned.

"What's your recommendation?" I fired at him. *You're* the credit man. I want to know what *you* think we should do. If I don't agree with your judgment, I'll say so. If there's a problem you can't handle, I'll help you work it out if I can. But I want *your* opinion. I want *your* thinking on the subject."

Get the point? My credit man did.

"Don't come to me with problems," I tell my people. "Come with ideas, actions, alternatives. Bring me answers."

When you force a man to tackle trouble, he develops the knack for coping with it.

The more troubles you tackle, the less formidable they appear. My philosophy is this. If you regard each trouble as a character-building and savvy-building experience it will bring out the very best that is hidden within you. That goes for you. It goes for your people.

Trouble-shooting recap—pot shots to remember

1. Switch from negative to positive thinking. Remember the old adage: "A problem is nothing more than an opportunity in work clothes."

2. Shirtsleeve management pays off in trouble-busting achievement. So, if you're cooped up in a cubicle, climb

down from that "ivory tower" and padlock the door. Get out on the floor and into the act.

3. Trek through your department like a Master Snoop. Nose out trouble signs like a prospector searching for gold. Undiscovered trouble multiplies like fungi. Pinpointed problems are readily uprooted and eliminated.

4. Don't ignore complaints, or react to them with the "mañana" approach. Complaints are the harbingers of trouble. Trouble-shooting rule number one is to apply the grease where you hear the squeak.

5. Keep a curious eye peeled on the competition. Find out out where they have the edge over you. Then scrutinize your own operation to find out why.

6. Pay King Customer his royal due. When the King's unhappy, it's time for you, his good and loyal subject, to get on your horse and run down the source of his dissatisfaction.

7. Be specific in scouting your operation for profit leaks. Don't settle for surface appearances. It's the underlying core that counts. And don't settle for the answer, "Fine," in response to your question, "How's it going?" The question elicits little. The answer divulges less.

8. Don't concentrate on simple problems, and sidestep the complex ones. Your value—*and compensating reward as a manager*—will be based on the scope and size of the troubles you are qualified to tackle and subdue.

9. Get out into the field from time to time. Observe how the other fellow solves his problems. But don't attempt to superimpose another man's system on your own operation. The idea is to *selectively* adopt and modify what is useful to you.

10. Take care when investigating outside use of systems or equipment to determine its value to your special case. (a) Educate yourself on the subject, or employ the services of an expert to assist with your decision. (b) Select the company you visit on your own; don't ask the supplier to do it for you. (c) Visit the company alone, not accompanied by the supplier's representative. (d) Get the

opinion of the host executive whose function it is to assess the system or equipment with the profit motive in mind.

11. Saddle your people with responsibility. It's a way to cut down trouble and pinpoint leaders. Make key subordinates defend their actions—and their inactions as well.

12. Develop the professional investigator's deep respect for questions. The well-phrased and well-directed inquiry is the most powerful tool in the trouble shooter's kit. Start today, and build an inventory of "Leading Lines" derived from your own observations and experience.

13. "Objectivize" your trouble-shooting campaign. Develop the powerful technique of "climbing into the skin" of the customer, the supplier, the subordinate, the associate, even your boss. Once you can view a problem from the other person's vantage point, the solution becomes that much easier to work out.

14. Don't permit misunderstandings to pass by unclarified. De-muddle confusion, de-fog doubts. Ignorance is the breeding place of trouble. Brighten up those dark spots and troubles will scoot from the light like rabbits at the sound of buckshot.

13

How to Translate Your Thoughts

into Action

A sage once said, "You are today where your thoughts have brought you; you will be tomorrow where your thoughts take you."

Your thoughts will take you far if you develop the ability to translate them swiftly and efficiently into action.

Seventy per cent of a manager's time is spent communicating

This is a fact of business life. Another fact is that communications is the lifestream of any organization. Through good communications problems are solved, decisions made, profit goals attained.

The question is this. How can you get your thoughts translated swiftly and efficiently into profit-directed action? Here are five tested techniques. They won't give you *all* the answers. But, in mastering them, you will be off to a fine start.

Communicate in "shorthand"

The poet, Robert Southey, once said: "It is with words as with sunbeams—the more they are condensed, the deeper they burn."

This is another way of saying: Communicate in shorthand. Cut out the bushbeating. Get right to the heart of the matter and you'll get your message across much faster and with much more impact.

Shorthand is the art of condensing words and thoughts. It's the art of boiling down a problem or a situation from two or three paragraphs to two or three sentences.

Here's an example. The other day one of my people came to see me with a delivery problem. "This customer called," he began. And he went on to tell me that the customer needed a special shipment because of a last minute change in his building schedule, and that the customer realized he had ordered the frames too late, and so on and so on.

At that point I stopped him.

"Look," I said, "get to the point."

He frowned. Then he gave me the gist of the situation in about one minute. I gave him his answer in two sentences. And that was that.

There are usually a bunch of whys and wherefores tied to any situation. Sometimes you need the detail to make a decision. More often, you don't.

That's the point. *Summarize first.* The detail can come later if you need it. If you can manage without the song and dance, look at the time and effort you've saved. That's shorthand.

A manager should train his people to think in fundamentals when they work with problems. He should teach them to pull out the essence and to focus on the action that is required.

Take memos, for example. Some of them ramble on and on and on. I insist on two things for every memo I issue, and every one I am given to read. First, the main theme of the memo must be summed up in a sentence or two at the start. Next, I require the word ACTION to appear at the bottom of the memo, followed by the action itself spelled out in simple language.

This disciplines the writer to keep his thoughts on the beam. It sets the stage for quick fulfillment of the memo's purpose. And the reader gets the message fast.

One of our engineers went out of town to look at a piece of equipment. On his return he wrote a beautiful two page memo describing the equipment, its features and the costs. After reading this very detailed memo, I took a red pencil and wrote across it the words "so what" and promptly returned it to the engineer. The next day, a new memo appeared on my desk with four sentences. 1) This machine will do the job we want. 2) It costs $5,000 delivered and installed. 3) Based on production forecasts, we can save $5,000 in 14 months. 4) I recommend we purchase the machine today. Our vice president of manufacturing agrees.

ACTION: I promptly approved the purchase.

I don't have to read all of most of the memos I receive. By just glancing at the ACTION I find out all that I need to know. If this doesn't satisfy my need, chances are that the summary portion at the beginning of the memo will.

Try this with your people. It will conserve precious minutes of management time. It will help to translate your thoughts into profitable action a great deal faster.

Tune out the noise

Two people are engaged in conversation. Anything that comes between them that does not relate to the subject at hand detracts from the effectiveness of the communication. On Madison Avenue they refer to this as "noise."

Noise takes many forms. The more obvious distractions—strange sounds, other people's conversation, telephone interruptions and the like—don't warrant our consideration here. Needless to say, these should be minimized.

Another kind of noise is caused by thoughtlessness, lack of courtesy. You're talking to someone and his attention wanders. Or he permits cigarette smoke to drift into your face. This, too, will weaken the communication. How can you control this? Lord Chesterfield has a pertinent comment which comes to mind: "A man's own good breeding is his best security against other people's ill manners."

Another kind of noise is particularly destructive. Most often, you don't hear it, or see it. *You feel it.* It's the kind of noise that is present when one part of the communicating team—and good communications is a team effort—is uncomfortable, self-conscious, ill at ease.

If you talk with a subordinate, for example, and part of his mind is taken up with how to impress you because you're the boss, or how to hide his nervousness, it is going to decrease his degree of concentration.

Some time ago a key job opened up in our company and I decided to interview one of our plant people for it. I knew this man's record. I had talked to other managers about him. I was half sold in advance that he was the right man for the job. But the moment he walked through that door I could sense his nervousness. And it was understandable. This was his big chance. He was worried about blowing it.

Sensitive to his feeling, I decided to play it slow and easy. The first thing I did was to offer him a cigarette. Then after we both lit up, I took a photo out of my desk drawer and showed it to him. There was nothing especially significant about the photo, except that it was a very good picture, and this man was an amateur photographer. Within two minutes we were talking about photography. Within five minutes his nervousness was gone.

The noise was tuned out.

Then we were able to communicate.

Often, to tune out noise, or to set a proper mood, you have to play a role. As I already pointed out, every savvy manager is a good actor. He adjusts to his surroundings. You play one part when you talk to a man in the shop. You play another when you talk to an assistant, a customer, a salesman in the field.

This doesn't give you license to commit the cardinal sin of talking down to people. Or acting unnatural. Or pretending to be what you're not. The point is this. A good manager is a little bit of everything that goes into management. He is part salesman, part production man, part public relations man, part human relations counselor. The trick is simply to wear the proper hat at the proper time.

The trick, when you are engaged in face-to-face communications, is to talk to the other person's reactions.

I had an economics professor in college who appreciated this and it made him a great teacher. He worked on the principle that each of us understands words in a different way. Therefore, as he spoke, he would try to say the same thing by the use of different words in order to capture the thoughts of as many people as possible. When we took notes in his class, this presented a very serious problem.

When we asked this professor to repeat a particular point, he would never repeat the message in the same way as originally stated. Although this made it difficult to take notes, we were able to enlighten ourselves on the subject matter. His standard comment was, "It is more important to thoroughly understand the subject than to merely record it," and he provided sufficient *feedback* to make sure that the meaning came through.

Put feedback to work the next time you explain a situation to somebody. Or when you give instructions to one of your people. *Talk to the other person's reaction.* Make sure that your message is getting across. Don't be afraid to express the same thought in a variety of ways.

Take the Talker's Pulse

What is he *really* saying? How well are you gauging his reactions?

One way to gauge a man's reactions is to listen to him. The Roman philosopher, Epictetus, once said, "Nature has given to men one tongue, but two ears, that we may hear from others twice as much as we speak."

How do you listen well? With your ears, of course. But there's another way, too. I like to think that I also listen with my eyes.

There's a mine of information in the way a man smiles, the way his lips move, the way his eyes respond. Watching a man's expression while he listens and while he talks is an important part of communication.

Horace Mann refers to the face as "the artless index of the mind."

Watching a person's face is another way of gauging his reaction. It's a tip-off as to how well you are enacting your role. A failure to respond with a smile at a given time may tell you to soften your approach. A shadow of skepticism in his eyes may tell you to act more authoritative. An uneasy expression may be a tip to become less formal.

A friend of mine owns a chain of men's shops. He is a brilliant businessman and an ace salesman. One time he visited one of his stores in Cincinnati. Standing in the background, he observed his salesman talking to a customer. The customer was well dressed. He had class written all over him. He was interested in some fine shirts, and the salesman was "yes sirring" him to death. He did all but salaam.

After the customer left without making a purchase, my friend gave his salesman a valuable lesson in communications.

"Look," he said, "you're not a servant. You're an authority on shirts, an expert in your field. That's why the customer came to see you, and that's what he wanted you to prove to him. If he wanted a valet he would have gone to an agency for domestics."

My friend is trained to gauge the other person's reactions and respond accordingly. He was sharp enough to spot what his salesman had missed completely. Maybe it was in the curl of the customer's lips, a flicker of annoyance in his eyes. But what my friend spotted was his loss of respect because of the exaggeratedly deferential treatment. The salesman had made a mistake that is quite common to the unskilled communicator.

He had failed to take the talker's pulse, and respond accordingly.

Treat each letter as a profit opportunity

Whoever said that opportunity knocks one time only wasn't talking about the mail.

Scarcely a day passes that I'm not able to pick at least two or three profit plums out of the morning correspondence. A brochure comes in from a supplier. "What can this new product do for us?" I ask. Can it improve systems, boost production, cut costs? An inquiry arrives from an unknown company. Could this mean potential business? A letter is received from a job applicant. Can we use this man in our operation?

I find profit opportunities in my morning mail because I know they are there and I look for them. I have trained myself to *relate whatever comes to my attention during the course of the day to our company's profit goals.*

What steps can you take to make the most of your mail? How can you train your people to do the same? The trick is to create profit awareness in yourself, and to keep it stirred up in others.

A young manager came to me recently with a letter he had received. He wanted clarification on some point.

I took one look at the letter and saw that it was signed by the district sales manager of a hardware manufacturing company. It was a request for information about our fire doors and frames.

"Charley," I asked, "what was the first thing that struck you when you read this letter?"

He frowned. "I don't know. I wanted to give the man the information he is looking for."

"Pretty routine, would you say?"

"Well, I guess so," he said suspiciously.

"All right," I said, "here's the point I'm trying to make. This letter is from a hardware manufacturing company, and as you know, some of our most profitable working arrangements are with hardware companies. Also, the letter is signed by a district sales manager. He is obviously interested in our products. How many other district managers are there in this company? Could they be interested too? What about the sales manager? And the general manager?"

Charley nodded. He was beginning to see the light.

The main idea is this. Since we are all creatures of habit, *why not make profit-directed thought a habit too?*

If you do, it will cause you to read your mail in a new light.

"This letter is anything but routine," I told Charley. "It deserves very special treatment. A personal long distance call, perhaps. A reply that is signed by a top officer of the company. Follow-up action to make sure the opportunity is milked to its full potential."

The idea, when you spot a profit opportunity, is to make a big deal out of it.

Our company receives hundreds of inquiries each month. We handle them promptly, referring them to our distributors in the field. No matter how hard we try we never are able to get the proper feedback of results of the referrals. Therefore, each week my brother and I take some of the inquiries at random and telephone the people requesting information. This is often a very rewarding and profitable experience. It is packed with "multiple value" and often helps to formulate management decisions.

Here are some typical benefits from this one act alone:

1. It brings us closer to the selling point of our product, enables us to talk to a customer who is interested in our product.
2. We get a chance to make a personalized impression on the customer, something few executives take the time to do.
3. We sharpen our own skill in evaluating sales opportunities and making sales contacts.
4. We uncover interesting market trends and learn more about the use, needs, and applications of our product.
5. We get a chance to discuss our distributor in the field and evaluate his treatment and service.
6. We get the opportunity to reinforce the distributor's selling message and help him to make a personal contact.
7. We appraise our advertising and promotion by learning the source of the information inquiry.
8. We arm ourselves with data about the saleability of our product and gather valuable information for use in sales meetings.

A magazine writer once asked the old classic question of a top business leader. "What do you consider to be the main ingredient of your success?"

His reply: "I've been conditioned to jump at every opportunity."

"But how can you be sure that an opportunity exists?"

"You can't. The idea is to keep jumping."

Your morning mail is as good a leaping-off place as any.

Get to the Point

The French mathematician and philosopher, Pascal, once told a friend, "I have made this a rather long letter because I haven't had time to make it shorter."

Brevity is not an easy art to learn. But if you practice brevity often enough it will become a habit. If you apply it to your business correspondence you will more than double the effectiveness of your communication.

A key distributor wrote us a letter. He wanted to run a color ad in a magazine, and the cover of our catalog appealed to him. Were the plates available? Could the cover be adapted in some way to his purpose?

An assistant dictated a two-page reply to the letter. He went into the complications that would be involved if we complied with the distributor's request. The catalog cover was an offset job. There were problems involving the paper, the equipment, the plates, and a dozen other things. Because of the expense it wouldn't be practical to tackle the job.

After spending more than two hours on the letter, my assistant showed it to me. I skimmed down the two pages.

"I can see you went out of your way to get the answer just right," I observed, "because this distributor is so important to us. But," I pointed out, "he is also a very busy man." I reached for a yellow pad, and hastily penned these lines:

Dear George:

We are flattered by your comments about our catalog cover, but frankly, there would be so many complications involved in trying to reproduce it for your purposes that we feel the cost would be prohibitive. I hope we can be of more service next time.

Sincerely,

Use meetings to solve problems and spark decisions

In my view the meeting is a powerful communications tool. I know I am putting my neck way out when I say this.

There's much talk these days about the value of individual thought as opposed to group thought. And you have probably heard the claim that the Ten Commandments are so short and to the point because no meeting was held to formulate them. Well, I think there's another side to the coin.

I think you can derive great value from meetings if you don't permit them to deteriorate into a meaningless routine.

Every meeting we hold must have a specific purpose. And every meeting we hold must begin with a statement of that purpose.

It thus becomes the leader's job to keep the group zeroed in on that purpose at all times. Without good organization a meeting will quickly bog down. All it takes is one person who is permitted to run off on a tangent.

There's an old Chinese proverb: "To talk much and arrive nowhere is the same as climbing a tree to catch a fish."

I think this is what most of the controversy about meetings is about. Some time ago I was invited to sit in on a meeting at one of our suppliers. They were discussing a new product that was of interest to us. The purpose of the meeting was to develop a plan for handling the component parts involved. The meeting was running on target until somebody mentioned a part in the new product that was made of a certain kind of steel. Somebody else wanted to know if a different kind of steel would do as well. From here the discussion got into sizes, suppliers, and steel in general. At this point the meeting leader, who was a savvy manager, stepped in.

"Hold on," he said. "This subject is important and it's something we should talk about. But not here and now. Our objective now is to get this new product moving. Dave, why don't you make a note, and we'll pick this up again at another time?"

Get the idea? Running a meeting is like guiding a missile that must constantly be kept on course.

The ultimate goal of a good meeting is action. The idea is to come to a firm decision and a firm definition of who is to be responsible for what.

There's one technique I use with great effect. It's to have the person who is most affected by the decision wind up the meeting by stating the proposed action in his own words, and in front of everyone else. This puts him on the spot. It commits him personally to the fulfillment of the action that has been decided upon.

At this point the meeting is quickly adjourned. It ends on a high note and everyone leaves, satisfied that the purpose was accomplished. There is no lingering about, no petering out.

Spice Your Meeting With Variety

A president I know thinks it is a good idea to hold regular weekly staff meetings just to "talk things over." I don't agree with him. At times there is nothing significant to discuss. Also, such meetings tend to follow a set pattern. Week in and week out they're the same. There are no surprises. People know what to expect. As a result, they are bored.

At Steelcraft, our aim is to throw variety into our meetings. As an example, we don't always announce them in advance. This may be cheating on the book a bit. But we find there is much to be gained from this technique. It's another way to cash in on multiple benefits from a single action. Here are some of these benefits.

1. Word of an unannounced meeting immediately triggers interest and excitement. People want to know: What's up? What is it all about?
2. The unannounced meeting also interrupts the daily routine, which we like to do from time to time. It gives people a welcome breather, a new perspective.
3. The impromptu meeting also doubles as a powerful development tool. It trains people to think on their feet. It sharpens their persuasive powers.
4. The unannounced meeting provides planners with off-the-cuff reactions to key problems and ideas. A person's first reaction can be very instructive.
5. It can help a manager bring his own views and goals into sharper focus.
6. It can pinpoint areas that weren't analyzed in sufficient depth, or were overlooked entirely.

Here's another way to make meetings produce profitable ideas instead of weary yawns. Use the "stand-up" technique. The stand-up meeting is just that. Participants don't get comfortably ensconced in chairs.

We developed this technique at Steelcraft, and our managers are all for it. With good reason. It's a way to minimize talking and maximize action.

At times too much deliberation tends to muddle a manager's thinking. The stand-up meeting means business on the run, and it's all business, with the formalities and trivia cut out. It shortcuts problems and pins down decisions faster.

There's only one caution to be noted in putting a stand-up meeting to work for you. That's the danger of working off the top of your head when more intense concentration is called for. The technique has to be used selectively. And flexibility is a must. If a participant is unhappy with a snap decision he must be free to voice his objection, or reactivate the issue at a formal meeting.

Put your literature to the firing line test

"The idiots!"

How many times have you hurled this invective at a company because its catalogue was fuzzy? Or its brochure didn't tell you what you needed to know? Or a set of assembly instructions struck you as senseless and confusing?

Many companies produce top quality products. They go all out to achieve the best in materials and workmanship. Then they blunt the effect by following through with literature that undermines instead of enhances the effort. They fail to communicate effectively to the most important audience of all—the customer and the prospect.

The trouble is that company literature is too infrequently subjected to the "firing line test." The job is done subjectively instead of objectively.

Just what is the firing line test? It's simply a matter of making sure your message will be meaningful to the person who is going to read it and act on it—the merchant, the housewife, Mr. Average Citizen, or whoever.

A few months ago our advertising and engineering departments issued a set of instructions for putting door frames together. They wrote some copy, and had the artist draw some cartoons.

A friend of mine was in the office when they showed me the result.

"Tom," I said, "do me a favor. Here's a set of instructions. See if you can put a frame together."

Tom reluctantly gave it a stab. In the end he did much head scratching, but little assembling. I called in one of the accountants and gave him the same chore to do. He was "all thumbs," too.

We went down to the shop. Without giving him the instructions, I asked our master carpenter to install a door frame for us.

He put the frame together methodically and efficiently, a step at a time. I turned to the advertising boys and the engineering boys. "There. That's the way to install a door frame. *That's the way it's really done.* Get that into your copy and cartoons."

Granted, theory does have its place. But I've found this to be true time and again—it won't stand up against the real thing.

Vice President Humphrey once said, "I learned more about economics from one South Dakota dust storm than I did in all my years in college."

It's the old story. Theory versus the firing line.

Wrapping up the package

Now for a capsulized rundown of the tested communications techniques spelled out in this chapter.

1. *Communicate in shorthand.* Don't hem and haw when you speak or write. Get to the heart of the matter. Boil down problems. Condense situations from pages to paragraphs, from paragraphs to sentences. Pinpoint key ingredients for the reader or listener so that he will be able to bypass the detail if he wants to.

2. *Tune out the noise.* Minimize distractions when you communicate. The more obvious message spoilers are strange sounds, outside conversation, interruptions. Add to these: inattention, table drumming, cigarette smoke, plus the kind of "noise" you don't see or hear, but *feel*. Make it a habit to *talk to the other person's reactions*. And use *feedback* to test his reactions. Have him repeat *your* message in *his* words. You think four times as fast as he talks. Use this speed advantage to listen effectively with your ears and *your eyes*. Weigh his words. Observe his gestures. Watch his face. Take the talker's pulse and respond accordingly.

3. *Treat each letter as a profit opportunity.* Relate each piece of correspondence you send or receive to your company's profit goals. Train your people to do the same. When you spot a profit opportunity, blow your horn. *Make a big deal out of it.*

4. *Use meetings to solve problems and spark decisions.* Make sure the purpose of every meeting is clearly and unmistakably stated, and keep participants sharply zeroed in on this purpose. Be objective when you lead a meeting. Organize. Plan. Combat group tedium with variety. Work in surprises. Keep your people guessing. Try unannounced meetings as one way to achieve this end. Use stand-up meetings to spur decisions, bypass red tape, provide an added dash of variety.

5. *Put your literature to the firing line test.* Use the nuts and bolts approach when you communicate with the most important audience of all—your customers and prospects. Don't tell about your product or service from an ivory tower. Get down to real

cases in real surroundings. Talk to the housewife in the kitchen, the salesman on the road, the production man in the plant, the architect on the building site. Use on-hand facts, not dreamed-up theory. Test your literature on the average user, the average buyer, before sending it on its way to act as a representative of your company.

14

Change "It Can't Be Done" to

"It Will Be Done"

"What a man can imagine or conceive in his mind he can accomplish." So says Henry J. Kaiser. "Impossibles are impossibles as thinking makes them so."

It's a thought worth pondering. *Today's successful manager is the realist who shoots for the "impossible dream."* Sound paradoxical? It's not.

The manager with the forward thrust to hack his way through the competition and emerge at the top is the man who possesses the savvy to instill *"Yes Determination"* into himself and into his people.

What elements are needed to change "It can't be done" to "It will be done"? The five key factors are explained—and dramatically proven with live examples—in this chapter.

1. Replace *Can't Do Skepticism* with *Must Do Urgency.*
2. Refuse to take *No* for an answer.
3. Master the *Simultaneous Equation.* Get all wheels turning at the same time.
4. Gun down the *Hold-Up Man.*
5. Keep the motor running with *On-Hand Fueling.*

1. Replace CAN'T DO SKEPTICISM with MUST DO URGENCY

Hammer home the stake involved

A man will often tackle a task with limited vigor because of a question mark in his mind. *How far does the boss want me to go? To what degree can I commit myself in terms of time, money and manpower?*

As head man, it's your obligation to clarify the limits and the plan of action. The point to get across to your people—*and yourself*—is how, precisely, getting this job done will affect the profit objectives of your company.

Some time ago we developed a new sliding door. Its success hinged on a patented idea to use a spring-loaded device to pull the door closed. The product was important to us. We wanted it ready in time for our big sales meeting in two weeks to help trigger a major promotional campaign.

The door itself was completed. We installed the spring device and tested it. It worked just as our engineers predicted it would— the first time, and the second time. The third time it failed. We checked the device and found the reason. It was neither big enough nor strong enough.

Two weeks to go. I asked my chief engineer to contact the supplier. "See how fast he can come up with a sturdier model."

Later I learned that he did my bidding by writing a letter.

A letter! That's when it came crashing down on me. *I* knew the importance of having the door in time for that meeting. But I hadn't communicated the importance to the chief.

Donning my actor's garb, I dramatized the cost of not having the device ready in time. I blew up the problem, made a big deal of it. Right then and there we got the supplier on the phone.

"Send down the model," he suggested. "We'll check it out and see if we can come up with something."

"*Send it down, nothing!* We've invested thousands in this project. Without that spring device, it's worthless. Look, I'm flying my man down on the next plane."

Next day I got a long distance call from the chief. They could come up with the model, he told me. But it would take three weeks.

"Hogwash!" I demanded to talk with the president. "If we don't have that model in ten days it'll be worthless to us. We'll call the whole deal off."

There was a pause. "Hold on a minute." He came back on. "If we commit ourselves to ten days, will you foot the overtime costs?"

"Agreed," I said. "Put the chief back on."

I spelled out the arrangement to my chief. "Your job is to stay on their backs until they get this thing rolling. Give them any help they need."

This time the message got through because I had translated the urgency of the situation. The telephone calls, the plane trip, the extra cost commitment. The target *had to be achieved* at any cost. The chief understood this now. He knew he could go to the limit in fulfilling the objective.

Spark the Support of Your People: Don't Take it for Granted

Behind almost every contention that a job can't be done is somebody's lack of concern over its achievement. In discussing world competition General Electric Company's Vice President Virgil B. Day stresses the importance of getting your people personally involved in your goals. "The difference between success and failure," he says, ". . . lies in the way we manage our human resources."

Day cites a particular GE experience. Starting in 1957, the Japanese capitalized on an American invention, the transistor, and within five years captured half the U.S. transistor radio market.

In early 1960, GE launched a determined effort to regain its hold on the six-transistor shirt pocket radio segment of the market. Its retail price at the time was about $36. The Japanese-made sets were selling for $19—and projections indicated a probable price of $12 by 1970. It was this price that GE decided to shoot for. Representing a two-thirds reduction, it was a formidable task. Not many in the Radio Receiver Department thought it could be done.

At this point, instead of handing down a management dictum, key GE people were brought into the act. The challenge was presented, the need made clear. It was a question of either succeeding, or "exporting jobs abroad."

There is no greater competitor in the world than Joe Doakes, American. GE not only made the target, but by 1965 the price was brought down to $7. Remarkable achievement? Perhaps. But in Day's view, the people-ized approach made all the difference.

2. Refuse to take NO for an answer

Ever hear of George Francis Train? He was an eccentric American millionaire. In 1870 he circled the globe in 80 days. Later, Jules Verne used Train's remarkable feat as inspiration for his famous novel, *Around the World in Eighty Days.* Another time Train decided he could shorten the trade route to the Orient by running a transcontinental railway across the Rocky Mountains. Cornelius Vanderbilt was among the many who told him he was out of his head. Train ignored the scoffers and the no-can-do men. He got the U.S. Government to help finance the project. He persuaded friends to invest the then gigantic sum of $1,400,000. And he boldly predicted that his railroad would be completed in seven years.

It was finished in six.

"Impossible!" The French statesman, Mirabeau, once said. "Never let me hear that foolish word again."

It's a sentiment that is shared by the savvy manager. Anything is achieveable to the man who knows when to refuse to take "no" for an answer.

Find the Key to Open the Door

Often it takes a meeting of two or more minds to achieve a goal. But if one mind is a closed door, the attempt at achievement becomes futile.

Example. Some time ago we had our eye on a distributor in a major city. We wanted him to handle our line. "Not interested," my sales manager told me flatly. "The guy wouldn't even talk to me."

Why not, I wondered? We hadn't ever met with the man. He didn't know who we were or what we could do for him. What we needed was a key to his mind.

It took a bit of checking, but we found one soon enough.

I got the man on the telephone. "Look," he began, "I thought I made it clear to your sales manager—"

"You did," I said, "but I don't think you're being fair. I think you can help us and we can help you. Wouldn't you say we were at least entitled to a hearing?"

"Well—" I had brushed against his conscience.

"Look," I said, "are you familiar with . . ." and I named a certain trade organization. His interest perked instantly. "Why, yes. In fact, I've just been named a vice president."

"Congratulations. But here's something you may not know." I started reeling off names of officers of the association, present and past. "These people are all doing business with us on a very profitable basis."

He told me he didn't know that. "There's a good deal you don't know about us. Why don't we both sit down and chew this thing over a bit?"

He agreed to at least sit down and meet with us. Today this man is one of our most productive distributors. Because we had found the key—his deep and prideful involvement in the association—to open the door.

Before Giving Up, Try a Second Look, a Third, and at Times a Tenth

Too many goals are defeated for the simple reason that men give up too soon. Here's a potent savvy tip. When people say, "It can't be done," refuse to accept it, unless you yourself are *personally convinced* that it can't be done. Example. Some time ago the Martin Company in Orlando, Florida, purchased a microwave oscillator tube from a French company for $19,500. Some time after the warranty expired, the tube failed. The manufacturer claimed that it couldn't be repaired. Martin contacted a number of American tube producers. They said the same thing.

One savvy manager refused to accept this contention. He felt it *could* be repaired. He decided to keep trying until someone convinced him he was wrong. Finally, he got in touch with a Japanese firm who agreed to work on the tube on a no-cost, no-promise basis. Their objective, to gain experience.

Martin paid $400—the company's only cost—to send the tube to Japan. Weeks later it was returned, as good as new.

It's a point to remember. When someone says, "It can't be done," if it's his word against your conviction, challenge him to prove your conviction wrong. If he can't, proceed on the premise that it *can* and *will* be done.

3. Master the SIMULTANEOUS EQUATION. Get all wheels turning at the same time

Some years ago, we bid on a government job to manufacture arch-rib prefab steel buildings. We were low bidder but we had to present a sample of the product before a contract could be awarded. At our staff meeting, we began to plan. Not just an ordinary plan, but one that would involve three or four methods to accomplish the goal. Our main problem was to produce an arch steel section that forms the main structure of the building. First we ordered rolls. Simultaneously we got our tool room to hand-make a small press brake die. And we got a local company to start making a Kirksite die (a temporary plastic-like material). In other words, all three projects were started at the same time to make sure the goal was met.

The "Simultaneous Equation" is the savvy manager's way of getting started and keeping going on schedule. Step one is to assign the right job to the right person. Step two is to build into the assignment the proper check points or bench marks so that the task can keep moving. Step three is to know the right questions to ask to check on the project's progress. Step four is to keep the channels of communication open up and down the line.

4. Gun down the HOLD-UP MAN

"Tomorrow, and tomorrow, and tomorrow," Shakespeare said, "creeps in this petty pace from day to day, to the last syllable of recorded time; and all our yesterdays have lighted fools the way to dusty death."

What this means in simple savvy English is that indecision and delay can scuttle goals and deaden deadlines. Want to remove the IM from the word "impossible?" Then rout the waverer and divert him to a steady course. Here is a brief rundown of typical "hold-up men" who specialize in blocking goal achievement:

- The person who takes the long route instead of the shortcut. *Example:* In getting that urgently needed spring device remodeled, one "hold-up man" decided to write a letter instead of getting on the telephone.

- The *mañana* advocate. The individual who fails to seize an opportunity when it's hot. Instead, he postpones it for another day.

- The closed-minded resister. At times it takes two or more to make a deal, resolve an action, get a program underway. *Example:* The distributor we wanted to handle our line who closed his mind to our offer and ideas.

- The time killer. He spends his time showing why it "can't be done" instead of finding ways to do it. *Example:* The manufacturers who tried to convince the Martin Company engineer that the defective tube couldn't be repaired.

- The indecisive roadblocker. He's timid; he lacks confidence; or he's afraid to venture out on a limb. Result, he can't—or won't —make up his mind.

- The lazy goal defeater. To produce action would require an effort he's not willing to put out—such as cracking a book, putting in some extra time, performing an unaccustomed task.

These are some of your more proficient "hold-up men." The alternatives are clear. Either convert them to your way of thinking—or gun them down. You have no choice. If they succeed in their objectives, you will fail in yours.

Now YOU. Pinpoint Your Personal "Hold-Up" Men

The procedure is simple. First, take a pencil and pad. Then spell out in writing every objective you can call to mind that you are trying to achieve, both on and off the job. When this is done, write down the name of each individual who, for one reason or another, is standing in the way of your goal fulfillment. These are your personal "hold-up" men. Now it is simply a matter of working out some way to either win them over or to gun them down.

5. Keep the motor running with ON-HAND FUELING

Ever watch a top flight rigging crew chief organize and direct the hoisting, hauling and relocation of a heavy piece of equipment? It's a sight to see. There are three or four men on the crew, each assigned a series of functions. The unit being moved weighs five or six tons perhaps. But the man to focus on is the chief. Constantly, he's right there at the heart of the operation, gauging, measuring, estimating, barking rapid-fire instructions at his men.

"Tighten that rope." "Shift the dolly." "Lower the lift." "Let out the slack." "Reset those plates."

Never a question of what to do next, or how to do it. Result, the job moves forward, steadily and positively towards its goal.

Why? Because there is never one molecule of doubt. The chief is in control at all times. If a problem crops up, he's there to cope with it. If a lag occurs, he's there to step up the movement. If a crewman wavers, he follows through with clear and decisive action.

In short, he plays the role of leader, motivator, pace-setter. He keeps the operation on target and on time. When he's needed he'll be there, where the action is taking place.

And so, the job gets done, the unit gets moved, difficult or not, two tons or ten.

It's a thought to take with you. Executive, supervisor, foreman, crew chief—or savvy manager. ON-HAND FUELING will get you through the toughest task. It doesn't let the motor die.

The Cuban crisis

A Case History Example of CAN-DO MANAGEMENT in Action

The date was October 29, 1962. Among the more newsworthy events of the day were the blockade to prevent war materials from entering Cuba, and the sudden call-up of reserves on the United States mainland.

It was, as you will recall, a time of grave national crisis.

9:05 Monday morning, my telephone rang. The U.S. Army Engineer Procurement Office was on the wire. Some special parts were desperately needed for the construction of bridges.

Years back we had done this kind of work. But in more than four years we had not bid on a single government contract.

The caller's voice was crisp and tight. "We know of no other supplier who can do the job in the allotted time."

My automatic impulse was to refuse. We were in no position to tackle that kind of work. But something held me back.

"Is this a matter of national emergency?" I asked bluntly. It was.

"Let me take the matter up with my people. I'll call you back."

FACTOR ONE: THE MUST DO URGENCY. At the time, I was general manager of Steelcraft. I discussed the matter with Al Levinson, my father, who was president, my brother Charles, who was executive vice president. We obtained drawings of the parts in question, and an erection manual from the local Corps of Engineers. Reviewing the situation, we agreed on two things: (1) The job couldn't be done in the time specified. (2) The job *had to be done* in the time specified.

I called back the Procurement people and set up a Chicago meeting. While enroute, our people at the plant went over the plans, and talked to suppliers.

I called the plant from Chicago at 10 AM and spoke to my people. They were skeptical, but unwilling to say no in face of the emergency situation. That was good enough for me.

"I can't tell you what this job is going to cost," I told the Procurement Officer. "We don't want the job, and we're in no position to do it. But if you have nobody else it looks like we're elected."

A contract was drawn up on a cost-plus basis.

FACTOR TWO: REFUSE TO TAKE NO FOR AN ANSWER. The stakes were high. Higher, perhaps, than even we could imagine. The Engineering Procurement Office (EPOC) was betting that we would manufacture—without special tools, dies, or previous experience with these parts—over 1,960 pieces for 32 different items, weighing some 80,000 pounds. And they were betting that we would ship them by noon Sunday, November 4, 1962. This would give us six days for the entire job.

Our people were superb. Managers, supervisors, engineers, production and office people. They pitched in on an all-out around-the-clock basis. Many of them lived, ate and slept at Steelcraft. And yet it was only natural that some said, "It can't be done."

The words fell on deaf ears.

Our subcontractors worked under similar conditions. They lacked the special dies and exact tooling. To state it bluntly, the entire contract was produced on a "hand-made" basis. And all this time, with very few exceptions, our normal commitments were being met on schedule.

FACTOR THREE: THE SIMULTANEOUS EQUATION. All wheels turning at once. This was achieved from the very outset of the operation. Even before the actual production got under way.

Step one, you'll recall, was to get the planning under way.

At the same time I was in Chicago in conference with EPOC.

At the same time our plant executives were rallying our people to the cause, setting up schedules, working up plans.

At the same time contracts were being drawn up.

At the same time materials, parts, tools were being obtained.

No time was lost. No lag between one operation and the next. No waiting for instructions or materials. Everything was anticipated, all functions overlapped to the maximum degree.

The "Simultaneous Equation." It saves days, hours, minutes.

And in this situation, every minute counted.

FACTOR FOUR: THE HOLD-UP MAN. Hold-up men? There weren't many on this job. Our people were inspired. Our subcontractors, bless every one of them, were just as inspired.

Still, it was a rough time for all of us. Everything was new, everything strange. Decisions had to be made, swift decisions, sure decisions. And from time to time a man would waver.

But behind every waverer, there stood a decider.

From time to time a man would grow discouraged.

Behind every skeptic was a "confidence man."

Sometimes a man would get scared. "What if I make a mistake? What if I'm wrong?"

We checked and rechecked. We left no margin for error. We removed all justification for fear.

Hold-up men? They can scuttle a goal, thwart a deadline, replace "go" with frustration. But only when they're "armed." Take away their weapons, and they're helpless.

FACTOR FIVE: ON-HAND FUELING. During our own small segment of the "Cuban Crisis" there were times when "On-Hand Fueling" made *all* the difference. Once a subcontractor of an especially critical item pressed the panic button. "We can't possibly deliver on time!" My brother Charles flew to the contractor and stayed with the operation until it was out of the woods.

They delivered on time.

Any time a contractor, a supplier, or one of our own people ran into a roadblock, one of us was on hand to pitch in on the problem or bolster morale. Sometimes we hardly knew ourselves how we achieved what we did. But somehow or other—knowing the job *had* to get done, it *did* get done.

FINALE. Noon Sunday, November 4, 1962. That was the deadline. Had we made delivery on the fifth, we could have thrown the 1,960 pieces in the river.

This, bear in mind, was the job that couldn't be done!

Yet on Saturday, November 3, at 6 PM, we started making delivery. By midnight the remainder of the contract was loaded— *12 hours ahead of schedule.*

The commendation sent to us by Colonel J. H. Jackson, commanding officer of EPOC, could as well have been sent to each and any of our 15 subcontractors. They too had proved that when you put your mind and heart and will into the act, "impossible" or not, the job can be done.

What if it's REALLY impossible?

Does all this mean if you apply unswerving resolve and "Yes Determination" to each and every goal that confronts you, somehow or other it always will be achieved? Unfortunately not.

Some goals *are* impossible, really and truly impossible. The trick is to differentiate between the seemingly impossible, and the genuinely impossible.

I recall once we were trying to develop an idea for a new kind of supermarket door product. It appeared to have an excellent potential, and we had hired the inventor to work with us for several months.

But time proved some of our judgments to be wrong. Things weren't working out as we had hoped. Market studies weren't living up to our original expectations. We found our organization was not as ideally suited as we had thought to distribute this kind of product. We decided that if we continued trying to buck the mounting odds before us, it would mean pouring too much money into the venture.

The project was abandoned.

The trick, of course, is to measure the potential benefits against the realistic costs. You have to keep evaluating and re-evaluating. Business at best is a gamble. You have to keep asking yourself: "What do we stand to gain? What do we stand to lose?"

When You Back the Wrong Horse

What happens when the cause you espoused turns out to be the wrong one? Admittedly, it's hard to admit you've been wrong. But the sooner you face up to reality, the better. Holding off can only compound the mistake.

Once we opened a branch plant. I had planned this plant. I had pushed for it and helped to get it on its feet. It was my baby. But the baby never started to walk on its own. Unforeseen obstacles developed. Finally—and to this day I can remember how much it hurt—I went to my brother, who was also my boss, and I said, "Charles, I think we should close the plant."

All he said was, "Thanks."

That's when it came crashing down on me how much better it was that *I* had made the suggestion, and not he.

The point is this. The sooner you can swallow your pride and face up to your defeat when the task *is* a truly impossible one, the more of a man and manager you will be.

Self-Evaluation Time. Your Personal Project Rundown

How many truly impossible tasks are *you* espousing? Step back now and evaluate some of these projects you have been struggling over, pouring in added funds, added effort, added manhours. If you have already done an evaluation, re-evaluate in the light of latest developments. Ask yourself: "What do we stand to gain? What do we stand to lose?" If the figures don't tally up to a definite profit plus, abandon the project now. Admit you were wrong.

"Can do" achievement factors—summary roundup

1. Spell out for your subordinates exactly how far they can go to achieve any given task. How much money can they invest? How much time? How much manpower? Self-imposed limitations can make an achievable task impossible.

2. Translate the urgency of the situation to your people. Blow it up into a big deal. Don your actor's frock to dramatize its importance.

3. Achieving a seemingly impossible goal is often a teamwork objective. But don't take for granted that others involved share your motivational drive. The idea is to work with them and through them to spark and sustain their enthusiasm.

4. Lincoln once said, "Determine that the thing can and shall be done, and then we shall find the way." Step one is to determine that your personal faith in the project's fulfillment is unshakable. Then, when somebody claims that, "It can't be done," if it's his word against your conviction, challenge him to prove that your conviction is wrong. If he can't, proceed on the premise that the job can and will be done.

5. Many tasks are tagged "impossible" only because somebody's closed mind is blocking the way to achievement. But there is a magic key that will open the door to any man's closed mind. If you can find that key and turn it at the right time, it may make all the difference between failure and success.

6. Quite often it is only the whole that seems unattainable. Considered one at a time, the parts are much less formidable. Try breaking down each presumably unreachable goal into its component parts. Then tackle the project a piece at a time, and watch that no-can-do notion dissolve.

7. Overlap operations to overcome that seemingly deadly deadline. Allow no time lags, no waiting between steps or functions. Get as many wheels as you can spinning at the same time. Use the "Simultaneous Equation" to trigger and sustain action.

8. In tackling a rough and challenging task, move quickly to disarm the "hold-up men" in the way of fulfillment. Crack down on the slow mover, the long-way-around man, the closed-minded resister, the "mañana" advocate, the indifferent roadblocker, the fellow who can't make up his mind. Don't permit any individual to slow the forward

thrust. Use the needle where you must, the ax, or the shotgun, whatever is necessary to keep the project moving.

9. Change talky-talk into can-do action. You know the old story. One person explains in painful detail why the job cannot be done. Nearby works another person who is not paying attention because he's too busy doing it.

10. Don't walk away from tough and demanding projects. Don't assume because you planned it, organized it and got it under way, that from this point on it will continue moving ahead on its own steam. The rougher the task, the more important your "on-hand fueling" will be to its achievement. Be there when needed to help your people cut problems down to size, to stave off discouragement, to prevent decision paralysis from setting in.

11. No player can blast the ball out of the park every time he gets up to bat. At times you will judge wrongly or decide incorrectly. At times you will reach the crossroads of determination: to go ahead with the project, or to abandon it. There is only one factor involved: "What do you stand to gain? What do you stand to lose?" When the minuses add up to more than the plusses, it's time to "give up the ghost."

12. Finally, and most important, in attempting to achieve the "impossible," there is always that extra ounce of guts, that extra inch of "go." Or, as some unknown sage so aptly put it, "When you get to the end of your rope, tie a knot and hang on."

15

Make Savvy-Building a
24-Hour Job

A waggish observer of the business scene complains that the modern employer is out to hire men 25 to 30 years old with 40 years' experience.

There is much truth in the jest. The most sought-after manager today is the well-rounded master generalist. Bluntly stated, today's savvy manager is the human computer of his organization. He can speak with reasonable intelligence on any business subject. He may not know all the answers on a detail-by-detail basis, but he does know how each function and subfunction ties into the overall planning and goals of the organization.

In short, the savvy manager is not restricted by boundaries of technology, or walled in by the limits of a single function. He remains aware. He knows the score.

Perhaps you've heard the Sam Levenson story (no relation to the author) about the father with six youngsters in tow in a museum. Irritated by the slow rate of progress, he barked at his brood, "Look, kids, if you're gonna stop to look at everything, you ain't gonna see nothin'."

In a sense, the well-rounded savvy manager is a lot like those youngsters. He stops to look at *everything*. He wears awareness like a pair of eyeglasses that he sheds only when he sleeps. *He makes savvy-building a 24-hour occupation.*

Make your personal life an asset to your business life

Savvy-building doesn't start at nine and end at five. The skilled generalist develops off-job techniques for strengthening his business skills. He expands his savvy management to include: (1) His family. (2) His community. (3) His personal living habits.

FAMILY. I have no patience with the dedicated workhorse who arrives regularly at the job at 8 AM and gets home at nine or ten in the evening. I don't subscribe to the concept that the longer the day, the better the manager. The savvy manager gets others to do things for him. He guides. He trains. He directs. He spots and develops talent and ability. When I see a man working long extra hours day after day, my guess is that he's not delegating properly.

The manager is, after all, a special breed of professional. This implies certain *reasonable* demands on his time—the unexpected business trip, the occasional after-hours meeting, the midnight oil session in response to a business emergency. But 11 or 12 hours a day as a steady diet—this I can't see. It adds up to family neglect. It leads to all kinds of problems. The truth is that your family as well as your company needs your management expertise.

I recently came across a 12-year-old's impression of a happy family. "A happy family is like a baseball team, with Mom pitching, Dad catching, and the kids fielding, with everyone taking a turn at bat."

At our home, we try to give each member of the family his "turn at bat."

One night, for example, I expected an important call. The caller needed certain information, and then, depending on his response, he needed directions for action. This person was traveling, so I couldn't call him. That same night a meeting was scheduled that my wife and I had to attend. Obviously, I couldn't be in two places at the same time.

I took a deep breath and put my son Jon, who was only 15 at the time, on the spot, just as I do with people at the plant. I explained the situation and went over the instructions until I was reasonably certain Jon understood them. "When you take the call," I advised, "simply put yourself in my place." "Sure, Dad," Jon replied noncommittally. Crossing my fingers, I left with my wife.

We arrived home at 11:00 PM and were greeted by a smile Jon was not quite able to contain. Yes, the person had called, he said with an overdone casualness. The information? "No problem at all." It had been a breeze. The next day I talked to the person on the phone. He complimented me on the way my son had handled the call. "That boy of yours is a real pro," he said. That evening I passed the compliment along to Jon. His buttons were popping. So were mine and my wife Phyllis'.

It was a gamble, of course. Had Jon fouled up that information, it would have produced premium-size headaches. Still, training and then doing by example is the only way to learn.

At our home, we try to live as a team and help each other whenever necessary. We have several company parties each year. At these affairs the whole family is invited. My two sons have learned that we are the hosts at these affairs and that they should conduct themselves accordingly. I must admit that this is some-times tough to do. Last summer we had a company picnic. I guess about 1,500 people attended. So did my family. Jim, my other son, who was seven years old, knew that he was supposed to be a host. He said he would help out with the children's games. At one point he was asked to be in one of the games. He certainly had his eye on the prizes. He didn't win the game, but I did notice that he really wasn't trying too hard. Afterwards I asked Jim what he was doing and he said, "I didn't try too hard because I wanted the other kids to win the prizes." Here again, Phyllis and I were proud as punch! Jim was a real trouper.

My wife, Phyllis, always displays a unique characteristic of being able to adjust to the circumstances. She is able to make people feel at home and tailor her conversation. Her memory is unbelievable. She can recall first names on the spot. People like her because she is sincere and it really shows.

COMMUNITY. Want to become a local hero, and serve your own ends at the same time? It's easy.

Become actively involved in the affairs of your community!

Here again, the *Multiple Value Concept* comes into play. The community gains; you gain too.

The payoff comes in a variety of ways: For example, community service:

1. *Sharpens your organizational abilities.* Talented organizers are in short supply. Experience you get in planning community programs and getting them under way will serve you well on the job.
2. *Smooths your personality rough spots.* A manager on his way up can't afford to be backward and shy. The community is a good place to develop your powers of persuasion, acquire poise, make your personality more dynamic.
3. *Helps you handle responsibility with greater assurance.* "In the community," says one company's newly appointed executive vice president, "I was handed top-level assignments. The experience helped immeasurably; one of the best training grounds I know."
4. *Hones motivational skills.* Your success in the community or on the job will depend largely on your ability to get work done through others, and to inspire them to excellence in their performance. What better place to test your motivational strategies than at the local meeting room or council chamber?
5. *Cultivates your speaking ability.* It takes the gift of gab to sell ideas and convert them to action—in the community or on the job. Speak up, and you won't be left out.
6. *Develops you into a master evaluator.* Is Smith sincere in his desire to be of help? Is Clark qualified to handle the job? Will Kellogg's program work as outlined? These questions come up at work and in the community.
7. *Builds the idea-generating habit.* In the community, there are always new programs to consider, new wrinkles to iron out. The stimulation of new ideas is a direct by-product of the diversified problem-solving challenge.

PERSONAL LIVING HABITS. The well-rounded manager lives a well-balanced life. He sleeps enough, but not too much. He drinks in moderation—most of the time.

His chief overriding interest is *people*. He's concerned with how they act and how they react. He knows that only with people and *through* people can his life be rich and rewarding—both on and off the job. Thus it is one of his primary drives to expose himself to as many people as possible, and to a variety of people-ized situations.

The savvy manager gets around and makes it a point to broaden his savvy during his travels. He reads voraciously about people and things. He involves himself in all kinds of problems, and evaluates judgments and decisions from various points of view. He is part lawyer, part clergyman, part entertainer. Up to a point, he is part psychologist without infringing on the territory of the professional psychologist.

In short, the good manager is alert. Curiosity is more than a passing fancy with him. It is a burning passion. He cares. He's aware. He wants to find out as much as he can about everyone and everything. Most of all, he knows that if he serves people better on the job and in the community, they will almost invariably respond in kind.

GENERALISTS MORE WIDELY WOOED. It is possible that a slow and gradual double awakening is in progress in America: company-generated, people-generated. We're still very much enmeshed in the so-called "age of specialization." But the natives are growing restless. Thoughtful managers are beginning to wonder if ultra-specialization isn't really self-defeating in many respects, mainly from the standpoint of growth. And many top level corporate officers are disquieted by the same thought.

Is this a portent for the future? Perhaps. In any event there are whispers in the wind. And some companies are starting to respond with positive action. A typical example is displayed in an employment ad recently run by the Friden Corporation: "WHAT IS A SPECIALIST/GENERALIST?" the ad was headlined. "Are you one?"

The ad went on to say, "A specialist is a fellow who works within the limitations of a specific problem or field of interest. He seldom gets involved in the 'big picture.' (Perhaps that's you now.)

"A generalist is closer to the overall job. He sees how the work of many specialists fits together. But he often misses out on the thrill of being an expert in something specific. At Friden R & D these two functions are combined. Because research teams are relatively small, you do get involved with the project as a whole, in addition to your specialized work. . . ."

Does this mean the "age of specialization" is beginning to wane? The prospect seems unlikely for a long time to come. But it does mean, perhaps, that there's no better time than now for a dynamic manager-on-the-climb to hop on that generalist bandwagon.

Keep your personal PR mirror defogged

A young man I know was a manager in a medium-size insurance company. He's sharp, intelligent, pleasant, personable. But for years he was moored fast at one level in his company. The employer was not at fault. For all his talent and poise, the young man's PR mirror was fuzzy. He dated half the girls in the place. Any time the name Harry came to mind, the association of "wolf" came with it.

Two years ago Harry married a fine girl. He settled down and changed his job. Today he's notches ahead of his former position, and climbing fast. There's no question that Harry has the stuff to get ahead. All he had to do was clean his mirror.

What about *your* mirror? It is time now to evaluate each adverse characteristic with *you* in mind.

1. How do you look to others? Right or wrong, like it or not, people tend to judge you largely by your appearance. Are you careful about the aspects of your appearance that are under your control? Do you keep your clothes fresh and clean? What about your personal grooming and physical appearance? Are you permitting yourself to develop a flabby face and a paunchy middle? Do you get enough sleep to banish that worn and dragged-out look?

2. Are you a good listener? The man who can listen appreciatively to a story or idea is in great demand. The one who stomps inconsiderately on a "punch line," or responds with sick disapproval, is usually the fellow you can well live without.

3. Do you talk too much? Often, the bum listener and the man you can't get to shut up are one and the same person. Chances are that the individual with *windbag* chalked across his PR mirror won't go far. Almost invariably he's a bore, a project stopper, a production stumbling block.

4. DO PEOPLE THINK OF YOU AS "THE CHARACTER"? Are you the company's practical jokester? Do you resort to zany, unpredictable actions in a bid for attention? Here's a savvy tip for you. Any characteristic that subtracts from the respect you command will hinder your growth and development as a manager.

5. ARE YOU A GOODY-GOODY SUPER-VIRTUOUS LOYALIST? Or, to put it more bluntly, are you the "teacher's pet" operating under the guise of "master politician?" Do you say "Yes!" any time the boss presents an idea, invites a reaction to a decision, or blows his nose—just because he's the boss?

6. ARE YOU YOURSELF? On the job, or off, the artificial flower doesn't grow. The man who makes the biggest hit in his business and social life is the one who acts naturally and unpretentiously. Try to be the kind of person you yourself would like to be with, and you won't go wrong.

7. ARE YOU "EASY TO GET ALONG WITH"? Everyone enjoys the company of a pleasant, friendly person. The fellow who argues constantly triggers resentment and irritation. Stand up for what you believe in, of course. But don't build yourself a reputation as the perpetual dissenter, the fellow who is anti-everything.

8. DO YOU WEAR "A SMILE FOR YOUR UMBRELLA"? A warm friendly smile has a magic magnetic appeal. It draws people out. It encourages them to respond.

9. ARE YOU OVER-AGGRESSIVE? There's nothing wrong with ambition, if it's kept properly in check. But ambition that is too apparent, or carried to extremes, can be self-defeating.

10. ARE YOU TRUE TO YOUR ROLE AS A MANAGER? As boss of your section, department, or division, certain standards of behavior are expected of you. Admittedly, it's tempting at times to lower the barrier between you and your subordinates. The urge to "let go" may be strong—to be just "one of the boys," join in on a too social get-together, have a few drinks too many with members of your staff. How can you tell where to draw the line? It's simple. Be a "regular guy" by all means, *but never at the expense of your people's respect.*

It's YOU-Evaluation Time

The main trouble with the mirror-marring traits is that they're not always so clear-cut and easy to pinpoint. The trick is to bring those negative traits out into the open. There's nothing complicated about the procedure, but you may need the help of at least one other person.

Marshal Foch once said, "Every young man should know well at least one old man to whom he can go when he wants the teachings of experience rather than sympathy."

Your confidant doesn't have to be an "old man" necessarily, but he should be someone you trust and respect. He could be a business acquaintance, a relative or neighbor—even your wife. Especially your wife, in some cases. An ancient proverb says, "Write down the advice of him who loves you, though you like it not at present."

That's your objective—to elicit the advice and opinion of somebody close to you. Consider the ten mirror-marring traits already cited. Add to this list as many other traits as you can call to mind.

Stretch your imagination. If a trait touches off even the remotest doubt that it might apply to you, write it down. Then urge your confidant to be completely candid with you, to pull no punches.

Steer clear of "socialized management"

There's nothing wrong with joining the boys at the bowling alley once a week. But give this savvy tip some well-considered thought. *Steer clear of "socialized management!"* Don't get too chummy with the people in your office or shop. The reason is clear and simple. You never know what tomorrow will bring.

Problems are sure to come up, judgments and decisions on your part that will affect these people's lives. It's not easy to act objectively when a close friend is involved. It throws your business and social responsibilities into conflict. It leads to misunderstanding, bitterness and resentment. The windup is that you hurt your friend and you hurt yourself in a way that often can't be repaired.

I know a sales manager who ran into a situation like this in his company. A juicy branch managership had unexpectedly opened up. The manager's close friend, a veteran salesman, was so sure the appointment would be his, he went out and splurged on an expensive new car. But the salesman wasn't right for the job, and the manager knew it. Another man was given the nod. The salesman was stunned, and resigned in an irrational huff.

I recently spoke with the manager. He confided in me vehemently, "I never want to go through an experience like that again."

Sometimes a closer-than-casual relationship is impossible to avoid. A man who is already a close friend is hired by your company. A subordinate is your neighbor. Of course, you don't disown an old friend, or snub a subordinate. But you can and should divorce your job activities from your social activities. Stick to business only on the job; and steer clear of discussions about company personalities, plans, money matters and the like, while out on the town.

Get your wife into the savvy-building act

As any wife will tell you, the "little woman," if you give her half a chance, can help develop you into a "big man," and speed the savvy-building process.

Or it can work the other way, if you don't take care. What it boils down to is that the savvy manager will go farther faster if he's lucky enough to have a cooperative wife working with him instead of against him.

The "simpatica" wife can be a powerful career booster.

The non-cooperative wife can be a powerful career buster.

The fact is that whether a wife hinders or helps a manager usually depends as much on him as it does on her.

Here's the question. How can you and your wife work together and plan together to help build *your* family's future on a sound and constructive basis? Hopefully, the following CAREER BOOSTING and CAREER BUSTING factors will help you to establish some meaningful guidelines.

• ENCOURAGE YOUR WIFE TO BE HERSELF WHEN SHE MEETS THE BOSS. Every manager is anxious for his wife to make a hit with the boss. The best way you can help your wife make a hit is by encouraging her to act naturally so that her real self shines through. It's strictly a joint effort on her part and yours.

The truth is that pretention shines a spotlight on our flaws.

Phyllis and I threw a small shindig some time ago. Among those present was one of our new young managers and his wife.

The manager was a capable and intelligent comer. His wife was *probably* pleasant and smart. I never found out for sure. Her eyes pierced mine with undying interest. She hung worshipfully on every word I said. She was unnaturally and embarrassingly over-attentive. It was obvious to me that she had been coached down to the last syllable.

It's a mistake new managers commonly make. When your wife is going to meet the boss, don't give her a step-by-step rundown on how to be "nice" to him. Chances are if you just give her the opportunity to be herself, she'll bring it off in a way that will make you proud. But when you shower her with directions about how to act and what to say, what you do, in effect, is to put her in a deep freeze. She winds up dreading the affair which was designed for her enjoyment. She gets so nervous and distraught that it would take extraordinary poise not to blow the whole performance.

Want to help your wife prepare for that affair, dinner, party, or whatever? You can do it in only one way. Get her the lowdown on what type of dress she should wear. Formal, semi-formal, or what? This is one of her biggest worries, and if she guesses wrong, it will ruin her evening.

But the main point is this. The girl your boss wants to meet is the girl you know so well. Not some artificial version who bears small resemblance to the real person.

• THE CAREER-BOOSTING WIFE PLAYS THE CHARMING HOSTESS— EVEN WHEN IT HURTS. The wife who enjoys meeting people and is naturally gregarious helps immeasurably to fuel her husband's upward thrust. The problem is that maintaining professional standards in the home is often tougher than maintaining them in the shop. Take a typical example.

Little Billie, who is just learning to walk, has been knocking things over all day long. The washing machine broke down. The cleaner ruined an expensive dress. Everything's in a turmoil. Then, all of a sudden, a call from the dynamic conquering hero down at the office. He'll be home for dinner in forty minutes with a customer in tow. Nothing, thinks the little woman—*nothing* at this moment—could be more irritating than the sound of that cheery businesslike voice at the other end of the line.

The wife hangs up. The house is a mess. She herself is in

complete disarray. And dinner for five instead of pot luck for four presents a seemingly insoluble problem. What to do now? Here's where you separate the boosters from the busters.

The buster—and she's not to be judged too harshly—would probably give vent to her feelings with a shrill mournful scream, or flop down on a chair and start to cry. But the booster would tighten her lips, tuck in her chin, and take the situation in stride. She'd work swiftly and efficiently, and achieve the impossible by converting that "pot luck" to a luscious feast. When the guest arrived she'd be the model of graciousness and hospitality. The pretzels and potato chips would be ready along with the warm interest and friendly conversation that is expected. (At least that's how it works in my home.)

The moment the guest left, of course, it would be a different matter. At that point she would lash into her husband (with complete justification), and give him the seven furies of Hades for not giving her more notice. But, if she's a real booster, the guest would have never suspected a thing.

• THE REAL BOOSTER LEARNS TO TAKE THE KNOCKS WITH THE BENEFITS. Every manager is called on to make personal sacrifices from time to time. Business "fires" of one kind or other are constantly in need of quenching. A customer fumes. A production process goes wrong. An important deal is on the block. Often, at a moment's notice, a manager is required to fly out of town, or stay late to sit in on a crucial meeting.

Sometimes the business trip or special meeting conflicts with important social or family plans. And more often than not, it can't be helped. The situation won't fix itself. That's what the manager is there for. That's why he's a manager. And it's at this point that his life will be made a lot easier if his wife is a booster instead of a buster.

The buster grumbles and groans; she's angry and bitter.

The booster says, "I understand."

It's not always easy to say, "I understand." But to the hard-pressed manager, those two little words make all the difference.

• THE BOOSTER LETS THE DRIVER DRIVE. The savvy manager runs not only his job and his people, but his own career as well. With some misguided females as running mates, this can become a man-sized job. The devoted wife often has an inflated opinion of her husband's ability. In her eyes, he can do anything better than anyone else. Add to this a dash of over-ambition and you wind up with a dangerous situation. The wife can become a *Back Seat Manager*. She can tip the "career growth scales" further than they're meant to be tipped. ("Go after that job, darling. I know you can do it.")

But does she know, really? The fact is that only YOU know if you can do it. The healthiest strategy for your wife to take is to level with you soberly and intelligently. ("Darling, I'm not familiar enough with the situation. I have confidence in your ability, but you're the one who's on the job day in and day out. If you think you can do better by changing, I'm with you all the way. And if you decide to stay put, it's all right, too. But the decision is yours alone. Because only you are qualified to weigh the factors and determine your own capabilities.")

It works the other way, too. A friend of mine who runs a mill recently told me about a maintenance man in his plant. The employee supervises four or five people. "I'd been following his progress," my friend said, "and I put him to a few tests. I was convinced this fellow was good management material. One day an opportunity arose at another location. I needed a man to run a fair-sized maintenance department. I offered the job to this fellow and he jumped at it."

But, my friend continued, next morning he was completely deflated. His wife had talked him out of the job. He made some halfhearted excuses about too much responsibility and an alleged lack of experience. My friend was of no mind to buck a "family decision." He gave the man a week to change his mind. After the week, he appointed someone else to the job.

What about that maintenance man? Today he's still a little man in a little job. He may be at the wheel. But his wife does the steering.

● How do you rate your wife—"consultant" or "sounding board"? There's a good therapeutic value at times in just organizing your thoughts on a knotty subject and letting them out in talk.

What better listener in such a case than the little woman? PROVIDED she can resist the impulse to suddenly transform into an inspired and knowledgeable "consultant." This is one temptation many otherwise charming and desirable females are totally unable to resist. As one wag puts it, "The reason God made woman *after* he made man was that he didn't want any advice."

I can think of at least one female who might have prompted this comment. On the rare occasion that her husband suffers a mental lapse and mentions a business problem in her presence, she feels obliged to solve it for him. Which only compounds the original problem by the injection of a new one—getting her to come down off the speaker's rostrum.

If your wife is a skilled and understanding "sounding board" type, consider yourself lucky. Milk that sympathetic ear for all it's worth when the spirit moves you. But if the better half is a natural-born "consultant," ask her advice about the house, the youngsters and your social life—but never about your job.

• YOUR CAREER-BOOSTING WIFE CAN BE THE BEST "PR MAN" ON YOUR TEAM. Your wife can help you to up your PR standing in a hundred different ways.

Sometime ago Phyllis and I took four or five of our distributors and their wives out to dinner. One couple was from Hawaii, and for them a trip to the States was a grand event. Phyllis sensed this instinctively, and went overboard to cater to their holiday mood of excitement. She made a big deal of their presence and gave them extra attention. She didn't do this with any ulterior purpose in mind. She just felt it was the friendly and hospitable thing to do. But it takes a special kind of sensitivity and awareness to respond naturally and instinctively to the situation at hand. These people sensed this special treatment. They thoroughly enjoyed it and couldn't do enough to show their appreciation.

Of course, this is a small and isolated incident. But now multiply it by 20, 30, 50 incidents involving customers, suppliers, business associates, community people. The net sum is an important supplement to your managerial PR image.

Career booster or career buster? Rate your wife

Rate your wife. But keep this in mind. When you rate your wife, you rate *yourself* at the same time. Your wife can help you in many ways to thrust ahead in your career. *But she can help you only if you help her to help you!* With this in mind, sit down with a pencil, a pad—*and your wife*—and answer the following questions as honestly and objectively as you can.

1. Is your wife herself when she meets the boss and your business associates? Or is she six other people?
2. Can you count on your wife to play the impromptu hostess and pull it off without any apparent hitch?
3. Is your wife sympathetic and understanding when you explain that you have to take off for Oshkosh on the next plane?
4. Does your wife encourage *you* to make the vital decisions concerning your career on your own? And right or wrong, does she stand behind your decision?
5. Is your wife useful to you as a "sounding board" for problems? Or is she impatient for you to wind up your discussion so that she can take the floor?
6. Does your wife take positive steps to boost your personal PR image among the "influentials" with whom she comes into contact?

Now that you've completed the quiz, ask yourself this one final question: Are you still on speaking terms?

Summary roundup

Your Personal Savvy-Building Checklist

1. Savvy-building doesn't start at nine and end at five. It's a 24-hour job. Scout constantly for new off-job techniques to strengthen your business skills.

2. "Work fascinates me," a wit once said. "I can sit and look at it for hours." The savvy manager doesn't share this philosophy. He is also fascinated by work. But he doesn't "look at it." He wades in and gets it done—but on a rational, reasonable basis; *not on a regular ten-to-twelve-hour-a-day basis*. Unduly long hours may make a tired businessman; but they don't make a successful businessman. The truly savvy manager works "smarter," not harder. And he does this by delegating.

3. Serve your community, and multiply your savvy-building input at the same time. For you, there is no more effective proving ground in which to sharpen your personality, develop

and implement ideas, assume added responsibility, learn to speak more forcefully, and gain experience in training, motivating and evaluating others.

4. Take positive action to expand the scope of your off-job activities. Travel as extensively as you can. Read as voraciously as you can. Participate as often as you can. Expose yourself to all kinds of people and all kinds of situations. *In short, generalize!* You'll be a better man for the effort. And a better manager.

5. Take care to keep your "personal PR mirror" defogged. Picture yourself through the eyes of others. Take a mental excursion to your boss' desk. Picture yourself from his vantage point. Ask yourself with a mental outlook of cold critical appraisal: "How do I sound to others? How well do I listen? Do I talk too much? Am I known as 'the character'? Do I smile enough and make my smile genuine and sincere? Am I anti-everything? Am I noticeably over-ambitious? Do I ever step out of character as a manager and invite loss of respect by my bearing or behavior?" Consciously, or unconsciously, the people you deal with are aware of these things. All the more reason for you to be *doubly* aware of them.

6. Steer clear of "socialized management." Don't become too chummy with your associates and subordinates. The time will come when the buddy-buddy relationship may backfire, leaving a nasty smudge on your career. It's difficult to act and react objectively when a close friend is involved. Don't permit your social life to prejudice your business judgment.

7. Get your wife into the savvy-building act. It's going to take a bit of bend on both your parts. But if you work together and plan together, you can help her to help you in a variety of ways. Make savvy-building a partnership proposition at home as well as on the job. Work as a team, and the reward is inevitable. The "profits" will roll in and multiply. Your "profit-sharing" arrangement will benefit yourself, your wife, your entire family.